EFFORTLESS BELONGING
The Lost Science Synchrony

OSCAR WILLIS MITCHELL

A DIVISION OF HAY HOUSE

Copyright © 2022 Oscar Willis Mitchell.

All rights reserved. No part of this book may be used or reproduced by any means, graphic, electronic, or mechanical, including photocopying, recording, taping or by any information storage retrieval system without the written permission of the author except in the case of brief quotations embodied in critical articles and reviews.

Balboa Press books may be ordered through booksellers or by contacting:

Balboa Press
A Division of Hay House
1663 Liberty Drive
Bloomington, IN 47403
www.balboapress.com
844-682-1282

Because of the dynamic nature of the Internet, any web addresses or links contained in this book may have changed since publication and may no longer be valid. The views expressed in this work are solely those of the author and do not necessarily reflect the views of the publisher, and the publisher hereby disclaims any responsibility for them.

The author of this book does not dispense medical advice or prescribe the use of any technique as a form of treatment for physical, emotional, or medical problems without the advice of a physician, either directly or indirectly. The intent of the author is only to offer information of a general nature to help you in your quest for emotional and spiritual well-being. In the event you use any of the information in this book for yourself, which is your constitutional right, the author and the publisher assume no responsibility for your actions.

Any people depicted in stock imagery provided by Getty Images are models, and such images are being used for illustrative purposes only.
Certain stock imagery © Getty Images.

Print information available on the last page.

ISBN: 979-8-7652-3574-4 (sc)
ISBN: 979-8-7652-3575-1 (hc)
ISBN: 979-8-7652-3573-7 (e)

Library of Congress Control Number: 2022919649

Balboa Press rev. date: 11/15/2022

DEDICATION

To all those who have known suffering.
To all my sons and daughters throughout the world.
Fare thee well

CONTENTS

Foreword by Joanne Mitchell xi
Introduction xiii

Part 1: Core Concepts

Chapter 1   Thesis 1
Chapter 2   Lankavatara Sutra 4
Chapter 3   A User's Manual for Being Human 11
Chapter 4   This Book Is Not the Lanka 20
Chapter 5   The Path of Meaning 27
Chapter 6   Enlightenment 36
Chapter 7   The Five Aspects of Sentient Beings 45
Chapter 8   Esoteric Science 64

Part 2: Nature's Interdependent Co-Arising

Chapter 9   Disposition 77
Chapter 10   Our True Selves 88
Chapter 11   Loving-kindness 105
Chapter 12   Impermanence 112
Chapter 13   Three Marks of Existence 120
Chapter 14   The Cycle of Life 130
Chapter 15   Intuition 139
Chapter 16   The Observer Effect 149
Chapter 17   Ubiquitous Life 156
Chapter 18   Quantum Entanglement 162
Chapter 19   Observer Synchronicity 169

Chapter 20   Field Theory 173
Chapter 21   Alaya-Consciousness 188
Chapter 22   Sudden Awakening 201
Chapter 23   Synchrony: A Different View of Consciousness 218
Chapter 24   That's All, Folks 224

Part 3: Lankavatara Sutra, Chapter One,
Transcribed Sequentially

Chapter 25   The Awakening of Ravana 237
Bibliography 267

CONTENTS

Secret Koans xiv
New Relationship with Self.. 3
The Choice of Consciousness 14
Mind-only.. 18
Separateness 23
Beyond Knowledge 39
Free Will.. 42
Collection 47
The Endless Loop 56
Thou Art That... 73
Generosity: Gratitude's Expression 81
Solitude.. 85
The Central Oxymoron 92
Life in Balance 103
None Other Than Self 109
Life Consumes Life 117
No Story: No Suffering..124
Noble Wisdom 129
Boundless...133
Your Hidden Power...138
Self-realization...147
Thou Art Life...154
The Awareness of an Electron 159
Secret Koans Excerpt...160
The Wave...165
The Living Air 176
Soup..184
Never Surrender 196
Seeds of Change 199
Only This Awareness 230

FOREWORD BY JOANNE MITCHELL

This book is a passion project. I have witnessed many years of perseverance and untold patience, with more rewrites than I could possibly count. My husband is a highly intelligent man, and the difficulty that he faced trying to grasp and understand *The Lankavatara Sutra (Lanka)* and its translations brought him to his knees in humility as it wrote him and evolved his being. Much more than a simple challenge, it may better be described as a calling, his life's work, and he could no more give up than stop breathing.

I confess in the beginning, I did not get it, but my love and admiration for my husband kept me engaged and curious to see what so inspired him. This book seeks to make accessible an ancient work that tells a story, reveals many a truth, and shows scientific understanding we are only proving today. Science is anyway always a work in progress, and it takes imagination and curiosity to even start the scientific discovery with the necessary proof needed. As science evolves, so do we. Can we move from competition and individualism? I'm attracted to anything that strives to unite rather than divide us. This is where mythic and scientific fields meet; as we recognize things we label mystical may simply be things we can't yet prove or understand.

Power, humility; wisdom; truth, rational thought, analytical processing, integrity, self-realization, clarity, equality, reverence for life, unity, passion, choice, and free will, our ultimate gift. So much wisdom is held for us to discover here. Perspective is everything; it determines how we view the world. Are we turning back or turning in? I see it as almost turning ourselves inside out. From this inner knowing, we get it, seeing all outside as an extension of self.

When the unfathomable fabric of our existence becomes impossible to describe with our limited language, I find evidence that poetry can touch a place and hold a space within which my own recognition of truth can emerge. The proof of the magic held in this work for me culminates in the final poem *Only This Awareness*; I get this with great clarity. I realize that over the years watching this book unfold that I, too, have been changed and am now able to recognize what these master teachers of old found worthwhile protecting and preserving for posterity.

INTRODUCTION
BECOMING CURIOUS

Most of us question the nature of existence and feel what it means not to fit in at some point in our lives. These are the ultimate issues of our time that show our lack of purpose and social discontent, which curiously promotes war as an economic necessity. But this curiosity only serves to leave us with more questions.

This book will reveal an ancient science as documented at the end of the Buddhist golden age (500 BC–400 CE). As my most excellent teacher, writing this book has surprised me thousands of times, so I've tried to capture it where I could. Though researching a long-forgotten book may sound boring, it has opened many doors to creating a new life. Have you ever stopped to question "who you think you are" and how that's serving you? Or maybe you wonder about the unexplainable power of manifestation. Is it just wishful thinking, or is it grounded in understanding?

But there's no free ride. Understanding will require learning new concepts and perspectives. As these old ideas will be unusual to you, it is valuable to have a trick to recognize them, or you'll lose the enthusiasm to carry on. Learning always replaces some previous assumption, and this displacement can only be verified when we are surprised; otherwise, you're not learning! So, in reading something entirely new, you'll need to suspend doubt and stay open. This openness will prove its value with each new surprise, and recognizing one will lead to another.

I will share extraordinary practical magic from a marketplace perspective. Unlike more contemplative texts, this book relates directly to worldly existence. My view is one of a simple yogi-householder, well-grounded in scientific materialism. My most kindred Zen teacher says it best.

> *Without any intentional, fancy way of adjusting yourself, to express yourself as you are is the most important thing.*
>
> **Shunryu Suzuki Roshi,** *Zen Mind, Beginner's Mind*

You won't find meditation or spiritual practice taught in this book, though they are central to my life and this study. That is a personal choice, which generally comes out of need when you are ready. Also, many others are far more qualified to teach than I am. However, if you don't already grasp a certain sacredness as a life-giving refuge, you have the possibility of great adventures still ahead. But these methods are technical and depend on the school. They are the subject for someone else whose qualifications and lineage fit the specific teaching. My offering is simply trying to share the understanding of a shocking body of work.

I wrote this book for myself, but I'm publishing it for you. Meditation, yoga, and mindfulness practices make my life better from two standpoints. First, it gives me an increasingly optimistic, accepting, and often humorous world perception. Second, I'm a kinder, more giving, and loving person, which can be quite a challenge for one raised to be a cowboy. Frankly, I like myself better with this aspect of life. In this way, I show gratitude for those who choose to share life with me.

Thirty-plus years ago, I wrote the following prose inspired by Harry Nilsson's video *The Point*. If you feel some sense of surprise, this book may be helpful. It may help you understand what this book has to offer.

> *I see what I want to see;*
> *I hear what I want to hear,*
> *accountable for interpretation*
> *and Creation, I am.*
>
> *My undisciplined mind sees reality*
> *through the reruns of experience.*
> *My habitual thinking calls*
> *a self-fulfilling prophecy.*
>
> *Thinking habits must change,*
> *past emotions must corrupt*
> *my present perception no more!*

*Not controlled or offended
I see you, eye to eye.
No one other than self
is ever responsible.*

*Hobbling fear, wondering desire
or discipline understood,
all thought is prayer,
all prayer is answered.
I call my soul's desire in
quiet moments.
I call other things unaware.*

*Demonstration lifts me,
grace detonates my self-will,
consuming reservation.
Faith is to do, not just believe.*

*Our fathers blamed desire.
Following that way,
I've made myself a hypocrite.
Better to be honestly flawed,
as desire always finds a way.
But in error, I've grown also
to desire less naturally;
falling away as they seem.*

*Selfish desires mature; exchanged
replaced with selfless desire.*

Higher for lower,
mind is the choice and the work.

Desire is the vehicle and source,
commencement of Creation,
God desires us.

Truth spoken is not the whole truth.
Truth is a place beyond my mind,
where I cannot be right
if it makes you wrong.

Love described is hardly its shadow;
relationships invent each moment,
if we are both in this place
there is only one of us here.
In love, there is no other than self.

Joy misunderstood at root,
the only gift I have for you, me.
Joy, more than my right,
is my purpose and my duty.
Finding my own joys gift,
I have something to offer you.

I see what I want to see.
I hear what I want to hear.

Secret Koans, OWM

The Irresistible Desire

Studying the *Lankavatara Sutra (Lanka)* has been an extraordinary gift in my life. Understanding life in our essentially crazy culture was always an irresistible desire. And subconsciously or consciously, I've recreated my life many times, by whatever means necessary, to pursue this one goal.

My advanced years mean I'm probably already dead if this book has any reach beyond my immediate acquaintances. This fact allows me to share the magic just as I see it, no holds barred or stone unturned. Without concern about being accepted or what others may say, this book is for those who can hear it. Today is an opportunistic time when wisdom's seeds have blown from every source, cross-pollinating and growing into something new that may not be so new after all.

> *While our ancestors knew of only one true way, we have a cornucopia of spiritual and physical possibilities. More is known today about the diverse practices and insights of all cultures and religions of the world than at any time in history.*
>
> **Paul Ray, Ph.D. and Sherry Ruth Anderson, Ph.D., *The Cultural Creatives*: p170**

Teachings of the *Lanka*

Finally, this offering is not a translation or presentation of any school of thought. It is not a philosophy, nor is it religious by design. I intend to extract from it an understanding of its science, which existed before Buddhism became a religion in China. My resource, the *Lankavatara Sutra*, first appeared as a Chinese translation in 443 CE. It evolves a detailed understanding of the human condition in scientific terms, which addresses the most common problems of humanity at the source.

So, this book isn't a doctrine asking you to believe anything or sign up for a specific lifestyle. It is only my understanding and discoveries in studying D.T. Suzuki's work. However, I have derived many surprises and insights not commonly found in the orthodox Buddhist perspective.

However, the wisdom content of my writing is ninety percent D.T.

Suzuki, presented in my words from a western perspective. Our two voices became one in the process of translation, editing, and rewriting. So, rather than monotonously, give credit to D.T. on every page. Please understand this fact and keep it in mind.

Also, the original translation is academically tricky for many reasons, but two basic ones dominate. First, the English translation, interspersed with undefined Sanskrit names and terms, requires a glossary text to be readable. Second, in achieving his masterpiece, D.T. left out no detail and spared no description. So, I have rewritten or transliterated only the most relevant passages to fit my thesis, with no Sanskrit and minimum overhead. But it is a technical topic, and it was very challenging not to follow his lead, so when things get too academic, try to move quickly through and return if interested.

The venerable D.T. Suzuki, the Lanka's translator, points out two formal views of knowledge as explicit within the text, formulating my first decision in scope.

First, Right-knowledge, gained by experiencing and grasping the absolute, is the focus of Zen and most mystic traditions. This instruction is specifically beyond my qualifications to teach, except within the practice of Raja Yoga. As experiential knowledge, words and concepts can't express it. Right-knowledge and all the methods leading to it are beyond this scope. But we will have to touch on them lightly.

Right-understanding is the other view of knowledge. It isn't the ultimate experience but makes life better by offering a sane view of existence. This idea is my primary goal because it is approachable in words and, related to my yoga practice, is a practical guide to success in all aspects of life.

Using This Book

There are three parts to this book.

Part 1—Core Concepts
Part II—Nature's Interdependent Co-arising
Part III—*Lankavatara Sutra (Lanka)*, Chapter One, Transcribed Sequentially

Part I focuses on the pathway of first-order concepts necessary to understand the basics of waking up. It will develop more advanced ideas, like understanding why not fitting in is an evolutionary gift.

Part II explores the full range of human potential, advancements, and finally, the Seven Stages of consciousness, or seven first natures as the *Lanka* calls them. It is unlike anything you've heard. It is understood only in a spiraling logic, where each step leads to the next.

In Part III, the first chapter of the *Lankavatara Sutra (Lanka)* is completely transliterated. The first chapter is a template that presents an example of sudden awakening and realizing our full potential.

PART I
CORE CONCEPTS

CHAPTER ONE
THESIS

The most penetrating concept I understood through the *Lanka* is that we live in an utterly not-separate reality. I will begin exploring how I came to this conclusion, the framework of human potential, and where it originates in nature. I'll review common ground supporting existing philosophies and look at the limits of prejudice we've been taught as misconceptions. Because understanding human potential is the *Lanka's* reason for being, I will clarify the boundaries without arguing against either point of view.

Today's problems are so numerous it's challenging to agree on what is most important. In a recent magazine article, millennials ranked ten predicaments in order of importance[1]; they named:

1. Climate change
2. War
3. Inequality
4. Poverty
5. Religious conflicts
6. Political corruption
7. Resource insecurity
8. Educational inadequacy
9. Safety/security/wellbeing
10. Lack of opportunity

Behind all this is the elephant in the room—overpopulation. The good news, these challenges can't be solved in isolation by any one nation or culture. So they force us to work together or pay the consequences. This commonality or not-separateness may be our greatest gift or our only chance. The crisis is a platform for solutions.

---

[1] Loundenbeck, T. (2016, August 30). Science Alert. *These are the World's 10 Worst Problems According to Millenials.* Retrieved from https://www.sciencealert.com/the-world-s-most-dire-problems-according-to-millennials

Getting closer to home are the cultural ills: crime, discrimination, racism, juvenile delinquency, poverty, drug abuse, depression, family disintegration, and social unrest. We see lack of meaning in confusion, disconnection, and displaced values. In some countries, suicide is near pandemic. It demonstrates that our old stories no longer work, and our old beliefs no longer serve us.

Consciousness and Awareness

However, these problems have one thing in common. Humanity's state of mind, central to all our predicaments is self-interest. External control only improves appearances. But, what I don't know about the future and its potential gives me tremendous hope.

Shortly after the 2016 US presidential election, futurist James Burke made a statement on the BBC's *Beyond 100 Days*. His predictions from 1985 accurately showed our cultural changes through connectivity in an eerily precise way. In this interview he revealed our limited thinking, relative to internet technologies as it impedes our progress today:

> *The future possibility that everyone would be educated by it (the internet-Avatars) and that there would be more direct democracy because of it, has not yet happened. And I think that's because basically we live with institutions that were created in the past, with the technology of the past, to solve the problems of the past, according to the values of the past. And we still live with those strapped around us and they tend to hold back quite a lot of things, like the two I've mentioned.*

This is the inertia we have inherited but also sustain. It is the habit which challenges mental wellbeing. The ancient sciences were developed to understand our natural limitations and how to overcome them. We've just forgotten that they were the leading scientists of their time, though disguised in their monastic tradition. Not understanding their language or their worldview, we don't realize they were concerned with our primary problems. The following chapters will introduce their ancient psychology of objective, self-determined, individual choice.

Right-understanding is critical in seeing how we got here. It applies to everyone and can reveal fresh possibilities and new relationships with self. Presented in a western frame of reference, we can address cultural confusion and the modern world's lack of purpose.

> *Crushing vastness created the diamond*
> *in pressure, heat, stress and pain.*
> *Here abides the individualist world,*
> *Creation bleeds in every limb,*
> *though not yet surrendered to extinction.*
> *Recycled values held as sacred, true, and moral*
> *solved problems of comfort with unhealthful sustenance*
> *and unconsidered wellbeing diseased.*
> *Self-interest rules all: exposed absurdity,*
> *indecent prejudice, systemic discrimination,*
> *poisons of the multitude, our crushing vastness.*
> *But I am the multitude and the masses are me;*
> *focused on the particle, I miss the wave.*
> *But you are the particle and we are the wave.*
> *Thou art connected,*
> *separation the delusion, destroys humanity.*
> *Turning back from compulsion and ignorance,*
> *one person at a time is the revolution.*
> *Out there is really in here.*
> *Ours is the problem.*
> *Thou art the only solution.*
> *Thou art the diamond.*

New Relationship with Self, **OWM**

CHAPTER TWO
LANKAVATARA SUTRA

The Indian subcontinent was the world's leading home of science, encompassing psychology, biology, and physics, two thousand years ago. The monks dedicated to objective observation built their science on Vedic foundations and proved their theories in colleges of debate for nearly a thousand years.

The first universities were monasteries founded by some of the most objective, rational, and wise people to have ever lived. They thrived for hundreds of years. Through public debates between the masters, they revolutionized human knowledge by delineating the relative and the non-dual.

But then, unthinkable murder and destruction arrived with the invasions of barbarians from the north, the White Huns. Monks hurriedly gathered their scraps of wisdom in a collection of fragments called the *Lankavatara Sutra*. It has survived in a handful of translations from the original Sanskrit, but its lack of social acceptance protected it from popularity, misuse, and distortion.

Many vital ideas were misplaced as ancient knowledge was translated and transliterated to accommodate each culture's ruling dynasty and religion. But around the year two hundred CE, invading armies destroyed their culture at the pinnacle of Buddhist development in science. Fortunately, they had completed documenting a science of being. These were the ancestors of modern Buddhism, all but erased from history in India and finding refuge in other countries. [2]

The Buddhist teachings parceled out to monks were transplanted across Asia or assimilated into the local religions. The texts that survive were rewritten or cherry-picked for cultural and political acceptability. Some fit the political whims of leaders; others did not. However, due to the ancients' extreme diligence in saving the *Lanka*, we owe an enormous debt.

Buddhism evolved to influence many cultures as it was scattered to the wind or annihilated and assimilated. Partially recognized, the *Lanka*

---
[2] Allen, C. (2003, revised ed. edition). *The Buddha and the Sahibs.* John Murray

was often used to create new scripture, though its scientific content was obscured by cultural interpretation. However, as ancient books go, few predate this one, which was protected, transported to China, and used in religion and philosophy over the generations. The *Lanka* found little popularity outside the library, as it is very challenging to understand and does not comply easily with any doctrine.

Two common aspects of transplanted Buddhism are entirely absent in the Lanka. They are concepts that make forgiveness or salvation accessible to religions worldwide. The first is gaining spiritual merit by serving others or doing good deeds to develop better karma. The second is being forgiven for past sins through suffering for others. In Christianity this second idea is the fulcrum from which the miracle of salvation derives. As the basis for most religious redemption, this may be revolutionary heresy and people who questioned it in the past, have met with the rath of believers. Defining this question as one of belief instead of religion, we will look at Dostoyevsky's short story *The Grand Inquisitor*. But to reiterate the question, these concepts of good works and martyrdom are culturally significant, but completely excluded in the *Lanka*, where rigorous logic is applied to human existence as a science of self-determined awareness.

The Lanka does not directly address the concepts of redemption, except in their absence. But the first Patriarch of Zen apparently referred to them as wishful thinking to the horror of Emperor Wu of Liang (504–49 CE). I think his point was that awakening is a personal experience and is not about cultural acceptance or even religion in these terms.

This discernment is the *Lanka's* razor edge of objectivity, where self-determination and full responsibility for oneself take the place of moralizing and rationalizing. Rather than submit to the convenience or displaced accountability, the *Lanka* demands reality just as it is and psychology we might call behavioral self-determinism.

Emperor Wu is said to have chastised a holy man for a self-serving translation of the *Lanka*. But, legend also has it that in seeking credit for his patronage of Buddhism, he alienated himself from Bodhidharma, the first patriarch of Zen. Told his good works meant nothing to his awakening, the Emperor sent the master packing.

The Lanka also upset the nobles of ancient China by challenging the prevalent slavery system, as it left no room for class discrimination. This dark underbelly of culture was hidden by protesting the *Lanka's* non-religious practices and the displacement of religious doctrine, which served the masses almost as well as it did the masters. So, the *Lankavatara Sutra*, set aside around fourteen hundred years ago, appears as many points of brilliance in later scripture.

A Fresh Perspective

The *Lanka* is critical today because it offers an objective take on humanities' state of mind. Though less glamorous than media, its perspective is practical and not sugar-coated. What sets it apart is its integration with life sciences. This viewpoint sees quantum theory and metaphysics as reflections of nature. But, in case of doubt, you should always take only what is worthwhile to you and disregard what is not helpful.

The ideas of how life works best took root in the *Lanka* but sprouted into Zen several hundred years later. My take is pragmatic and psychological, which D.T. Suzuki might say is idealistic.

> *Some say the world is illusion,*
> *but it is as it is, quite real.*
> *Our perception is the illusion,*
> *as the world is our creation*
> *and Mind-only is its source;*
> *mind created illusion.*
> *Some say thought is delusion*
> *but thought like reality just is,*
> *and the delusion is we are that thought*
> *and its outcomes, the world.*
> *Quiet the mind, the world and thought*
> *are neither illusion nor delusion*
> *without preferences, it just is.*

***Reality*, OWM**

Mind-only is the next foundation stone in the *Lanka's* architecture, psychology, and mysticism. It is the source of reality, which requires ultimate responsibility for everything in the individual's life. Metaphysically, Mind-only is also a growing awareness of life's conscious fabric, which moves gradually toward broader levels of belonging and effortlessness.

Practice and Discipline Over Doctrine

Fundamentally, the *Lanka* prioritized objective reasoning and self-determination over religion and salvation doctrines, which is identical in many respects to Rene Descartes' "I think therefore I am" in the Age of Enlightenment, as it also addressed the suppositions of religion.

Much of the most valuable life science was de-emphasized over time except among the initiated inner circle of Buddhism. What remains to assist the masses was thought more accessible as cultural philosophy. However, our ancestors' down-to-earth science remained hidden for safekeeping, which D.T. Suzuki brought to light after seventy generations. D.T. also emphasized that understanding is useless without breaking from compulsive, habitual thinking to realize we are the awareness we create.

However, Buddhist teachings, such as mindfulness, are sound science, even by today's standards. This guidance was the ancients' intention. At that time, theirs was the most objective science on the planet and studied from an objective perspective; modern science has validated their findings for the first time in human history.

Buddhist sects such as Zen, Chan, and Tibetan Vajrayana have direct ties to an ancient Buddhist group called Yogachara, which appears to be the Lanka's source. The name, Yogachara, leads us to think it reflects Yogic science combined with the Buddha's wisdom.

> *Ancestors saw through the delusion,*
>
> *the misdirection, religion, and*
>
> *philosophy, once upon a time.*
>
> *What thou art?*
>
> *The lost science of being human.*

Understanding is your first step;
quietude the method.
Thou art enough.
Thou art allness and oneness.
Millions followed as great stars shown for a thousand years,
reaching far beyond the mind to return again.
Driven underground, exported, morphed,
recreated in our image to our needs.
Lost science or hidden understanding
reformed as religion and philosophy.
But where did it start?
What have we missed?
What is there for me?
Thou art that, in what thou art.

Can the Insanity Be Cured? OWM

Understanding the *Lanka* isn't easy, laden with monastic dictates and harsh judgments. This smokescreen may be another reason the *Lanka* didn't reach popularity, saved on a dusty bookshelf until the time was ripe. Its message is beyond knowledge, belief, and imagination. Its perspective supports every form of creativity and scientific discovery. Its magic seed, carried by Bodhidharma to China (470 CE), defined the starting point of mindfulness, which eventually grew into Zen.

A theory or idea only establishes
a possible source of reality;
suchness is the quiescent nature of mind,
which grasped
gives the yogin certitude of Mind-only.

Lanka, Sagathakam, sloka 270

I begin with this first transliteration from the Lanka as its most central principle. It clarifies that your ultimate and most profound answers always have been and always will be only within you. Suchness here isn't just the natural state of a quiet mind; suchness is the mind's serene nature. The *Lanka* calls it self-nature. There is implicit magic between the two perspectives—the first looks from the outside-in as becoming suchness by quieting the mind. The second is more Zen-like, seen from inside-out as being suchness as one's essential nature. I attempt the second viewpoint wherever possible.

Furthermore, this sloka or song identifies Zen's mindful heart and every faith's still quiet voice. Applying this one sloka reveals the source of unchanging knowledge, which is the only resource necessary for an authentic, fulfilled life.

Certitude will require much deeper penetration to understand fully. It is a leap beyond the ordinary certainty of belief because it doesn't depend on knowledge, understanding, imagination, or even thinking. Certitude comes only from direct experience of the non-dual or absolute, which may sound completely off the wall. But if you bear with me, it will make sense.

D.T. says all this is accomplished in discarding discrimination, which sounds like a good idea in our everyday usage. However, it is much broader than age, sex, or racial discrimination. It is the intellect regarding the world.

To summarize, the mental state of suchness is first a quiet mind, which doesn't validate prejudice, opinion, judgment, or even preference. Though subtler than thought will grasp, everyone experiences it in stillness. This first step of listening intuitively is to encounter the unchanging knowledge at our core, our still quiet voice. By reducing the focus on what we think, we face the wave action of what we feel and understand without labels. As mind-bending as that may seem, it opens the door to a whole new world.

> *Thou art the mind's quiet center,*
>
> *where no disturbance may enter.*
>
> *Your nature is apparent in effortless being;*
>
> *ineffable, unflappable, and peaceful.*
>
> *Comprehending this one thing; sitting in it, resting in it,*

striving ceases for love of harmony,

center of the universe and creator of worlds,

your part is the world's reconciliation.

Not Larry or Sue, not Mom or Dad, not master or slave.

Center of the cyclone is your quiet eye of being.

You are the peace which no-thing can disturb.

This suchness is the nature of your quiet mind.

Thou art that! Tat twam asi!

Suchness, OWM

These foundational concepts will come pretty fast. So to reinterate, we've just touched the surface of:

- Not-separate reality: missing this point we live in delusion of separateness.
- Mind-only: Our reality is the creation of mind and engaging this leads to greater levels of belonging or awareness.
- Suchness: The mind's quiet nature.
- Certitude: Certainty born of direct experience, unrelated to belief.

CHAPTER THREE
A USER'S MANUAL FOR BEING HUMAN

The *Lanka* challenges us with esoteric symbols and mystic secrets. Its work describes the inner workings of being born and becoming human. Though, often defensive, presumptuous, and out of step with current literary tolerance, it isn't easy.

So, the rest of Part I is a user manual for being human. In modern terms, it is being true to yourself and learning to live without games, masks, or stories.

To research this book, I studied two English translations of the *Lanka*. The main one was translated from Sanskrit to English by D.T. Suzuki. I also read a translation from Chinese to English by Red Pine to clarify difficult sections. Because of the complications of reading the text, I will explain how my work came into being and use it to introduce a sequence of essential concepts.

My work wasn't a linear translation. D.T.'s translation was available online, accessible to Microsoft Word. So, using computer search correlations, I built a glossary of untranslated Sanskrit terms and concepts as they appear throughout the text. Then I edited the text to include my translations and modified various ideas around context. Over the previous decade, I created a contemporary understanding with multiple references, translations, and extensive online study.

Sanskrit names of people and things were very challenging, as the text uses them as metaphors for vague ideas of the context within a Vedic cosmology. To understand, I followed individual concepts from beginning to end, cutting out relevant sentences to compare in glossary documents. But eventually, it led me to a deeper meaning in simpler terms. This work isn't a translation because I can't separate my conclusions from the original text. It is transliteration or simplification of arcane text. So, all I provide is an intimate vision of its gift to me.

In the following quotes, the Lanka addresses the primary modes of consciousness available to us. It is from the *Lanka* as translated by D.T. Suzuki and Red Pine with commentary. Judge the difficulty for yourself.

> *D.T. Suzuki: "[Further,] three modes are distinguishable in the Vijnanas: (1) the Vijnana as evolving, (2) the Vijnana as producing effects, and (3) the Vijnana as remaining in its original nature."*
>
> **Lanka, Chapter 2, section IV**
>
> *Red Pine: "And the different forms of consciousness, Mahamati, have three aspects: an unfolding aspect, a karmic aspect, and an intrinsic aspect.*
>
> *Commentary: The unfolding/transforming aspect (paravrtti) aspect is produced by causes, the karmic (karma) aspect produces effects, while the intrinsic (jati) aspect remains free from causes and effects. The Sanskrit here for "aspect" is also lakshana."*

Red Pine, *The Lankavatara Sutra*, Translation and Commentary

After several years of study—expanding, cross-referencing, defining terms, and listening to my intuitive voice— I understood the same text to say the following:

> *Our understanding is that consciousness has three modes. First, it indiscriminately collects concepts, experiences, emotions, and things.*
>
> *Second, it creates cause and effect; doing tasks; taking action.*
>
> *The third mode of consciousness remembers its inherent nature, unaffected by collecting or doing.*
>
> **Lanka, Chapter 2, section IV**

This section from the Lanka is a brilliant statement of suchness as remembering one's inherent nature. But more importantly, it points out the essential functions of awareness, which is our first clue on how the mind works.

We begin with indiscriminate collecting, which provides our reference for future thought, programming the subconscious with memory, actions, and consequences. Here we build a sense of identity, but it is with the collections rather than our inherent nature. So, we interpret life by what we do, what we own or what other people think, etc.

This external identification makes all our interactions subjective, based on thoughts and feelings rather than facts. In this way, circumstances control our lives. As we operate in reaction, habit, or compulsion, finding what we want is everything, and others are irrelevant unless they serve our desires. Life, in this way, is a matter of fixing the outside world to suit us, though it's constantly changing beyond our control. But the tremendous loss is an authentic connection with others, rather than being fully present and available. This unavailability is our soul-killing misfortune.

The second mode of consciousness is doing which includes objective reasoning. It interacts in two distinct ways, either open-minded, impartial and even-handed or cold, uninterested, and unemotional. The first manner of interaction resolves many problems in consciousness based in collecting as the self-interest is balanced with good manners. But the second manner of interacting with the world creates the perfect storm for dislikeable people, as they show the world its irrelevance in a nasty aloofness.

However, besides the obvious advantage of being nice, the objective doing consciousness can be used as a gateway to the third form of consciousness, remembering one's inherent nature. Here we have walking meditation methods, the rigorous ceremonies of the Zendo, and yoga in various forms, which work on developing suchness.

Countless temporary fixes allow us to step beyond the subjective mind, such as dance, music, singing, gardening, making love, etc. But their effectiveness is limited by long-term misidentification. So, we often embrace the temporary fixes and become addicted, but the root problem persists. The actual shift from subjective awareness is where we begin to move away from the logic by which we have created a tangible reality.

It may be uncomfortable to consider because what seemed solid might be realized to be fragile and illusory. This view is what it means to experience the absolute or non-dual; our constructed reality is seen for its imaginative qualities.

When we can touch on mindfulness as no-thought, through relaxation and concentration, we are liberated from collecting and doing as judgment disappears. Though these methods work in isolation and with focused intent, they are disciplines not suited to ordinary circumstances. Most people cherish the experience without understanding it, but others are so insecure and afraid that they may become violently emotional. And unfortunately, outside the group's control, objective and subjective minds deceive each other and fiercely defend ego identification in their natural relationship. Which is another way of saying we can't just think ourselves into suchness.

Besides the process of using the objective awareness in "doing" to entrain mindfulness, another doorway exists in grasping the non-dual essence of life. It is a shift into non-dual awareness, the disposition of Mind-only.

On the surface, this statement conflicts with the previous "not thinking our way into suchness," the distinction is that the essence of Mind-only occurs as a sudden awakening within the subconscious and the method is whatever path you choose. But it's harder to comprehend, though more sustainable in everyday circumstances.

It may already be apparent, I have the disability and gift of dyslexia. It makes writing extremely difficult and linear progression impossible. But it's probably why I could parse and collate the massive *Lanka* into a dozen or so dominant concepts, which have been misconstrued through philosophy and religion. They might be lost otherwise. You will need to bear with my challenges to grasp an amazing opportunity for human understanding. In practical terms, it evades even our wisest and most enlightened. The Lanka reveals a powerful perspective shift, which can give the reader the power to create life as the best expression of themselves. But first you must push through the challenge of my rambling abstraction, which may serve to exhaust the unprepared. To make it a little more accessible, I've created poems to say, insinuate, and telegraph what my limitations can't express otherwise.

> *Thou art human being.*
>
> *In survival sense-consciousness is always busy*
>
> *collecting and doing.*
>
> *Dominating ordinary life, the human-collecting covets*
>
> *thoughts, experiences, feelings, and things.*

Served by the human-doing, taking actions, thinking, or talking.

But thou art human being, meant to be the quiet master,

remembering each moment.

Nothing sticks to mindful suchness.

Here thou may orchestrate conscious collection and artful doing.

If freedom is thine vision all relaxes its hold,

empty unaffected by outcomes,

neither collecting, doing, judging, nor controlling.

Serenity to see the fabric of life,

oneness is the suchness of all things.

Thou art that!

The Choice of Awareness, OWM

Non-dual Awareness

The *Lanka* embraces our world driven by self-interest but with a non-judgmental perspective. What seems like compassion and open acceptance is actually the vastness of non-dual awareness as seen clearly in nature. The wind blows, water flows, and the sun shines without judging our worthiness for its gift. There is no right or wrong, no good or bad, just nature, wild and free. In non-dual awareness, life struggles are like a butterfly emerging from the pupa. The pain and difficulty must be accepted and go unmolested because to assist the butterfly in its escape is to cause its death. The art is when the pain and difficulty are met with acceptance and gratitude.

Mind-only is the Lanka's primary gateway to the non-dual because it addresses everything we see and experience. It is the naked awareness of being but without the mind's modifications in prejudice, opinion and judgment.

What we usually experience is modified by what we already think before the event even happens. Experience is colored and maybe warped as we hold onto opinions and preferences. In this distortion we identify with thoughts and hang onto them as truth, acting as if we are the outcomes of thought. In this delusion, the world appears to be separate and alien.

However, since our mind creates this reality, we have the power to reimagine our life at any time. We can reimagine it at any moment by pausing to observe the circumstances as our own creation. Identifying our complete responsibility is the creative spark of ignition.

An exercise might help. Pause and examine what you are, not who you are. Try to find that part or function which is you. In honesty, it naturally feels like we are these thoughts and attributes or maybe a function of our thinking. But, that's the misidentification of every animal. We have a chance to see beyond it.

We are the one who controls thought and is aware of existence. But the magic is we can re-identify at any point, taking control of our discernment and changing life's experiences.

My insight is I am essentially an awareness. It is waking up to who's in charge by taking a new view of personality as a delusion. And as I master the mind, I engage free will when my view is undistorted. This is my most natural state, beyond being offended or external manipulation. It is a non-dual awareness, where, like nature, judgment, opinion, and preferences are no longer in control, as in non-discriminating. It's fair to say I've replaced many beliefs with one belief or viewpoint, which with exercise and experience, becomes a new perspective.

In his last years, Ram Dass (Richard Alpert) liked to say his mantra to keep the mind clear, "I am loving awareness." He pretty much hit the nail on the head for me.

Of course, I've begun with Zen's core principle, mindful suchness. Then, in this section, I've expanded into the cornerstone of *Lankan* psychology, conscious choice as collecting, doing, and being. But these concepts are not as philosophical as they may seem. They are practical observations as to the nature of our existence. In this same way, we will begin from central concepts throughout the text and work our way to higher-order ideas.

Rudolf Steiner may have described the *Lanka* when he said: "The best books are those we have to take up, repeatedly, books we cannot understand immediately but have to study sentence by sentence." This aspect is why we get something new every time we read a great book. Because we've gained a fresh perspective and grown in understanding, we can grasp what we missed before with each read.

> *Suffering, which comes from discrimination*
> *and identification of self*
> *with form, desire, and thought.*
> *It ceases in non-discriminating awareness, suchness.*
> *In this realization,*
> *there is an end to ignorance and craving,*
> *often masked as accomplishment and achievement.*
> *Where judgment, opinion, likes, and dislikes*
> *no longer control,*
> *here the observed world is seen as the creation*
> *of one's mind itself.*
>
> **Lanka, Chapter 2, section VI**

Here, the *Lanka* lightly dispenses with discrimination and the effects of worldly preoccupation to reveal the logic we've been talking about. This section also points out that even accomplishments and achievements derived from misidentification are ignorance and craving. It's interesting to find the achievements or accomplishments which were not derived from separateness.

This point doesn't disregard a good work ethic; it just prioritizes health over industry. But, failing to see our control and responsibility for thoughts, we are asleep. The other way round, we react out of habit under the control of circumstances. So we never see things just as they are, and we are never free.

However, the shocking reality is that most of us have very few moments outside of our identification with form, desire, and thought. We are constantly projecting meanings that may not serve us. Even when we get too busy, we get sucked back in. When that happens, we can refocus on who's actually in charge and gain a little peace of mind. But this is where the method comes in. Like Ram Dass's mantra, "I am loving awareness," we need to be prepared with something that naturally brings us to the present moment. I can't over-emphasize the importance of coming back to the present.

An old T-shirt of mine says, "Don't just do something. Sit there." But it's not so simple as a curious mind wants to explain this paradox. If it's so easy, why doesn't everyone get it? First, everyone doesn't want to get it. But the answer to why is that it is naturally how every other animal and we are programmed. We will explore ego development per the *Lanka* from conception to maturity to understand it. Maturity means emotional development for more profound levels of belonging. So, we can call it awareness.

Realizing quiet mind, effortless being.

Displaced in preference, discrimination, and prejudice.

What you think and what you want;

labels, stories, or habits blind you.

But desires and humanness are just the syllabus

in this life's lessons, repeating till mastered.

This is the doorway to effortless being,

as suffering burns out compulsion and false-imagination.

Replaced in connection

by joy, love, compassion, and peace.

Right here, right now,

Thou art suchness

where judgment, opinion, likes, dislikes

and even imagination no longer control.

Here the world is as it is.

Projection ceases as Mind-only is observed.

Thou art not the mind.

Mind-only, OWM

Tucked away for hundreds of years, the *Lanka* provides missing links between ancient and modern psychology. The structure of consciousness is fascinating, explained as coming out of the subconscious. That space behind the mind is where memory is stored, and dreams form. Unlike cognitive psychology, it is available to healing as we stay awake, fully present, right here, right now. This connection is already allowing modern psychology to consider simple practices and new models of treatment side by side with mindfulness practice.

As we will see, the *Lanka* embraces a holistic view of science derived directly from nature. Only in the last hundred years has quantum mechanics and particle physics given us the tools to consider its science which embraces ubiquitous life and its entanglement. But these verifications are only the tip of the iceberg, where the ancient science lays out a new paradigm on what it means to be human.

CHAPTER FOUR
THIS BOOK IS NOT THE LANKA

This chapter will share a few challenges aimed toward the vision of not-separateness, which come from a deliberately chaotic and convoluted text. Though its challenging form may be all that saved it, only D.T.'s translation of the original *Lanka* allowed me to understand. Without his work, comprehension would have been impossible.

But, the *Lanka's* message began long before the venerable D.T. Suzuki, and it leaves me in awe that so many generations spent their lives creating it for posterity. It was a miracle that they gathered the pieces together before their persecution became murder. Though forced to collect details hastily and smuggle them away, we did end up with a library of information. My explanation of the process should aid your grasp of its essence or give you the tools to inquire independently.

Buddhism was a significant player before its displacement from India. A couple of hundred years before its destruction, it was at its zenith with University-level education and a whole class of people dedicated exclusively to expanding the knowledge of humankind. Buddhism was probably the state religion of India for an extended period, as Emperor Ashoka (268 BC to 232 BC) built monuments to the Gautama Buddha and his successors. Many monuments stand today, but western science proved out much of the historical record, which was previously second-hand, was compiled in China, generations after the Indian conquest. During the occupation, it was rediscovered by self-trained archaeologists, mainly the British. [1]

Buddhist non-violent principles may have led to its downfall, as religious forces and the White Huns invaded from the north. Buddhist monks wouldn't defend themselves, and it made them soft targets. Those not murdered or brutally silenced fled to save their lives and sacred teachings. My fascination begins with the unsung heroin named Prajnatara, who I imagine to be central in gathering the *Lanka's* fragments and secreting them away. It is uncertain, but likely it was a female monk or nun, rather than a male, entrusted with safeguarding this ancient treasure.

Prajnatara, the twenty-seventh matriarch or patriarch of Indian Buddhism, fled to southern india, leading a group of monks and devoted followers. The Huns conquest failed to penetrate all the southern states, where remnants of Buddhism survived in places like Tamil Nadu and Sri Lanka.

Buddhists don't all agree that Prajnatara was female, however. But in times of mass murder and war, treasures are hidden in creative ways, so the Korean perspective on Zen history inspires me most. However it is widely accepted that Prajnatara was Bodhidharma's teacher, and it was she who instructed him to carry Zen's seed to China. Years later, it is also documented that Bodhidharma gave his heir, Huike, the patriarch title, and the *Lanka* recently translated into Chinese.

The Intended Reader

It is vital to remember the *Lanka's* intended audience. It was compiled for monks and teachers within Yogachara. As you might have noticed from earlier examples, the most significant challenge with existing translations is mixing English and Sanskrit within the text. Because of this, I have translated Sanskrit terms entirely, giving only a few reference points.

The second challenge is the text is more akin to Hinduism than modern Buddhism, coming out of ancient India. This point is apparent in the *Lanka's* first chapter, where the setting is Lanka, as in Sri Lanka. The primary characters create a sequel to the Hindu Ramayana, where Ravana is no longer a demon stealing the wife of Ram. He is the inflated ego representing us all. In the sequel, where his demons and nature spirits join him, Ramayana tradition introduces the characters and scene. I've sought the middle road, drawing on yogic lore, Hindu scriptures, and Buddhist traditions to seek out the essence. A thousand words are about fifty in transliteration. So, at least, I've greatly simplified your effort in reading.

Besides the difficulty in language structure, the imagery is often degrading. The following example compares the habitual ignorant mind and false-imagination in an array of unflattering comparisons, from which the more offensive adjectives have been discarded. You may ask why sharing this is important, and the answer is to clarify the central problems that we don't know how to relate to the brutal descriptions of our condition, and we need it simplified to understand.

> *Consciousness in habitual thought*
>
> *and the delusion of separateness;*
>
> *sees existence changing continually,*
>
> *like a river or clouds in the sky;*
>
> *like a monkey mind, always restless,*
>
> *indiscriminately feeding, and never satisfied,*
>
> *like a fly in search of unclean things and defiled places.*
>
> *So, life goes on reanimating dead beliefs, memories, and experiences,*
>
> *in an endless cycle of compulsive consumption*
>
> *and unconscious fantasy.*
>
> *Compassionately understanding these tendencies,*
>
> *one bears witness to the common patterns of life and*
>
> *the insubstantiality of ego-identification.*
>
> **Lanka, Chapter 2, section XXIV**

This verse is extruded from esoteric and negative connotations. Besides being condensed and distilled, the scope is soft-peddled to make it accessible.

In the introduction, D.T. points out that there were only two kinds of people for the ancients: the enlightened and the ignorant. The ignorant people live ordinary lives dominated by collecting experiences and ideas while seeking pleasure and comfort. But they're missing the meaning and purpose of life.

I am soft-selling with terms such as the "cultured" or "modern" in regard to humans and cultures, where D.T. Suzuki accurately translated Sanskrit as "deluded" or "ignorant." My word choice is audience driven, since everyone is subject to separateness, the blunt negativity does not serve our potential. So I've tried to give credit for two thousand years of education.

It also must be admitted that the *Lanka* is a religious and specifically a monastic treatise. So, where a monk might see D.T.'s "egolessness of persons" with reverence to the Buddhist doctrine of "no-ego-soul." I avoid arguing whether or not the soul exists.

To make the ideas available to the broadest audience, I've focused on the ego's formless nature. This idea also appears in the *Sagathakam*, where the *Lanka* supports the soul as a necessary construct while arguing no-ego-soul in the next breath.

> *Your separateness is the illusion, not the world.*
> *Thou art not alone nor disconnected.*
> *Only habitual thinking makes it so.*
> *Collection and consumption dominate but never satisfy.*
>
> *Stop experiencing life at the whim of emotions and compulsion.*
> *Throw out belief and disbelief; and the many possibilities will amaze.*
>
> *Thou art the unchanging knowledge.*
> *Compassion recognizes ego's story as only story, lacking substance.*
> *The story, a theory of false-imaginations, is the delusion.*
> *Thou art one nature with all nature.*
> *Thou exists in everything and everything exists within you.*
>
> ***Separateness*, OWM**

Existing Translations

The existing translations of the *Lanka* from the original Sanskrit may be counted on one hand. They are mostly Chinese, with a single Sanskrit to English translation by D.T. Suzuki. The Sagathakam included in D.T.'s translation is usually omitted as it holds the most controversial slokas. Other translations also use different chapter structures because the original text was an array of fragments without organization, which was likely unedited.

D.T. Suzuki is probably the most renowned translator of Buddhist texts into English. But, even D.T. often admits confusion. His translation is readily available on the internet for more curious readers. But, his book is the only authentication for my work. As I've tried to explain, even that is a stretch.

My work isn't merely an explanation and not nearly a translation. What you read are lessons from fifty years of practice. I take full responsibility for all errors and misinterpretations. Every time I read my manuscript, it changes. It would never see publication if not for my wife's part as editor and muse.

The second English translation I've read is by Red Pine. His version differs in many respects but seems more in the spirit of mainstream Buddhism, with many eloquent and penetrating observations. It is much easier to read and expresses the grace of Buddhist scripture.

D.T.'s edition though rougher was translated directly from Sanskrit to English, giving me confidence because it passed through only one other person's understanding. However, Red Pine's translation helped clarify transcriptions, though it wasn't used in the analysis, lacking computer access.

Additionally, this book isn't Zen. That would require more thorough training and expertise than mine. My understanding comes from a synthesis of my experience, first as a Yogi, then a Zen and Sanskrit student. I rely on Shunryu Suzuki Roshi in *Zen Mind Beginner's Mind* for straight to the marrow Zen. As my primary companion and resource, it is joined by the *Hsin Hsin Ming*, translated by my late friend, Richard B Clarke. Both books have been the focus of lifelong contemplation. However, Suzuki Roshi best expresses the importance of a proper attitude in life and suchness.

> *In the beginner's mind there are many possibilities, but in the expert's, there are few.*
>
> **Shunryu Suzuki Roshi, *Zen Mind, Beginner's Mind***

Peeling Back the Layers

Another way of saying not-separate is interdependent co-arising. This description, coined by Thich Nhat Hanh,[3] came through Buddhism as dependent arising. As the *Lanka's* central problem statement, our delusion and cultural insanity are not recognizing oneness underlying reality . Interdependent co-arising is oneness in it's dynamic form. It conveys oneness in that life only exists within other life, as we will see explored in the physical world.

However, in not-separate, anything and everything is curiously possible. We are free to imagine anything we wish, and by connecting the dots, we can play in a world filled with synchronicities. This is accomplished with an open mind seeking the surprise of learning, as the ultimate treasure.

> *Truth spoken is not the whole truth.*
> *Truth is a place beyond my mind.*
> *Where I cannot be right*
> *if it makes you wrong.*

Secret Koans excerpt, OWM

I've requoted this part of my old poem to reflect the difference between relative and absolute truth. Truth as a concept should never be relative or how could it be truth? And being absolute, it must also be non-dual. So, there can be no opposites such as right or wrong.

The *Lanka* can leave the door open to all possibilities because it sees no truth is whole, complete, or constrained. It allows all facts their relative value but accepts no absolutes in dualism. Trying to explain *Lanka's* essential message, we will reveal and demonstrate its reflections on the science of living.

Structurally this book is peeling back layers of meaning for modern understanding. So far, we started with examples from the *Lanka*, which build a foundation for suchness and mindfulness. The basic steps present a spiraling logic that can reveal itself as we go along and prepare for profound

---

[3] Hanh, T.N. (1999). *The Heart of the Buddha's Teaching*. Rider

surprises. These are the highlights which demonstrate the conceptual base for mindfulness:

- *The quiescent nature of the mind, suchness* (*Sagathakam*, sloka 270)
- *Three modes of consciousness, collecting, doing, reflecting* (Chapter 2, section IV)
- *The observed world as a function of Mind-only* (Chapter 2, section VI)
- *The insubstantiality of ego-identification* (Chapter 2, section XXIV)

CHAPTER FIVE
THE PATH OF MEANING

I've looked for common sense understanding my whole life because the world around me seemed utterly nuts. But that's not the most evident approach to mindfulness. Seeking meaning is almost frowned upon in Zen; searching for the absolute as an experience. Luckily, the *Lanka* defined a meditation to explore meaning, which I've used as a template to create my understanding.

Quieting the mind to experience the absolute is a bit like climbing Everest to catch the air. Few people grasp that it's not there, it's here, and it's not something, it's nothing. But that's the problem; the subtlety of no-mind or the suchness of Mind-only are just words. Having spent fifty-odd years in daily meditation, the absolute hasn't been an absolute. It's been a surprise.

Since the *Lanka* provides a formula for what's essential and what's not, its definition forms the focus for everything in this book. Clarity is the most difficult, though no less critical, because words and meaning have little to do with our natural awareness. But understanding helps remove the blinders. We will only be looking at the qualities of two things from a few perspectives.

> *What is the meditation to explore meaning?*
>
> *It is practiced by those having broken the habit and pattern of unconscious life by understanding that ideas of self and other-than-self are futile.*
>
> *In this, one examines the meaning of not-separateness and the stages of conscious development.*
>
> ***Lanka*, Chapter 2, section XXXVII**

No Division

Though these stanzas may seem to be philosophy or psychology, they are much more significant than they appear at a glance. The *Lanka's* whole proposition is to show us that we are not alone and not separate. But there is a big problem right from the start. The stanza asserts that to explore meaning, we must have broken the habit of sleepwalking through life at the whim of habitual thought and already get that we are not-separate. But this is a work in progress for most of us.

As described before, the prerequisite is waking up and recognizing that what we are is awareness and personality is just a story we tell ourselves. However, this stanza further presents a perspective that ideas of not-separateness are futile, which is realizing what serves us and what does not. But, this is not fanciful or make-believe; it is practicality in waking up. But breaking old patterns is like collapsing a spell cast by the mind. The secret to recognizing a compulsive trance and learning to live each moment consciously is no small task, and getting it intellectually, is barely the first step.

Our challenge is to separate science from doctrine. Our observations may validate the theory but not prove its truth as it unfolds, deepening inquiry. However, verification will only be available in the practitioner's experience.

This path has two aspects: "why" as in meaning and "how" as in method. Since this book is specifically about interpretation, only one factor is significant. The practice doesn't require our explanation since techniques and styles come to light through various traditions, such as Zen, Chan, yoga, Vajrayana, and many others.

Luckily for a tenacious old practitioner like myself, the *Lanka* doesn't close doors on either doctrine or science. This openness allowed me a bias toward science and will enable others to continue exploring whatever their preference.

The *Lanka* emphasizes exploring "the meaning of not-separateness," bringing to light the development stages. It may seem as if we've already dug into this aspect of the path, where in fact, we have just begun.

Our growth journey begins from this starting point, redefining ourselves authentically as a tiny part of the whole and thereby understanding the stages and processes along the way.

The entire *Lanka* is the exposition of not-separateness whose focus is actualizing the intangible aspect of Mind-only. This concept may sound like the *Lanka's* enlightenment, and it may be as an arc of belonging.

> *The first principle and essence of awakening is self-nature,*
> *which arises in seven kinds.*
> *Stages from delusion to enlightenment,*
> *they range from self-isolation to oneness,*
> *struggle and suffering to transcendental bliss,*
> *Exclusive obsession to total inclusiveness,*
> *Self-centered struggle to no-other-than-self devotion.*
> *What's in it for me to effortless belonging.*
> *Dog-eat-dog reality to interdependent co-arising*
> *Ignorance to Noble Wisdom*
> *Intolerant discrimination to Suchness*
>
> **Lanka, Chapter 2, section VI**

At first, we belong only to ourselves, then others as in family, tribe, or team. Then shell begins to crack and we belong to no one. These are the stages of suffering or the first three kinds of self-nature. Beyond them, we enter the stream of awakening to grasp our self-natures of formlessness, non-dual rationality, certitude, and perfection. The path has no conclusions, but we may encourage it through right-understanding, mindfulness, and loving-kindness.

Learning Without a Teacher

The cornerstone practices of Zen, per D.T. Suzuki, present the most lucrative opportunity for an intuitive penetration into life. At the heart of Zen, gentle mindfulness and meditation practices work best in the shadow of a teacher, a group, or a partner. However, for most of us without a teacher, a group, or a partner who gets it, we must find what works for our sanity.

Another great benefactor of Zen in the 20th century, Shunryu Suzuki Roshi, made the most eloquent case in *Zen Mind Beginner's Mind*. His thesis goes back to the concept of the original mind, quiescent mind, or natural suchness. He presents the practice of mindfulness and Zazen as enlightenment itself, a moment-by-moment choice to unclutter our perspective. In his experience, enlightenment is sitting in stillness, listening to the breath, and let go of thoughts to experience our true selves. It couldn't be more natural and straightforward, though it evades most of us.

Not doubting the great Roshis and knowing from experience their truth of non-cognitive awareness, there is a time we must rise from the cushion and engage in everyday life. Immersion in life is where we need sustainable support. As a student outside the Zendo or Ashram, my sanctuary is trying to understand. It provides somewhere to nourish growth. This middle way is where the *Lanka* has been my user manual for being fully human.

Recognizing our limitations, the opportunity moves on to meaning, demonstrating not-separateness and the growing stages of awareness. We will look at experimental psychology, microbiology, and particle physics while laying out the elements of conscious development until we reach an unusual perspective. Though I doubt the experience itself is exclusive. It is somewhat unique in terms that may serve you. Still, it is a solitary journey that can only be alluded to in understanding.

The theory of "not-separateness" looks for sameness, connections, or resonance. This view rebirths an old paradigm that few have understood and even fewer experienced. So, we must turn the process of examination back on ourselves.

Many years ago, I was introduced to a story that was used to feed the fires of religious rebellion in the 19th century. A Russian named Dostoyevsky wrote it. It feels hazardous sharing this revolutionary tale because it's bound to be misunderstood, as it was initially used as a means to assign blame to destroy religious institutions of control, like the Catholic Church. But it's not only about the possibility of religious corruption, it points to the basic flaw of human psychology, which is bound up and limited by self-definition in systems of belief. I've come to understand this message differently to be a reflection of human nature fostering separateness, entitlement and exclusion. So, it is very useful in understanding conceptual difference between the *Lanka* and religious scriptures. Where our problems are systemic, looking at us is looking at systems.

I hope you can realize that to grasp a non-separate reality, we must understand the natural hypnosis of instinct, which is a problem that blankets all our cultures. My retelling of this story is straightforward, not sugar-coated, nor intended to raise descent, anger, or any negative response. It is looking at us in our darkest corners without assigning fault! It is the reflection that we all create systems of belief to control our children and subordinates, but it naturally comes from instinct. This story is a reflection of human nature, limited to the insanity of beliefs which justify any means to an end.

The Grand Inquisitor

My story begins in Asia but neither China nor India. My search for truth started long before Zen was more than a name to me. My story began in Russia.

The original requirement to read Dostoyevsky's *Grand Inquisitor* is lost in memory. Still, it is likely due to a young woman teaching freshman literature at a Florida University Extension in Panama (1970). At nineteen, several influences tried to redirect a dangerously angry young man, but the story gave that anger a systemic focus. It seemed to describe the mechanism of institutional control through religion and cultural misdirection, or that's what I incorrectly thought at the time.

Understanding systemic pretences are essential to any objective search for meaning. Otherwise, the redirection of cultural norms will obscure authentic meaning and replace it with subtle manipulative alternatives.

The Grand Inquisitor's story goes something like this:

Of the brothers Karamazov, Ivan tells his brother Alyosha a story in several thousand words, which I will summarize in a few hundred.

> During the most murderous part of the Spanish Inquisition, Jesus Christ decided to visit Seville. When he showed up, he was immediately recognized. People flocked to him to repent and be

healed. This wildfire went on until he raised a young girl from the dead.

But, as it would happen, the Grand Inquisitor was just then, passing through the street, and saw everything. His voice, still ringing in the people's ears from a hundred burnings the day before, commanded his guards to seize the man.

Locked away in the deepest, darkest dungeon, the Grand Inquisitor himself visited Jesus, angry for his disturbance. Christ was mocked, threatened to burn at the stake, and told he had no right to add anything to what was said some fifteen hundred years before.

The inquisitor intended to reveal the error of his ways in offering freedom to the struggling, suffering, sinful people. Couldn't he see that their mutinous selfishness prevented them from happiness outside of servitude?

Jesus was advised to understand his grave mistake in rebuffing Satan's three temptations of turning stones into bread, casting himself from a great height, and ruling the world. Because the same miracle, mystery, and authority had become the most successful formula ever, by which the debauched commoner could sacrifice their freedom for security and happiness within the church.

The Grand Inquisitor praised the deception and mocked Christianity, saying that the people, deceived by the *miracle* of Christ's sacrifice and forgiveness, embraced the church's generosity, which only returned them the smallest portion of their labor's fruit. The ruling elite maintained the deception as a great *mystery*, circumscribing redeemable sins and taking on everyday sin in a show of forgiveness. Lastly, the church provided the *authority* so the wretched masses, though weak and sinful, could love Jesus and serve as raw materials to the high and mighty.

However, the Grand Inquisitor also looked to the future, seeing that freedom, intellect, and science would one day break the spell of orthodox control. Leading many away from their respective communities of belief, human advancement would deliver the common man and woman into unfathomable mysteries, technologies, and discoveries that nullified the old ways.

And here we are

The older man continued by saying that these three subterfuges, miracle, mystery, and authority, were then used to leverage the people's strongest tribal instinct for a community of believers. This leverage separated factions to fragment their power, manipulate their fears, and set one belief against another, assuring sustained control. This separation left all people in cycles of restlessness, confusion, and unhappiness; the weak were controlled by fear, while the elite were controlled by greed.

In telling the story, Ivan was interrupted by his protesting brother Alyosha on numerous occasions. He was alarmed that his brother should suggest such a tale, much less consider publishing it. It meant their ruin. However, Ivan continued the Inquisitors damming rant at length.

The wicked old man said that the benefactors of Christianity had corrected Jesus' great mistakes and, in his name, actually served the evil one, and this lie was their secret. They had accepted what Jesus had rejected, all in the name of delivering the masses from their weakness.

Three types of disobedience received three types of consequences. The most disobedient would merely destroy themselves in suicide. The feebly-disobedient would destroy each other in war and conflict. The remaining feeble and unhappy people would return to the illusion of belief, irrespective of evidence to the contrary. Surrendering their freedom, they would say, "Save us from ourselves."

Gloating, the wretched villain bragged about the enslavement of humanity. Given the idea of undeserved happiness, shown to be hopeless and impotent, the people would rejoice in sins redeemed. Under the leave of a higher authority, they would confess their sins to feel a little better and cheerfully submit to the yoke.

Finally, the Inquisitor relished the irony of death and hopelessness in Jesus' name. The institutions would continue to lure and control the ignorant in the deceptions of miracle, mystery, and authority.

Ivan's story ends with the Inquisitor frustrated to hear nothing from Christ, who lovingly kisses his aged tormentor. Eventually, rather than burning Jesus, the old priest turns Jesus out into a back alley, with the threat never to return or face the worst possible end.

As Ivan finishes his story, his brother protests the indignity; such a story would mean ruin to them all. But Ivan argues that the higher truth justifies it even in a horror story. And he chooses to set aside personal consequences.

Dostoyevsky's work was used to feed violence in a ferocious time and he died shortly after the publication of *The Brothers Karamazov* in 1880, which included *The Grand Inquisitor*. Coincidentally, it is said that the Tsar's secret police had investigated a disturbance at a neighbor's residence the night before his death.

Though painfully obtrusive into the religious beliefs I grew up with, the story reveals what only seems like the architecture of subjugation. In every excruciating turn, it is seen in suicides, war, conflict, and domination worldwide. However, it's not a conspiracy or church corruption. It's human nature.

It shocked the world in the nineteenth century and was central to social revolution because people blamed institutions. But it's not something corrected with violence being a basic human survival instinct. It appears anytime anyone develops power over another. You can see it in our *miraculous* standard of living, the *mystery* of science and technology, and the *authority* to control money or resources. However, we've forgotten the lesson today, and it's still reflected through every form of institutional control. I could labor on and show this pattern in academics, medicine, business, etc., because it's in every person as the instinct of control.

You will also recognize systemic delusion in individuals around us. It presents itself as a wall of attitude, self-righteous entitlement among the affluent, and defensive armament among the oppressed; the reflections of greed and fear by different names.

Of course, the original formula still includes religiosity anytime it redirects from objective understanding and direct experience. So, I've had to apply it to the *Lanka's* transliteration, challenged to separate meaning from the legacy of religiosity.

Objectivity and hidden meanings required detaching from the *miracle* of enlightenment to look at relevance in the ordinary world. Translating from the *mystery* of Sanskrit gave voice to an accessible understanding. And separating it from the *authority* of Buddhism is the justification for my perspective as the unattached observer.

As an angry young man, I was assigned to read and study this work fifty years ago. I embraced a revolution of neither belief nor disbelief, which provided an openness that anything is possible. It developed as scepticism, understanding that miracles and mystery, not personally experienced right here and now, maybe veils to create control, which as a young soldier during the Viet Nam war, I clearly recognized. Though doubt is a necessary part of my rationality, it has also been the limiting factor of discovery. But in the case of my own limitations, it seems I must first doubt my own preferences and judgment to find what just is.

Lastly, I was fascinated by the inquisitor's visionary view of the future, which is specifically where I see the world today. As religion becomes secondary in the younger generations, we see a world searching for a new basis of meaning and purpose, which the *Lanka* has offered me.

Accepting the *Lanka's* thesis that humankind suffers from a delusion of separateness, we will take a scientific tack to show it fitting our conventional viewpoint, mostly showing up as nature's common sense.

CHAPTER SIX
ENLIGHTENMENT

Enlightenment isn't the most important thing we can learn from the *Lanka*. As our parents' and grandparents' beliefs no longer worked for us, we rebelled against their domestication. We naturally replaced a belief in religion with a belief in technology. The hypnotic sitcoms like *Father Knows Best,* and *My Three Sons* were replaced with video games and the funny, irreverent *Simpsons*.

However, we haven't solved anything. Our minds have only replaced old belief systems with contemporary substitutes, and the trap is even more fierce. The loss of anesthetic media and institutions of faith pushes more people into the disquiet of not belonging. Replacing belief is not a solution. So, we must look to examples that do work.

The awakened focus is on what is experienced directly, not filtered or interpreted through preference. Not held up to belief; it is seeing things just as they are. Though we might see it now, that's not enough for it to stick. It's not something. It's nothing. It is not a belief we can repeat and reinforce as we do with the sound bites of advertising. Removing obstructions of our domestication is only permanent in our subconscious, where the change is below the mind, in our fabric of being. Though difficult, this evolution of consciousness is the most important thing we can do for humankind.

My mother-in-law has a homily that sums up our modern confusion. "Often wrong, seldom in doubt." Our current narratives and assumptions create our disorientation.

Enlightenment and Oneness

An example of this confusion is much of what we consider spiritual. Let's look at our past definitions:

- The Age of Enlightenment points to our shift away from doctrine and superstition to rational discrimination and valid thesis as we broke away from religious domination.
- The hippy generation struggled with the misconception that enlightenment was becoming an all-knowing God-like consciousness.
- Today people promote abundance or fulfillment of desires as enlightenment. Or enlightenment is oneness, described as a stage of total joy and bliss within the endless peace of unconditional love.

According to the *Lanka*, all these definitions of enlightenment may be valid if they go beyond separateness. Surprisingly the closest description to the *Lanka's* perspective is our cultural norm, the Age of Enlightenment.

1. *the action of enlightening or the state of being enlightened: —spiritual knowledge and awareness, which frees a person from the cycles of birth and rebirth. (Buddhism)*

2. *a European secular ideology of the 17th and 18th centuries emphasizing rational analysis, verification, and individualism rather than the traditions of common belief. It was heavily influenced by 17th-century philosophers such as Descartes, Locke, and Newton.*

The classic Buddhist definition isn't a good fit. The description of spiritual enlightenment is accurate, but it barely concerns us as a guideline to escaping rebirth. Of course, it's the *miracle* that doesn't make sense in everyday suffering. Not to argue reincarnation, why do you want to escape? What's wrong with just making this a better place for incarnation?

A goal or focus would be more relevant if it removed suffering for humanity right here and now. Most Buddhist, Hindu, and Yogic schools focus on an individual's primary motivation for liberation or escaping reincarnation. It may be childish or unenlightened on my part, but it seems passe or out of sync with human desires and cultural development.

There are groups in Buddhism that focus on Nirvana, or sustainable bliss in life, rather than complete liberation. This idea is more valuable to our modern problems, but its limitations are unclear. Its methods appear to be more religious than my thesis. Rather than an understanding of existence, the method can be purely practice, like chanting to an altar or the worship of heavenly beings. Of course, I have deliberately not engaged the many sects, to maintain a healthy ignorance.

The second definition represents the Age of Enlightenment or western rationality: "I think, therefore, I am" (Descartes), which we will address in comparison. This framework is what I know best, and so it is what I will apply to understand our possibilities and potential.

My focus is not enlightenment but an understanding that allows the greatest joy in this life, just as it is. I will reveal my conception of enlightenment as effortless belonging, which I get from spiritual experience with the *Lanka*. But first, we need to understand what it means to be fully awake or self-realized and how we got trapped in the first place. Then we might look at absolute or non-dual aspects beyond our understanding.

The following sloka describes what might be the European intellectual movement a thousand years before its birth, along with some insight related to our human predicament.

> *The cultivated man or woman sees themselves standing on the truth of their own knowing.*
>
> *They profess brilliant ideas based on what can be known and sensed,*
>
> *but in this way ultimate truth remains beyond them.*
>
> ***Lanka, Sagathakam*, sloka 266**

The Age of Enlightenment is our dilemma and our salvation, without which we might still be burning people for witchcraft. Our breakthrough can be that we don't know what we don't know. We are not wrong to approach life rationally, expecting verification for what we call real, but evidence shows things are not working to our benefit. Furthermore, believing only in the physical world and beliefs as truth leads to crippling judgments in the silence of conscience, intuition, and inspiration.

I've come to see western enlightenment in slightly different terms. The *Lanka* points out that much more is unseen by the microscope and mass spectrometer than is seen. Real learning comes as a surprise that exceeds beliefs, existing knowledge, experience, and imagination. Otherwise, it's no surprise.

> *I think, therefore, I am.*
> *Not this body, not this mind, not thought nor their outcomes,*
> *not knowledge, nor any function of mind.*
> *I am this awareness.*
> *Thou art that, beyond your own knowing.*
> *Thou thinkest and confuse yourself with its outcomes.*
> *In this formless infinity, I am and thou art.*
> *Existing as concept, I gather and define, but it is not me.*
> *In formlessness, where I am, thou art also.*
> *Where does my concept end and yours begin?*
> *Could it be there is only one of us here?*
>
> **Beyond Knowledge, OWM**

Rational Objective Discernment

Truly honest rationality lets go of belief to grasp larger truths that current knowledge alone can't define and indeed restrict. The *Lanka* asserts rationality and objective discernment as the principal weapons of inquiry while warning against our burden of prejudice, which enslaves our view compulsively.

We might think the *Lanka*'s view of metaphysics would be at complete odds with the rejection of all things unseen and not understood. Where scientific materialism discounts supernatural phenomena, the *Lanka* generally gives minimal description throughout the text, except to open the possibility.

Descartes' argument was a revolutionary leap forward in the power of reason and free-thinking. His philosophy propelled the world out of darkness. His demands for pure reason, fuelled by the fires of the Grand

Inquisition, are synonymous with the *Lanka*'s rigorous objectivity, which was initiated by a profusion of gods, beliefs, and social chaos. Starting here, the *Lanka* also understood the enlightened human potential of free-will, beyond habitual thought based on obsolete knowledge, false-imagination, and self-delusion.

However, we have put belief on a high pedestal for many generations, equating it with understanding, knowledge, and truth. Belief based on separateness creates fear, prejudice, and discrimination. It may have been what Descartes questioned, casting doubt on the reliability of sense perception and preferring pure reason. We will examine this in the Five Aspects of Sentient Beings.

Descartes' *"Cogito ergo sum"* ("I think, therefore, I am") sits comfortably beside the *Lanka*'s central thesis of Mind-only. In a relative sense—or when definitions are limited to what is seen and known—Mind-only defines our perception of reality as the mind's manifestations (I see what I want to see, I hear what I want to hear.) So, the two philosophical axioms even resemble one another as sound bites, though they originate from vastly different western and eastern traditions. In a subtler context, both concepts may be the same.

If it were easy to have an open, unfettered mind, our usual preferences, opinion, prejudice, and judgment wouldn't govern most human interactions. The *Lanka* adds to western rationality because these barriers to connection are only in total control, as long as they are unseen or unconscious.

When we see that thought, personality, and desires are all self-creations or Mind-only, their impediments can be held accountable as potentially flawed. In this observation, the *Lanka* supports western rational enlightenment as a primary step to higher awareness.

This stage is the relative aspect of Mind-only, or what it does for us in everyday life. Here thoughts, opinions, and judgments can be moderated or discarded. First, we see the controlling aspects of our prejudice; then, we can change our reactions with a pause, open our minds, and consider what is clear of distortion. As a core practice called "the observer," this awareness reflects many aspects of mindfulness and the dawn of suchness.

The *Lanka* distinguishes unconscious belief as an obstruction to heightened awareness and free will.

The yogin is beyond the philosophies of belief, non-belief, materialism, and skepticism.

Grasp the cycle that everything we think we create;
everything we create we experience; everything we experience we discriminate.

Discriminating desire, we cling to it, clinging to desire we crave it;
craving highjacks all thoughts creating addictions.
Craven thinking amplifies suffering.
In this addicted cycle of mind,
there is no free will.

***Lanka,* Chapter 6, section LXXXIII**

Western enlightenment and the *Lanka* appear to coincide in freedom of thought and free will. In the east, people aspire to liberation, which is the highest level of self-determination in the west. This commonality is our cornerstone, and the *Lanka*'s gift points out our simple choice that freedom is just controlling our natural tendencies. Like delayed gratification, we must pause to enjoy the present.

In some Zen retreats, a bell is rung every fifteen minutes to have participants pause and mindfully consider this moment. It may sound academic, but these cycles are more relentless than physical addiction. The obsession is our craving experience, defined by body, mind, and what we think. To control craving, the normal solution is curbing our dependence on stimulation. However, trying to step out of it for a day may seem impossible. The panic of craving is the fundamental addiction, which sadly leads to an unconscious compulsion that we barely recognize doesn't match our aspirations.

However, the freedom the yogin represents may seem impossible: to live without a system of belief or disbelief. But, they demonstrate the critical definition of non-cognitive awareness or the quiet mind of suchness. With practice, we may decrease or even set aside who we think we are, but the undercurrent goes much deeper than intellect, and we must look at its source.

These ideas may even make sense, as we all have experiences of quiet reflection. But when taken intellectually, losing our definition of self can be terrifying. We desperately hold on to this sense of identity and panic if it gets disturbed by job loss, relationship failure, or losing whatever label we cherish the most.

Though we assume that thought and personality constitute who we are, the *Lanka* identifies beliefs as fluid and persona as a temporary abstraction. But, if we have no permanent definitions of identity, we may ask, "Who else would we be?" or "Who are we then?" The answer isn't simple. However, these ideas we call ourselves, act like an operating system, running silently in the background, filtering and controlling our thoughts until we take control.

Mind-only isn't saying there is no reality; it only means we will never know authenticity or true freedom, oblivious to the mind's natural operation. Oblivion robs us of free-will because it is unconscious of choice and alternative realities.

To be awake in this way is the *Lanka*'s psychology as un-conditioning. It is beyond the limits of natural evolution, the influence of the environment, and our cultural domestication. This self-determined awareness includes total accountability for reaction, interpretation, self-nurture, and optimizing our inherited nature. This view is also another way of seeing, "I think, therefore I am."[4]

In the simplest of terms, stepping beyond this identification with thought, to a thinking awareness, is what it means to be awake, but thinking is not enough by itself.

> *Free, free at last, not the shabby right to do as you please.*
> *Thou art free in each moment from the bondage of mind;*
> *compulsion, habit, and false-imagination.*
>
> *Thou are free in the truth of being,*
> *regarding emptiness for its unchanging knowledge.*
> *Not needing to know, control and prejudice vanish.*

---

[4] Descartes, R. (2008). A *Discourse on the Method*. Pomona Press.

All things past have loosed their grip,
habit, disposition, discrimination owned,
compulsive reaction curtailed.

Thou art free in solitude between thoughts,
in a space of being, emptiness, oneness, and allness.

Collecting, doing, being but letting go of outcomes,
unhindered by belief or disbelief, loose from predisposition,
co-creating with intention and selfless ambition.

Acceptance of inevitability, what is … is freedom,
not what was or will be.
False-imagination fades, preference loses sway.

Openness with all life, openness to joy, openness to love,
openness to effortlessness.

Thou art free as higher purpose makes it so,
all according to plan, just not my plan.

Free Will, OWM

To be awake is to be fully accountable for every aspect of life, so there's never anyone to blame or criticize. And though it may sound simplistic, staying awake is our greatest challenge and incredible gift as a species distinction. Other animals may have the advantage of not being deluded into separateness, but we can still claim an opportunity to awaken from a construct of our own making.

Just as Buddhist psychology primarily analyses the mind and its functions, the *Lanka* starts with the creation story of ego as the five aspects of sentient beings. To understand these concepts is to understand our limitations and opportunities for evolution.

I've come to experience that enlightenment isn't a fixed state or stage.

It is a path of increasing inclusion and belonging, which becomes effortless in a protected environment or sanctuary. Another way of seeing it is in relationships of effortless belonging. Like the first few years of passion, it feels delicious, but with a deeper partnership level and subject to far fewer ups and downs. It is sustainable in the mutual nurturing of each other's growth. This is the arc of my marriage.

So far, we have explored a few encapsulated points of the *Lanka*'s psychology and how they might relate to wellbeing. Summarizing where we've been so far, the four concepts of mindfulness include:

- The nature of mind at rest as suchness
- Consciousness modes of collecting, doing and being
- The nature of reality created in Mind-only
- The insubstantiality of ego

We've added to this the Lanka's core argument that we suffer most because we live in a delusion of separateness. So, the best way to explore a path of meaning is through non-separateness and describing the stages to grasp it.

Then we explored the archetype of institutional control. So, I introduced religiosity's test: avoiding miracles, mystery, and authority. And lastly, we've looked at the holy grail of western culture straight in the eye. Belief, which is confused with truth, may be the most enormous extinction effect since the meteor took out the dinosaurs sixty five million years ago. That is unless we wise up.

CHAPTER SEVEN
THE FIVE ASPECTS OF SENTIENT BEINGS

Now we've contrasted the *Lanka's* objective discernment to the Age of Enlightenment, whose wisdom has transformed the world well beyond the recognition of any previous generations. It's time to open Pandora's box with the *Lanka's* understanding of our animal sense consciousness and the entrapment it creates.

The story describes how we, and every sentient being, construct our unique view of reality and who we think we are. The process outcome is the ego-self. As every culture has a creation story, the Buddhist culture had the creation story of ego-identification. First, it is a map of becoming a sentient, self-aware animal. It describes how we accumulate self-image and personality based on collections of sense experiences and preferences that may or may not serve us. Understanding its implication is a key to conscious growth.

Assembling these fragmented concepts from the *Lanka* would have been much more complicated but for a story told by Chogyam Trungpa Rinpoche in *Cutting Through Spiritual Materialism*. His storytelling guided my exploration and created a framework for my understanding. Though his teaching was a Satsang with American Dharma students, my description is just a layman's view that examines psychological constructs from within the *Lanka*. In effect, we are narrating this story together.

> *Sentient beings, characterized by five aspects:*
> *form, sensation, thought, concept and sense-consciousness.*
> *Only form has physical substantiality.*
> *What is unique to an individual,*
> *exists only in the formlessness of mind.*
> *The wise recognize the aspects, including form;*

creations of mind and subject to impermanence. Mind creations obstructing view of one's true self, obsessed with individuality, caught in preferences, translated to self-centered belief.

***Lanka*, Chapter 2, section LII**

The five aspects of sentience are essential in demystifying the flow from form to formlessness. Just as life functions within the body, the habits we call personality are only ideas with no structure in physical reality. Of course, this means we are also only ideas, which we create and then must cling to.

The Crisis of Identity

It's like holding onto the side of a boat in deep water. But, being formless, we have no fixed sides to maintain stability. The inconstancy makes our self-image fundamentally insecure, so we cling even harder to external verification. The insecurity may appear as an underlying sense of panic, anger, defensiveness, or violence. It seems to be all there is, and all we have to define our lives. But in this construct, we are at the mercy of circumstances beyond our control, starting with physical appearance and extending to the delusion of what other people think.

To make it worse, these formless compositions that makeup sense-consciousness are mutually dependent. They can't discern this sense from that thought and how it creates awareness. So, they create labels and boundaries to defend ego identification, violently striving to maintain their self-image. This defensive uncertainty is where our first fear resides, not in letting go of ego but in misunderstanding how sense-consciousness works.

But it's a given that we can't function without ego in this world, and our fundamental insecurity becomes a huge cause of suffering. We are willing to die for our identity, but worse yet, we are also willing to kill for it. The clearest example is the fact that good men defend what they believe in, on both sides of every conflict. Then they destroy their goodness in acts of atrocity. This destructive cycle starts with our first crisis of identity.

Well, if I'm not the body, I'm the mind. If I'm not the mind, I'm ego, or maybe I'm a writer, a father, or a Yogi, and my list goes on and on. These are only my natural collection of labels that can be understood but not easily discarded because they don't exist anywhere. Besides being an ego creation story that only looks at the space of mind, this is also the creation story for our subconscious. It is another level altogether, as we will see. For now, the point is who is in control, my animal domestication, sense-consciousness or formless me?

> *Form to sensation gathering thought,*
> *building ideas, arranging patterns of concept.*
> *You like it, you don't like it or you don't care.*
> *Sense-consciousness is born of form but thou art not!*
> *Thou art born of formlessness as sense, thought, and concept*
> *and yet much more and less.*
> *Collection begins the substance of thought*
> *as pattern and habit, confused for totality.*
> *Repetition reinforces,*
> *preference confused with truth.*
> *Thou art not form, sense, ideas, or concepts;*
> *not habits of prejudice, opinion, and discrimination.*
> *Collection is living, to gather the wood, to collect the water.*
> *Collection is not life.*
> *Thou art life*

Collection, OWM

Though the story begins with form, everything we think we are, is a construction of the mind that arises from formless sensation, preference, and thought.

As every beautiful human being finds flaws in themselves compared to others, we naturally believe we are the body. Later we may have thought we were the mind, but eventually, we assume we are the outcomes of thought in response to an outer world. This gives us someone else to blame.

What's the Diffference?

This is the natural development of every animal operating in habit and instinct. A difference may occur in our rationality, but even that is unclear and unquantified. However, what may not surprise you is that the only difference begins with procreation.

> *Conception, subconscious life-force infuses first seed of consciousness;*
> *The fertilized egg, life energy mixes the red and white*
> *to create a sentient being.*

> **Lanka, Sagathakam, sloka 157**

Every sentient being began development by combining two life forms. Per the *Lanka*, cell growth begins from an immeasurable magic spark, a life-force that doesn't leave everything to DNA nor discount it. I will explain why this makes sense, talking about biological communications theory.

However, the most common excuse for the shortcomings of human children is, "It's my parent's fault!" And it is true that, based on living eggs and swimming sperm, our bodies are derived from our parents. But everything we do with it, is our responsibility. So, presented with the fantastic vehicle of human existence, we must choose either to understand it or continue to live life habitually. In driving the easy choice of habit is like letting go and closing your eyes, life is an accident waiting to happen.

Most of us are somewhere in between caring enough to understand or suffering enough to need it. An applied understanding can seem unattainable, but each of us starts out with everything necessary when we quiet the mind.

The outward characteristics that distinguish us from our animal origins is our level of rational communication and cooperation, which allows rapid adaptation, as seen in science, medicine, and technology. But the formless world is where we distinguish ourselves.

Sentient beings are anything that feels, perceives, and experiences a sense of self subjectively. Therefore, this concept applies to more than just humans. In Trungpa's story, his main character is a monkey, which can represent humans who are oblivious to anything beyond physical reality. As habitual beings, who rarely move beyond sense-consciousness, it's naturally the easiest thing to do.

How did it happen?

The process of ego creation starts with form. From conception, the fetus rapidly grows and begins to experience life through sensation, which is the second aspect of all sentient beings. So, the baby responds to sensory stimuli generating feelings and impulses even in the womb. These first reactions have three classifications: attraction, aversion, or indifference, which you will recognize as preference.

These basic impulses are seeds of thought, the third aspect of sentiency. Response patterns come from repeating sensations. Pattern recognition becomes a desire for pleasing sensations, rejection of discomfort, or apathy. The earliest organization of thought differentiates sense-feelings according to preference. "Do I coo, cry, or just carry on?" And so complexity grows with each sensory pattern and abstract identification. "This is my toe in my mouth. Oh wow, I have lots of them!" Well, not quite yet.

At this point begins the fourth aspect, concept-judgment and disposition patterns. It equates to creating and collecting reactive patterns to inform judgment and, eventually, opinion.

I use the word disposition to describe this fourth aspect of sentient beings, whereas D.T. uses "conformation" and Trungpa uses "concept." The primary reason for my choice is clarity regarding the collection of concepts, and the second is to identify the link to inherited tendencies. Disposition includes notions and the predisposition to be like our parents and grandparents. Non-physical traits are a strong validation for the concept of life-force, even if we never knew or had any other contact with our parents. Inheritance can come consistently through us as attitudes, behaviors, addictive inclinations, and mental health, but for which we never build concepts under parental influence. Of course, DNA may be used to explain physical effects, but the subtleties of disposition are a long way off.

Concept collection or disposition is where family inheritance kicks in, and the inherited traits can be overwhelming. However, shared personality traits or tendencies are easily understood by reviewing studies on identical triplets separated at birth and reunited as young adults. (If you haven't seen it, I recommend the factual events depicted in the film *Three Identical Strangers*.)

However, it may be unique for humans that the naming and labeling process goes through our first filter, categorizing likes, dislikes, or apathy. These sorting mechanisms are fundamental to most waking interactions but can indicate immaturity.

As a child, we don't pause to look beyond our compulsive responses. But as adults, we expect more understanding, openness, and acceptance. The enhancement of these characteristics is the most incredible gift and the primary sign of waking up. The signs of immaturity or sleep walking include:

- Blaming outside circumstances and other people
- or taking the guilt of the world on oneself.
- Making everything about me,
- making everything about you
- Being a victim
- or predator
- Being offended
- or offensive
- Being at the mercy of what other people think
- or acting out against what other people think

From the immature level of collecting concepts and developing disposition, we enter entrapped levels of discernment and discrimination, the fifth aspect of sentient beings, sense-consciousness. But, we choose to succumb to habitual thinking or we can question what's going on at this level.

*As the collection of sensations, the self arises
subjectively formed, subjectively controlled,
bound in hallucinations of desire and deed.
Without objective source, erroneous perceptions and
misinterpretations project a false-imagination
corrupting the awareness of reality.*

Lanka, Chapter 2, section XXIV

Sense-Consciousness

Our experience is like the painter's pallet, on which sense, thought, and concept create sense-consciousness. Seeing this is crucial in accepting our natural confusion and inconsistency. The source of discord or dissonance is between the two opposing aspects of the psyche, subjective and objective awareness. It is different from cognitive dissonance, between our actions and beliefs, which only addresses the most fundamental anti-social behaviors. What the *Lanka* points out is our choice or the internal argument between just living life as it comes or attempting to control one's destiny by recognizing an awareness beyond animal sentience, beyond thinking.

In this regard dissatisfaction is your friend. Even when we learn to align our beliefs and actions, thought is still subject to confusion. Fragments of sensation compile into intuitive understanding which often competes with preference and domestication. So, it is natural over time to not believe the story that we live, only going through the motions to maintain a comfortable habit. The disconnect can't be helped because the reality, of what we perceive intuitively, doesn't align with the story we hold up to support life choices, comfortable habit and even our checklist of identity. The suffering in life is nature's way of getting your attention.

We all acted out through emotional reaction and compulsive obstinacy as children. It would be easy to write this off as a child's first step. But this is also the first stage of human awareness, described in the *Lanka* as the first kind of self-nature. As a stage of awareness, it reflects social immaturity and narcissism and is the tendency to make everything about ourselves. Worst yet, relationships are treated as a means to an end, seen in transactional relationship failure.

The first three kind of self-nature lie within the aspects of sense-consciousness, by which we create and define separateness, identity, and the illusion of independent existence. Understanding our conceptual self-creation reveals our opportunity for sudden awakening from their physical limitations and the fourth stage of awareness, embracing our formless self-image.

> *Modes of identity are mutually dependent,*
> *linked to create habitual thought,*
> *solidified into personality and disposition.*
> *With no independence from sense limitations,*
> *elements, concepts and reactions exist in an ever-changing flow,*
> *without static reality, actuality, or fantasy.*
> *Understanding fluidity derives from their source.*
>
> *Personality has two sources*
> *Inborn tendencies and false imagination.*
> *It is the relation of self natures, pools of awareness.*
> *But this relationship of awarenesses is neither being nor non-being.*
> *It is only the imagination of who I think I am.*
> *Imagination does not become real with discriminating judgment,*
> *it is still only a mirage of my making.*
> *But in setting aside personality, clinging ceases*
> *though nothing is lost.*
> *This is to enter the stream.*
>
> *There are three tools by which to awaken.*
> *First is the view to set aside personality.*
> *Second is the questioning of one's projected reality.*

Third is progress in doing the next right thing.
These are knots which bind the delusion.
And when finally broken
Coveting, anger, fear and folly disappear.

Lanka, Chapter 2, section XLIX

This idea of personality is also an ever-changing function of abstraction or imagination. Like the river of Heraclitus, who said, "No man ever steps in the same river twice," for it's not the same river, and he's not the same man.

Personality may be the dreamlike process of compulsive life, commonly regarded as sleepwalking. It creates an illusion of reality, further complicated by our misidentification of self with what we assign as meaning. One such frequent hallucination we've all encountered is getting angry that someone has set out to hurt our feelings or offend us, which is later determined to be caused by some unfortunate circumstances of theirs, having nothing to do with us at all. This insecurity is the first fear response, anything threatening our fragile self-identity. But the whole idea of observing ourselves taking offense or realizing an impending compulsive reaction is a spiritual practice that we explore from two directions a bit later on.

How many sleepless nights have you experienced worrying about something you interpreted or perceived incorrectly? Life, as we naturally experience it, is usually full of mistaken meanings. Or, as Alcoholics Anonymous labels it correctly, "False Evidence Appearing Real," based on future events that may or may not occur. But what other choice do we have, and how can any different understanding make sense?

This entrapment is something that began long before our cognitive awareness. From conception and especially during our formative years, we build a subconscious foundation of imaginary ideas, concepts, or dispositions based on other people's baggage, unintended hurts, and accidents without cause. We make meaning from the random play of life. So, this same misinterpretation and projection process continues into adulthood, accounting for prejudice, opinion, likes, dislikes, and judgment. Many such errors also form our understanding of right, wrong, good, bad, love, hate, etc., but most critically, they control how we relate to others.

We project our version of things onto what is there, thus we become completely immersed in a world of our own creation. A world of conflicting values and opinions. Hallucination in this sense is a misinterpretation of things and events.

Chogyam Trungpa Rinpoche, *Cutting Through Spiritual Materialism*

Sense-consciousness, the fifth aspect of being sentient, is complicated and confusing, leaving us helpless in subjective reaction to an outside world. The issue here is our habitual thinking, in that unconscious responses rule us when we are unaware of their control. In this confusion, the compulsive tendency is to embark on fantasy, where we create lives tossed about under unexpected circumstances, searching for fragments of self-image.

In this way, most people's disposition is a dream creating projections of a world of their own making. According to the *Lanka*, when we generate delusion for ourselves or buy into the shared illusion of materialism, it is according to how we have misinterpreted reality. The trick then is to observe the natural tendencies and intercede, adding mindfulness before the point of reaction or mental response.

Our personalities are continually being built, beaten around by life, and constructed by external situations. Enlightening as the Five Aspects of Sentient Awareness are, they only show us the mechanism of ego development, not the cause of their entangling nature, which the *Lanka* also addresses in the eight forms or portals of consciousness.

Free will is "the imperative" to this discourse. We can choose to react unconsciously or mindfully. Our choice depends on prioritizing free will over being fooled by habitual patterns. There are four reasons why our senses predominate waking consciousness:

1. *We cling to the external world as the only reality.*
2. *Our clinging to form becomes a habit of false reasoning.*
3. *We protect identity through the security of likes and dislikes.*
4. *We are too eager for experience and its variety of pleasures.*

form *Lanka*, Chapter 2, section IX

The Five Aspects of Sentient Beings

These reasons for clinging to sense-consciousness are pivotal in showing how and why we maintain a tenacious hold on our story. Sticking to our narrative often derives from our fear of losing something, such as our sense of how life works. We fear what we can't see, touch, or haven't experienced. So, we cling to what we know—our comfortable routines and habits. Our version of facts helps us feel safe, limiting our potential and controlling our choices. And, of course, our story is most concrete if we see the physical world as our only reality.

It's scary to consider what we have to lose if we doubt our assumed reality of what we know and who we are. If we let go of our story, won't our lives and relationships unravel? The need to belong is a big one, but losing our sense of identity can be a complete nightmare for someone struggling with self-esteem issues or clinging to the importance of being a good husband, mother, etc. Even if we think about dissolving a made-up self-image, what's left? Usually, we cling to the physical form as self, and we are pretty attached to the drama as absolute and undeniable. The solution is beyond question and answer, in an awareness that my reality is not the whole story. As you will see, there are also many levels of reality and unimaginable perspectives.

But, the first response can be this marvelous brain as an ally in limited terms. Here we will touch on it briefly, but it is a much deeper subject with fantastic potential to be explored later. We learn to wear our identity loosely, like an actor who can take on new roles and wear different costumes. While an excellent actor is compelling to watch, they are never confused about who they really are.

> *Within sense-consciousness exists an objective aspect in a thinking brain.*
> *It distinguishes the world with distinct detached clarity.*
> *But thinking mind and sense-consciousness have no idea*
> *their parts are mutually and intimately conditioned from birth*
> *to deceive each other with representations of what is real.*
>
> **Lanka, Chapter 2, section IX**

We begin to touch on our rational limits and the mind's self-deception when considering sense-consciousness to have subjective and objective aspects. The subjective ego lives life as it comes, believing we are this body, mind and especially these thoughts. It deceives the objective ego, which may see a distinction and be aware that living life like a leaf floating in a stream, though comfortable, is surrendering life to the whims of circumstance. Though we wouldn't do this in business, we do it everyday in our minds. This choice, between living life as it comes or realizing we're fooling ourselves is the most difficult question, even if we get the distinction. But for most of us there is no question, as the game is not remotely understood.

The Five Aspects of Sentient Awareness act together, continually supporting, feeding, and recreating our sense of identity. Like the snake eating its tail (Ouroboros), we consume past prejudices to create a current judgment, all from subconscious impressions long since forgotten.

The egg impregnated with life-force.

Lub dub, lub dub, first sound, first sensation,

Sustenance variation, flow; yum, yuk.

Preference arises in differences. Duality is born.

Repetition to habit forms, concept arises

creating disposition, and you appear to be real.

Names arise separating this from that

Sense-consciousness nurtures identity to protect the life,

to covet pleasure, experience and excitement.

Insecure clinging becomes craving.

Addiction to who I think I am

becomes enslavement in desperation

"Holding on is all I have,"

limited by names, forms and ideas.

Untold lifetimes or just one wasted one.

However you see it.
Sense-consciousness serves survival.
But other minds arise inside the human child,
pattern recognition grows to see entrapment.
Objectively we discern clinging's' faulty judgment.
Intuitively we discern unchanging knowledge,
free of names, words or stories.
In stillness, in suchness beyond cascading thought, thou art that.

The Endless Loop, **OWM**

Defining Self: I Think, Therefore I Am

As children, we don't know what we don't know, but we define ourselves and the world around us at about seven years old. We live and find great pleasure in the products and achievements of thinking. This repetition and positive feedback becomes an infatuation with thinking, beyond our control, as we do what comes naturally. It is the subjective mind or this identification with thought that monopolizes our will and discrimination. And so, it is nearly impossible to let go and wake up. In the unawareness, attachment, fear and an addiction to thought outcomes controls everything.

> *116. Because circumstances vary, the levels of delusion in awareness differ by degrees. The characteristics of the sense-consciousness are will and discrimination to encounter the impersonal world.*
>
> *117. While the physical world offers itself to the five senses, the one dwelling in Right-knowledge and remembrance of the true self is unperturbed. Where abides intuitive mindfulness instead of cascading thought, there is little need for classification, comparison, and measurement.*

Lanka, **Chapter 2, section IX**

The slokas remind us again of the third alternative of consciousness. Beyond thinking and doing is reflective observation. I especially love its description as beyond the flow of cascading thought. It is nothing new but very compelling in experience. But that's not all I get from the *Lanka*.

Understanding the cusp of change is critical to facilitating human awareness. It is essential to realize that sense-consciousness doesn't damn us to our frailties, but it fosters them. What starts out as an infatuation with sense perception can ultimately be recognized as limiting our awareness, which can lead to real change.

However, a change in our thinking won't get it done. Like the knife that can't cut itself, mind can't see itself. We can only talk about abstractions. The idea of "who we really are" is only another mental construction, but where it comes from is completely in our control. Fortunately, our true nature or subconscious always abides in its self-nature, which basically means we can never be completely fooled by our own stories, so we spend great amounts of energy reinforcing the image, whether victim, savior or vigilante. As I have illuded to, the intuitive penetration of the subconscious mind is only limited by the chatter of and identification with thought. It always our choice.

However, the real change doesn't happen by thinking ourselves into objective awareness or suchness. The subconscious as our foundation for awareness isn't ever fooled but it's also not subject to most attempts at mental manipulation. So, our waking up is a fleeting thought until it occurs in the fabric of the subconscious mind, which may require existential pain or at least practices or methods to experience the unchanging knowledge which lies at the core of our awareness.

Infatuation becomes ignorance; becomes habit; becomes compulsion. No matter how natural it is to protect the fragile collection of self-identity, it becomes an addiction, which is minor or major mental illness depending on circumstances. But its recognition can also provide our opportunity for subconscious penetration.

Trying to support a self-image as a function of the physical world is all consuming, especially when that's all there is. Any change becomes a huge threat as we must redefine our construct by things outside ourselves and beyond our control. Sadly, it is the most common problem. Fear of change often creates a panicky disposition hidden in nervousness or mental instability.

This is the cause behind the cause of suffering and it's not about money, time, energy, health or relationships. Ego identification is all about maintaining the construct or lifeboat, we have created to hold onto, in the turbulent seas of life. Understanding this subtlety is usually blocked by the defensiveness of mind chatter. But to see it, is to hold a solvent for all other suffering.

Freedom from suffering is ultimately about releasing our awareness from self-image, which is constantly at risk and under threat, because its make believe. Crazy as it may sound, letting go of who I think I am solves all problems and is barely missed.

For most people, such a change is beyond control until a life-changing crisis, drug intervention, or tragedy destabilizes the mental construction of who-we-think-we-are, causing a level of breakdown and a fantastic opportunity. This deconstruction may be perfect, as our flawed dependence on things becomes apparent, and we see through our self-created delusion in a dramatic, inescapable way. This awakening is the third level of awareness or kind of self-nature, denoted by its sense of not fitting in. Many forms of mental illness and PTSD are being successfully treated with mind altering drugs and hallucinogens.

My own experience and conception remembers the streaming light which music became and can't help but think the LSD was activating a resonance in my DNA which perceived the entanglement of air molecules and their dance of vibration as sound. Science has identified this as the Serotonin 2A receptor, though what and how it perceives is vague. (Netflix series *How to Change Your Mind*)

The *Lanka's* term for the awakening is much more than beneficial drug experience. "The great turning back" D.T. characterizes it as a inescapable revulsion or disgust at the subconscious level with our infantile identity crisis. This moment is a sudden awakening for most, but there are also many other levels of realization with a sudden, shocking impact. However, without an accident, hallucinogenic drugs or a near-death experience, the slow path of influencing the subconscious mind starts with realizing our distortion of the "real" world and formless self-nature. Teenagers, renowned for not fitting in, rebel, and often damage themselves in the process, which is an indication they are ripe for mindfulness and education about their natural situation, true identity, and how life works. However, many of us are still teenagers, who have succumbed to various levels of domestication, but that's another story.

The *Lanka* shows the Buddha's way as remembrance of our mature, loving, and connected self. According to D.T. Suzuki, the Buddha exemplified transcendental knowledge and infinite compassion, which is also everyone's true nature, to see beyond the mundane with the eye of wisdom and love.

We want to feel awake and the rush of enthusiasm—interested, inspired, and curious. We may even want to be surprised when what we thought we knew and took for granted is shown to be misguided. But we don't want to feel stupid or wrong. Focusing on unity, what draws us and holds us together, is inherent, as is the primordial need for survival. Most of who we are (senses, thought, disposition, and awareness) exists only in the formlessness of the mind, but so does innate knowledge, which leads us to peacefulness and gives us meaning.

What happens if we accept that we don't know everything? Though it's easy to say, it's much more difficult not to identify ourselves with our knowledge. A shocking awareness is to grasp completely, at a core level, that "I am not what I think." It is the continual awareness that thinking is separate from the self. Thinking is a choice that combines projections, knowledge, and prejudice, including subconscious influence, to create the outcomes of thought, which we grasp as reality. However, thinking is valuable only when it serves us because otherwise it becomes calcified in habitual patterns. The calcification of habitual thinking is the cage.

If we loosen our grip, suddenly, "I think, therefore I am" changes from a self-limiting structure to a springboard, defining self and reality according to our best and highest desires. Reality becomes our creation without the ego story. It is the awareness that we are fully responsible for every action, reaction, and judgment.

Withholding likes and dislikes are the first steps to being fully present at the moment. This mindfulness addresses the dream-like quality of projection based on habit. Uncluttering of the mind lets things be just as they are. What may sound like passive acceptance is precise discernment and discipline.

Previously I mentioned waking up as identification beyond sense-consciousness. Though the statement sounds completely out-there, in our productive frame of mind, that's only because I am not pointing to another story, thing, label or anything as a focus. This mind boggling, lack of something to focus on, is why it's so difficult to grasp, much less to destroy self-identification as thought. It is self-reprogramming in every sense, though it is immediately available between every two thoughts. To contact the subconscious, simply pause cascading thought. It isn't an instantaneous fix to all problems but it improves with listening and life goes on, at a more measured pace.

Personally reducing the chronic habit of likes and dislikes, I address it as an opportunity, and I'm mostly past the idea of purely physical reality. But being eager for experience and its variety of pleasures leaves me personally guilty as charged. My attitude and partial discipline should be evident. My purpose is always to enjoy life more due to greater awareness and not miss out on any fun or even struggle too much. My affirmation is, "I am only this awareness." But then, this book is not done writing me yet.

Ultimately the only choice is to consider what lies beyond sentient consciousness. As presented, growth comes from breaking the mold at the subconscious level, which is our rite of passage. Alternatively, decreasing our identification with thought while mindfully destroying habitual patterns affects the equivalent change over time. These contractions of physical identification expand our connection with creation as a whole.

To understand where we're going we must understand where we are and have been.

The truth of one's own self-nature is the most purity we can attain.

Lanka, D.T. Suzuki, Introduction, Turning back

Our greatest challenge and opportunity is to perceive the fluidity of self-nature because we are never just this or that. There is no black and white. We may be predominately selfish, tribal, or disoriented. But the disoriented state is because our fallback narcissism and tribal belonging aren't working, though we might wish they did. The *Lanka* uses the term first self-nature in this way, it is the center around which we operate, in self-interest or loving awareness. It is an aspect of consciousness, open to rapid change but defining our fall back awareness.

We have the potential for all seven self-natures but may access three predominantly. The first self-nature is our dominant nature, like a center of gravity. We start and generally return to this stage, depending on the circumstance. This idea may be what D.T. refers to as the truth of self-nature, which would mean our purity is the level that we admit and accept our normal stage of conscious awareness with its self-obsessions. But looking clearly at our fallibilities takes humility, which also creates our acceptance of others' shortcomings.

The first stage of awareness or first self-nature is the childish ego identity, where everything is about me and I am defined by labels, appearance, possession and self-worth. At the most basic level, I must be the center of attention, or all hell breaks loose. These traits may grow into total narcissism with maturity and play out whatever the role, equally well as victim, predator, or savior. The mask is not as crucial as being the center of attention, be it the mask of drama queen, wimp, tyrant, or messiah. Me-me-me is the mantra of our first self-nature.

Another translation from Sanskrit for this first self-nature is suffering. This suffering is our own creation, usually defended as someone else's fault. Truth, lie, or exaggeration; honesty requires a diligent awareness to constantly examine what's-in-it-for-me in every role.

Coming out of an oblivious, self-centered focus increases our self-image to include others. The second self-nature begins our cycle of belonging. We enable social inclusion for security and its numerous benefits. This inclusion expands into transactional relationships, family connections, and tribal consciousness. What's-in-it-for-me is the dominant mantra for animal self-natures, but the more destructive mantra is us-versus-them when we engage the group.

Today, our second self-nature is on display in the positive aspects of team sports and family as the first sign of devotion. Still, the dark side includes nationalism, racism, sexism, war, and unimaginable atrocity. Most of the positive aspects we associate with the family, team, and tribal belonging, such as empathy and cooperation, come from our higher self-natures. However, all self-natures grow along the same lines of evolving inclusiveness in parallel with evolving awareness.

As you might guess, this is not yet the stage of being fully awake, necessary to grasp life's meaning. But, this stage's image is the family unit with happiness, sadness, loving, squabbling, pleasure, pain, judging, and defending. Its point of brilliance is the development of devotion, which can also be its restraining power as we define ourselves with the labels of us-and-them. But these are only the first two stages of awareness, still bound up in entrapment and suffering.

Realizing that there is a problem is entering the third stage of awareness, though still a form of entrapment. It is characterized by not fitting in and suffering from many psychological illnesses. Distinctively uncomfortable, we learn to let go of some habitual ways of relating and belonging but usually get stuck in modifications of the same old habits. If some change occurs, it might include new tribal structures but remains limited until we see beyond the limits of physical reality. Here many people stay caught, left bouncing between the three stages of suffering until they pursue the deeper meanings of compassion, honesty, and wisdom.

However, this stage of development is the most significant opportunity for all humankind. The growth path from suffering is the recognition of oneself or one's awareness as non-physical. Awakening a self-image as not defined by things, accomplishments, or relationships is the doorway to freedom.

CHAPTER EIGHT
ESOTERIC SCIENCE

In this chapter, I will provide a simple perspective of the remaining four self-natures and wrap up the introductory section of this book. It will begin with discussing esoteric concepts to give the required tools. Engaging esoteric knowledge is a primary means of expanding awareness by planting ideas in the mind that can then germinate into a new paradigm. But to nurture the mysterious takes immersion and repetition.

Teachings are esoteric for two reasons: it guards them for future posterity and ensures they are handed down without distortions. This protection was accomplished by several means, including limited audience and secret codes to preserve the original meaning.

There are no hidden symbols or secret codes in my writing, which aims to provide a contemporary understanding. The limited audience is not up to me because the reader chooses the book, and this book will seek out those who may comprehend it. As I've tried to say before, this book has been writing me and, as such, is my teacher. Anyway, not seeking the traditional path or a doctrinal understanding, we can focus beyond the teaching tools of the monk's way and look into what might be heresy to a religious person. Thus, we must consider the science that makes esoteric knowledge available to someone outside the monastery.

A long anticipated moment.

When we say that a quarter of all Americans have taken on a whole new world view, we are pointing to a major development in our civilization. Changing a worldview literally means changing what you think is real.

Paul Ray, Ph.D. and Sherry Ruth Anderson, Ph.D., *The Cultural Creatives*

The *Lanka* promotes the principle reality of "not-separateness" as before all other thoughts, ideas, and imagination. This is our complete dependence on the environment and all other living things in the delicate balance of a not-separate scientific view. Furthermore, this connectedness will take us into the fundamentals of quantum physics to provide a plausible relationship between experimental theory and life's actuality.

"Not-separate" seems straightforward only in the most basic examples, as in the food on my plate, which, as I eat, becomes me! Similarly, the air we breathe seems hardly separate since we can't see it and must make a conscious effort to perceive it as the function of our lungs.

However, what esoteric science, transcendental knowledge, or enlightenment looks like in words, can't possibly represent actuality. Shunryu Suzuki Roshi might sit in suchness, but we can only observe his loving-kindness reflected in penetrating wisdom. With a master's observable traits as the goal of practice, all spiritual wisdom becomes mindfulness to attain a loving awareness of the moment. If this is mystical knowledge, my grandmother was a master.

Our glasses influence how we see life; likewise, attitude, perspective, and cultivated disposition are primary life-enhancing tools. It is all about being ready, being empty to hear and see what is already there.

Esoteric science, commonly understood as secret teachings hidden by symbols and mysterious organizations, is only superficially correct. Something is also hidden when we can't get it because it's beyond anything we have ever known. Deep esoteric concepts, such as the *Lanka* alludes to and describes, can't be understood with the rational mind because one's experience lacks the necessary frame of reference. Just as if you've never flown, you'd have little sense of what turbulence might feel like. But if you're accustomed to flight in all weathers, just the memory can make your stomach go funny. That's what esoteric really means in this context.

This assumed disguise is employed in the *Lanka*. The esoteric, hidden in plain sight, will be unclear until you experience what it's talking about for yourself. What I share is only my perceptions and conclusions.

Esoteric concepts are also tricky without the fundamental ideas, in that culture, at that time. It is like understanding a foreign language without a dictionary or navigating a foreign culture without any introduction to local customs. You might notice the spiraling logic of this book is a structure to give you an introduction and a dictionary in simple terms. Because it's a new worldview, the language and the steps to understanding it must be sequential, building on each other. To make the next step, the challenge is that you must have a firm footing on the last few.

The subject of non-dual concepts is coming up now because we can't begin to understand the stages beyond the third level of awareness (not belonging) until we realize that non-duality is nature itself. Luckily we all have glimpses throughout life that allow us to accept an idea, having not fully actualized the experience.

This moment of change, the third self-nature is also translated from Sanskrit as the characteristic mark, like the old hippies label of themselves as freaks. For my brothers and sisters a whole new world opened up as they saw the fabric of reality with no frame of reference to understand. Their experience challenged everything that deluded domestication held as true.

But a serious look shows the optimistic potential of change; to awaken beyond sense-consciousness; to see beyond purely physical reality. During an hallucinogenic experience, the disoriented perception becomes a shock to the habitual sleep of physical reality. For a moment at least, habitual thinking is disrupted and the participants struggles to create concepts to understand their altered reality. It creates an opening which might allow the individual to seek a natural expansion of awareness.

This vague description of the drug experience is also what it means to be esoteric. It is non-sense until you have experienced yourself beyond labels, physicality, and thought. Experience is usually how we get that we are not only this body or mind. It is also the only way I can explain the stages of self-nature after the third, because they are the progressive awakening that we are also, not thought and not-separate.

Following is the *Lanka*'s next step in logic. Beyond perceived reality, it approaches the non-dual. It is similar to the nature of matter as understood in quantum physics, which describes the not-separate world.

> *Seeing the world naked and undisguised*
>
> *through unfiltered awareness and compassion,*
>
> *its dreamlike quality beyond intellect,*
>
> *contains neither permanence nor extinction,*

since the dualistic terms of subject and object no longer apply.

Lanka, Chapter 2, sloka 3

This is the wavelike intuitive perception of suchness. We hear described the hallucinatory raw awareness of non-duality, where distinctions no longer work. But it may sound crazy because our natural perceptions are loaded with prejudice and unprepared for expanded states of understanding much less consciousness.

However, seeing the non-dual without the filters of thought's prejudice, the expansiveness can cause disorientation. It is partially due to loosening the grip on concepts, but its wavelike nature allows me to recognize the vastness of what I do not know with an awareness that expands in subtle intuition. It is disorientating, like a hallucinogenic experience, but it is without drugs in the *Lanka's* description. One might ask, why would we subject ourselves to such horrors?

The answer for me is that it is our inevitable purpose, but for others, it may be not to suffer so much or maybe to enjoy the bliss of effortless belonging. For whatever reason, as awareness evolves, peacefulness and grace expand. Anyway, the not-separate subject-object paradigm is the unavoidable, mind-bending cornerstone within the ancient text. As we will explore, it represents non-dual awareness as the essence of quantum mechanics. However, it is also necessary to grasp that the natural laws are non-dual, which underlies the *Lanka's* science of existence.

An example of wind indicates that the *Lanka's* "not-separate" thesis isn't a simple construct or philosophy. It is a physical reality, like gravity, which must be experienced to comprehend. To see things just as they are, remove all blinders and the limits you would put on observation. So, the wind is not just air movement. It is the respiration of forests, the North Atlantic's thermal gradient, the tidal influences of the moon, and the mechanical turbulence of the Himalayas. The wind is not-separate, non-dual, without opposites, and has few defining characteristics except its' effects on the world. Such vague, esoteric descriptions aren't worth too much struggle, except to highlight that in the vastness of nature there are always countless unknown causes functioning interdependently. This is what it means to be esoteric and concepts which are non-dual can cause discomfort as the bodies reaction to confusion, where our concepts of reality no longer apply.

First Self-natures

The seven stages of awareness or first self-natures begin with ego creation. They are cumulative, where each awareness incorporates all previous steps. So, the Me-centric ego and clan member are within the person who is agitated in not fitting in, just not taking center stage. We move among the others at each step, but our center of gravity is the first self-nature, our most comfortable and broadest awareness.

The first three self-natures reflect the self-absorbed focus of suffering. Anytime we suffer psychologically, there is always an element of self-centeredness, clinging to definitions or feeling sorry for ourselves as separate, alone, and misunderstood. So, stepping beyond suffering is observing circumstance, body, and mind without being infatuated and lulled into thinking it reflects who we are. It is to recognize we are not the construction of thought or that our awareness is limited to physical reality.

The fourth stage of awareness or self-nature is waking up to the reality of ourselves as non-physical. As described earlier, it occurs as our limited identity in the physical world is shocked through disconnection of various sorts. Leaving us stunned and confused leads naturally to a state of contemplation or mindful awareness.

In my hippie generation and many spiritual lifestyles, you can see people celebrating a non-physical identity with its freedom from cultural norms. After the problematic third stage of not belonging, we may feel relief in letting go of labels and the rules of domestication. This step can be the beginning of a not-separate reality, including the potential of spiritual partnership and co-creation, where you can make or remake your life as you dream.

With the new identity as a non-physical being, begins the first great freedom, which is a step into liberty from our preferences. My favorite poem, the *Hsin Hsin Ming*, refers to it as a freedom from being offended, where we learn to observe objectively and holistically without reacting and taking things personally. So, people and situations no longer offend or upset us without our being aware. This consequence of relaxing the hold on self does not need to defend or prop up a story. The hooks of identification with the story dissolve gradually when we recognize the trap and aren't controlled by preferences.

Also, *The Four Agreements* has two primary points which present the same concept from a practical standpoint. Two of the agreements provide a straightforward method. Not taking anything personally while making no assumptions, in a given situation, is an equivalent opening of freedom, if you really get it.

If that sounds like absurd nonsense, this is your opportunity, and though you may not get it today, it is available as noted. To escape the cage of misidentification is not once and for all, nor complete at any time. It is the big first step, and the suffering will continue without it. The few that actualize this mindfulness are the peaceful ones.

An introductory esoteric statement is:

> *Not-separate awareness transcends thinking, belief, and memory perceiving the suchness of all things, just as they are.*

> **Lanka, Chapter 2, section XIV**

This idea exemplifies the outcome of fourth stage awareness, to step beyond mental grasping with a recognition of our emotional landmines.

Comprehending this reality through experience and application is a function of the fifth level of awareness, which is non-dual rationality. Thoroughly getting that we are not the body, mind, or outcomes of thought, synchronicity and connection become an ongoing perception, and deeper levels of observation demonstrate the ranks of cause behind the cause, behind the reason. The effects far exceed the physical, well into the mental, emotional, and interpersonal aspects of life. They rapidly take on a reverse priority, and the relations between people become the definition of ultimate value. Our connection to others feeds a new dynamic in everyday life in each situation.

The fifth awareness's freedom begins with letting-go-of-outcomes. It merges with a growing sense of synchrony and the effortlessness that interconnected awareness implies. It is the source of my personal daily mantra, "All according to plan, just not my plan." These concepts, along with many others, will be developed further as we go on, but it's too far to reach until I share the psychology, biology, and physics of our not-separate reality.

The next related non-dual transcription is that:

> *The not-separate relationship of existence and perception is mutuality as conscious awareness.*

Lanka, Chapter 2, section XIV

This conscious synchrony is the sixth stage of awareness, which is certitude, experiencing the synchronicity of interconnectedness without doubt about its reality. You might also call it Nirvana or just a life filled with peace and effortless belonging.

Certitude, first presented relative to suchness (Chapter Two), refers to a stage of near completion often regarded as the Boddhisattva's first self-nature. Here the individual faces a choice to stay in life and do some good, or effect a final release or awakening through imagelessness and transmission. Being aware of interdependent co-arising, the first self-nature of certitude gazes into the eyes of humanity seeing its chaos with compassion but still learning to set aside one's role and see every being as one's most beloved child. But that is the work of existing in one's potential.

My argument is that Nirvana, which arises from the self-natures beyond suffering, is preferable to enlightenment or religion, as it can be understood and taught by people who have right-understanding. This cultural paradigm shift goes beyond miracles, mystery, and authority. Instead of focusing of beliefs, doctrine or an unfathomable absolute, it is understanding our human potential to step beyond our petty offenses and learning to trust existence by letting go of outcomes.

The seventh stage of awareness is completion, and all I can do is provide its primary tenets in the coming chapters. These ideas will include impermanence, the three marks of existence, noble wisdom, and many others. Though no words can adequately describe it, we begin from a new starting point where the immediacy of things, just-as-they-are, is our crucial cornerstone.

154. Seeing the world clearly and without distortion;

that which perceives and that which is perceived are not separate.
No judgment arises.
Things are as they are.

***Lanka, Sagathakam*, sloka 154**

Here we touch on the non-dual nature of Mind-only, which might help grasp the other mind-bending concepts. What may feel like a radical departure from sanity, as in "the perceived and perceiver as not separate," might be understood in interconnected dependence as an aspect of not-separate.

If the perceiver creates a perception, the two are not separate as they are accountable for the conception. There's no external cause, no place for judgment, and no one else to blame. Even someone to forgive disappears. Subject-object awareness, challenged earlier under the mantle of not-separateness, becomes a little more explicit, as the perceived and the perceiver is seen as both creation and creator. This construction is to say again that the non-dual has no opposite.

Most people would associate Zen with esoteric knowledge, which is valid for the direct experience of absolute or Right-knowledge. Still, the Lanka's science presents Right-understanding as a basis for directing the best life can offer when examined as a process rather than a monastic doctrine. The science we will explore, taken for granted by the ancients, was culturally and verbally transmitted as common knowledge. However, it is foreign and often confusing because we don't share its cultural foundation and history. But, as a little-known science, it holds exquisite principles to serve modern understanding.

Don't worry about integrating an unfamiliar frame of reference; you need only a basic understanding. Although it may require some effort in practice, our role mostly requires patience and relaxing into who we are at heart. As the enlightened repeatedly emphasizes, "Your timing is perfect, as we are always where we are supposed to be." So, if you reflect on the steps that brought you here, their sequence should clarify that each one was perfect and necessary for the next.

The Ancient Buddhist Frame of Reference

The ancient Buddhists' vantage point still held sway from a few hundred years before Buddhism's destruction in India. The victors' history is generally recounted in violence and political agendas rather than the actual story's fragments. Authentic history has other avenues of discovery, albeit lacking hard proof. Hence archeology and threads of myth handed down through the ages often provide a more comprehensive view of what must have been.[5]

As mentioned earlier, the fourth turning of Buddhism equates loosely to the prophecy of the future Buddha, Maitreya. Some say the new age presupposes the loss of Dharma within humanity, which is an easy analogy given the current world economy fueled by weapons, oil, and unsustainable growth. This idea might also be reflected in the Buddhist world's political changes, such as in Buddhism's deconstruction in China and Tibet?

Another possibility is my optimistic thought that rational advances in science, culture and human consciousness will re-educate itself to include the pearls of ancient wisdom as contemporary awareness. This is happening today but without clear ties to modern science which leaves it on the fringe. It is this idea that drives my exploration. It also doesn't discount the myth and legend, encapsulating a science of Right-understanding as a handbook for the most fulfilled life.

Another part of this prophecy says that the future Buddha will be group consciousness, where many come to enlightenment from every direction. Some limit this idea to an enlightened community, but that seems problematic. I prefer the vision of humanity's awareness reaching a tipping point, not necessarily the commune, especially not the separatist cult. Tens of millions of people, enabling human potential were estimated a few decades ago. Today, these distributed groups' influence is seen everywhere in the progressive change of politics, natural health, environmental responsibility, and conscious capitalism. This wave of cultural creatives is another indicator that chimes the bell. Now is the time.

Thou art born of blood, bone, and tissue but not without lifeforce.

---

[5] Allen, C. (2003, revised ed. edition). *The Buddha and the Sahibs.* John Murray

You sensed, then you thought to recognize preference;
likes, dislikes, or doesn't matter.
Pattern became concept and sense-consciousness emerged,
collecting concepts, experience, and emotions;
taking actions to fulfill one's desires.
Supporting animal existence alone is me, mine, us and them.
What more could there be for human life?

What just is as it is?
What lies beyond a merely physical reality?
Freedom from compulsion's mind control
Freedom from taking offense, to see all things as not about me,
Freedom to learn effortless living and belonging.
Thou art being human, thou art suchness,
thou art between and beyond the senses, thought, and concepts.
In the inevitable present, awareness arises

Beyond sense-consciousness, beyond the discrimination and judgment,
beyond compulsion limited accomplishment and achievement,
no right, no wrong, no this nor that.
Thou art the still quiet voice within, to be fully present, to be still.
If thou art here, there is only one of us.

Thou Art That, OWM

These first eight chapters are like a user's manual for being human, with just a peek into what may come. The second part embraces the impossible task of describing how the precept of not-separate isn't metaphorical nor entirely metaphysical. Part II will share the limits of my understanding and speculation that, not-separate, rather than philosophical, is the physical reality of the universe and, therefore, a paradigm shift for many aspects of science and human potential.

This concludes Part I, which is the basic knowledge everyone should know and understand. From this point on, we move into higher-order concepts, which are more challenging to actualize. These ideas and their attainment were the Buddha's reasoning for preferring a monastic life for those devoted few who could step away from the world, its profusion, and suffering.

In today's world, we have undreamed resources and opportunities. So, we will go the whole way with our discussion, understanding that to attain the highest states and awareness may require stepping away from the world in various perspectives and attitudes. But the most important and often misunderstood choice is that the path is joy. In ever-increasing inclusion beyond the world's chaos, it evolves as a quiet heart. Renunciation is not necessarily pushing away the world. Renunciation is merely the rejection of the physical world as the only reality. Only a perspective shift, it is what we make it.

PART II

NATURE'S INTERDEPENDENT CO-ARISING

CHAPTER NINE

DISPOSITION

A cultured disposition is the reflection of Right-understanding in action. It is not inherited or learned through domestication, which is what we must often unlearn. It is the choice to exercise our power through the discipline of positive attitudes. It is being true to our primary gift, a loving nature.

But all the discipline in the world is meaningless unless it leads to awakening and a disposition of joy—or its relative version, happiness. Where material happiness is transitory, a nature of resonant joy is not. Cultured from the inside out, it always begins with gratitude, which more closely defines devotion than worship. Gratefulness becomes a joyful primary purpose, in and of itself. This is the devotion by which we serve others, becoming one's state of being for no reason at all.

Evolution starts by nurturing a disposition of joyful for no reason. This integrity with self appears in every wisdom tradition, especially those with organic connection with life, such as native American. Don Miquel Ruiz presented a fantastic description of individual sovereignty and integrity of word in *The Four Agreements.* Though from vastly differing cultures, his treatise of not taking anything personally and not projecting preconceived notions, fits perfectly with expressions within the *Lanka*.[6]

The disposition of gratitude, a prerequisite for the Lanka's science of a healthy mind, expresses itself primarily as generosity and compassion. Where we usually give lip service, this childlike willingness to give, serve, and love is essential to our true nature, Buddha-nature.

Being grateful for modern science, especially medicine, is easy for someone who could have died at thirty-five, forty-eight, or sixty when modern medicine saved my life. But it is a difficult shift for cultures based on self-interest. To develop such humility is uncommon, significantly, if you grew up on a farm in Texas. And yet, we can also appreciate that

---

[6] Ruiz, D.M. (2018, reprint edition). *The Four Agreements: Practical Guide to Personal Freedom.* Amber-Allen Publishing, Inc.

discovery comes through stretching beyond the known, testing theories, and thinking outside the box.

A humble awareness is to cut the mesh of thought identification, but usually, this requires a painful loss to create an opening. In this self-aware humility, even doing good must be questioned. But this isn't the humble, meek, or timid character traits we have seen in common usage; otherwise. This humility is the recognition of entrapment and a razor-sharp discernment, not to be fooled by base nature.

The *Lanka's* science, first and foremost, is about revealing the human path of conscious evolution as in the psychology of unfettered awareness. As seen in the following stanzas, the most challenging and sometimes incomprehensible parts of the *Lanka* drag even our good intentions into the light.

> *Humankind cling to and crave the positive signs of self-identity without realizing it mirrors the negative signs of separateness. In our self-importance, making the world a better place or achieving a higher purpose, we often degrade and devalue another's path because it looks different to our own.*
>
> *Like silkworms creating our own golden thread, enwrapping others in our charmed cocoon, we sleep to awake, not seeing the eternal, perfect solitude of everything beyond discrimination.*
>
> *Those of highest intention awaken to see there are no signs of self-identity and no distinctions of higher and lower. The essential meaning of awakening self is to recognize the awakening in everyone.*

Lanka, Chapter 3, section LXVIII

This inclusive awareness is the *Lanka's* heart science. Not-separate isn't just a concept of oneness; it is the meditative connection with the non-dual. The psychology of awakening recognizes our illusory rationalizations. Like misplaced charity, an unconscious choice makes us feel good but might not respect others' right of choice and free will. The key is to recognize our presumption or habitual thinking.

The Lanka's not-separate adamancy is an excellent leveling of honesty. It corrects our clinging to knowledge by reminding us; that we don't know and what we don't know, we don't understand. We are warned about judgment or opinion which fails to notice the essence or highest good for all concerned. We aren't aware of the essence in any given knowledge without direct experience, which puts every opinion and judgment in doubt. Even the accidental presumption that anyone is less-than because of appearances is critically flawed. Equally, there is no place for looking up to or down on anyone. The magic gift is when we focus on the awakening in everyone to the exclusion of ourselves, as others reflect to us that which we cannot see alone.

In the second stanza, the *Lanka* subtly catches flight in the line, *not seeing the eternal, perfect solitude of everything beyond discrimination.* We've all heard part of this statement, that everything is perfect just as it is, with some skepticism. Obviously, everything is not ideal in a relative sense. But this isn't about economies built on arms production, overpopulation, or desertification of our farmland. It is about perfect not-separate solitude or the interdependent sovereignty each individual has, to be precisely in the right place for their maximum development, which we cannot judge.

The *Lanka* introduces solitude as principal in character development and cultured disposition. Not to be confused with being alone. Solitude, in this usage, is our sovereign right of being. It's crudely an attitude that goes something like, "What I think is between God and me." It is sole mental determination rather than being a hermit or monk.

> *False notions are those which misjudge things as other than they actually are.*
>
> *They are nothing else.*
>
> *Reality is mistaken through clinging to the idea of independent existence, wherein essence is not seen, and actuality is drowned in prejudice.*
>
> *For this reason, penetration of formless essence outshines mere knowledge, freeing one from endless, bitter cycles.*
>
> *Formless awareness means the dismissal of discrimination.*

***Lanka,* Chapter 3, section LXXVII**

These stanzas give insight into formlessness as a primordial awareness of essence. Besides waking up from the story of our own making, stepping beyond conditioning and limited views of self, it goes back to objective discernment. At first, it may seem like letting go of the boat in deep water. The response can be fear and terror. It is also a problematic cultural shift. But it is only counterintuitive as we depend on our thinking, and this vision gets into the esoteric, which can only be understood based on previous experience. But in the end, it challenges us to trust we are enough and practice acceptance as life provides the buoyancy to sustain us.

In this ancient view, the evolutionary plans are the Laws of Nature, and Divine beings are expressions from within nature. However, this idea also includes a field of intelligence that consists of all sentient beings as its source. This path has been described as the "warrior's path" because its primary weapon is fierce discipline to see our limitations of mind, to encounter a boundlessness of self beyond definitions.

The Observer

In my own experience, it isn't enough to second guess or doubt my distorted view of reality; the challenge is to embrace not-knowing by witnessing life with an accepting attitude. This mindset is as much humility as I can muster. But it is distinct from a rational philosophy to hold judgment and opinions at arm's length. In this mindfulness, acceptance and discernment are that much clearer. But our cultural environment usually makes it difficult.

Our institutions and cultures direct us to agreed ideas and ways of living together. What can a responsible, caring person interested in discovery and improving the human condition do?

D.T. Suzuki points out that our ability to integrate learning depends on five primary aspects: propensity, understanding, prejudice, circumstance, and disposition. But learning itself doesn't take hold permanently. Except with exercise or testing and repetition, can a surprise awakening lead to a groomed disposition. First, propensity is our ability to do any or all of these five primary aspects. So to consider the integration of knowledge, we begin to address understanding of our natural prejudice and animal limitations. Then circumstance comes into play with a temporarily altered perception and our response to the change of attitude and environment. But disposition is the long game. Living in the world rather than in a monastery, I've found it necessary to re-train my habitual thinking with the repetition of mindfulness exercises. The reinforcement and repetition drive me to deeper levels of an altered disposition and ultimately, subconscious change. As my scope is only to reveal the *Lanka*, I can't instruct but only recommend other works which can help the seeker find a path. Joe Dispenza, D.C., describes the mechanics of altering disposition or personality in *Evolve Your Brain, The Science of Changing Your Mind*. His inclination is a good objective reprogramming, using the mind to prepare the disposition for further steps.[7]

> *Waking sleep identifies as thought.*
>
> *It follows a trail of outcomes, to color what is in masks*
>
> *good, bad, or irrelevant.*
>
> *Limited thinking makes it so, where ignorance and*
>
> *apathy may prevail.*
>
> *Throttled by self-imposed personality, are patterns of clinging,*
>
> *fiercely protected are ideas of who we think we are.*
>
> *Hungry for experience, addicted to excitement,*
>
> *gorged on pleasure, ultimately becomes dissatisfied insensitivity.*
>
> *What is this trap of sense-consciousness?*
>
> *Ascertain authentic joy; examine one's peace.*
>
> *Thou art not this mind.*
>
> *Thou art not this body.*
>
> *Thou art not this collection.*
>
> *Thou art not this story.*

---

[7] Dispenza, J. (2008, reprint edition). *Evolve Your Brain, The Science of Changing Your Mind,* Health Communications Inc.

Bars on a cage are discrimination, missing a sunset of colors,
flowers of life unseen, unsmelt, unloved.

Begin as one intends to carry on.
Gratitude is the starting point, not something you have or express.
Its something you exercise and develop with generosity.
Words are not enough, giving and serving is real gratitude
in words, deeds, and thought, but first generosity of spirit.

Peace is the guileless heart.
Magic accompanies listening and giving of oneself.
Thou art joy to love, always free
in blessed emptiness, acceptance, and faith.
The cage is not locked.
Thou art free.

Generosity: Gratitude's Expression, OWM

Solitude: A Recurring Theme

Happiness is the meaning and purpose of life, the whole aim and end of human existence.

Aristotle

Culturing joy may seem mostly about what we choose to do or not—as in listening to great music or not rushing through life. But it is first about being or making moment-to-moment choices, and second, doing what makes us feel best from within. This choice is solitude, being true to ourselves, as we've heard through the ages. It is a discipline of mind and free will, total acceptance of what is, and not trying to hold onto some things and push others away.

Our business is to be happy.

His Holiness the Dalai Lama

As our most outstanding teachers, relationships show their challenge in the simple joy of caring for others without expectations or judgment. But there is the problem; letting go of expectations and withholding judgment. Getting this point requires grasping the *Lanka's* subtlety; from a few paragraphs back, each path is perfect, and each track is unique, just beyond our understanding. Our solitude is to show up as the expression of love, holding space for another without dumping our collection.

We can learn from sincere and fulfilled people. Still, happiness is first and foremost being true to ourselves at the most innocent childlike level while exercising mature integrity, Mind-only awareness, and the suchness of no agenda.

For example, life's absolute joy often comes from caring for living things, gardening, or spoiling the most important people in our lives. Even washing dishes, especially if it's not your natural role, may become your best character trait, as it has for me. That's a personal observation learned from a movie. I remember Bill Murray washing dishes in a Tibetan monastery in the film *The Razor's Edge*. Serving life from a place of solitude adds the magic of ceremonial living to our state of mind. But just as the movie has been seen as Bill's least successful, finding our essential joy may not be popular.

> *Living beyond the chaotic changes of experience means*
> *living within one's nurtured disposition of solitude,*
> *as a presence of character.*
> *For this reason, reality is only known in cultivated discipline;*
> *living within oneself, true to oneself first and always*
> *as one's first service to humanity.*

Lanka, Ontology and the Twofold Egolessness

Solitude, logically the opposite of not-separate, is not exclusionary. However, it may sound like living a life separate from others, choosing not to be involved in many things. The *Lanka* uses solitude to describe a state of truth or awareness of being not-separate, which might seem to indicate monastic practices. But it isn't necessarily used in that way, except, as noted, to control involvement in activities that disturb the psyche.

> *As murky beliefs are cleaned and discarded.*
> *The seeker must recognize and make known*
> *the truth of solitude.*
> *In this not-two, he or she may truly*
> *begin transformation.*
>
> *Lanka*, Chapter 2, section LII

Not-two

Not-two is a perception shift of the non-dual. It appears within solitude as a discipline, inclusive of all beings in various stages of transformation. The frame of reference views life as devotion to the simple choice of authentic joy, whatever that means for you. It includes everyone, everything, and every experience, seen to have but one purpose, conscious evolution or transformation. And as said by others, the universe is conspiring for your growth. With this view of sacredness, we begin to fathom the Lanka's non-dual.

> *We are all connected to all that is, as facets of the one. All made of the same fabric, magnificently, uniquely individualized like every snowflake... If they melt, they lose individuation and return to source, water or vapor... demonstrating just a temporary illusion of separateness.*
>
> **Joanne Mitchell (my wife and principal editor)**

Solitude and the *Lanka*'s thesis that existence is not-separate, complement each other, though on the surface they may seem opposed. The *Lanka* defines a solitude of self-worth, linked to esteem for others, as a devotional internal awareness. In this awareness, interdependent co-arising is the expression of not-separateness. Because we depend on each other for life, this focus on individual character reflects our greatest gift. We can authentically express gratitude, generosity, and acceptance by being true to ourselves. Like Ram Dass would say, "We're all just walking each other home, holding hands." In other terms, you all are very dear to me, first because you are me, teaching me and giving me purpose, but also that none of us exists except for all of us.

Solitude is a construct to nourish stillness or suchness, like the door swinging gently with each breath is a construct of meditation. Like meditation, solitude is an early choice on a long path.

A few decades ago, I wrote a poem to express my secret life of solitude. It comes out of this perception shift, looking at life from within myself as the not-two nature of us all. In this view, everything—every experience and everyone I meet—may be taken as a teacher, whether they nurture or chastise. But personal integrity maintains the presence of mind, observing without allowing offense or flattery to create separation. I used the expression "God" in this poem because it felt right as all that is, but you are welcome to whatever term suits you.

> *We are alone, God and I, in all things,*
> *that I might hear his message.*
> *All creations dance her tune.*
> *Her principle in the rain and on the feather*
> *whispers yet softly.*
> *Governess nature chides my understanding.*
> *World's reflection my own, life the mirror, mind, and mentor.*
> *If I could but see and hear, not standing in my own light,*
> *remember it all, I would.*
> *We are one, thou and I, in infinities home,*
> *teardrops to the ocean we.*
> *Your expression is often his, though you know it not,*
> *as I purify to hear, I make it so.*

Earth is our greater self, on the organs of continent,
we the breathing cells.
Chaos is the misconception, synchronicity is design,
dancing for our own delight.
Supernatural is actuality, corporal world is the semblance,
relationships invent each moment.
If we both know the place, only one is here,
call it who you may.

Solitude, OWM

    Solitude and oneness, presented as synonymous in the poem, attempt to show a path between the two. We think of solitude as being separate, where it is the creation of the best circumstance for personal growth and service. Teachers such as Sadhguru Jaggi Vasudev instruct their students to create their sanctuary or sacred space rather than depend on some special place or ashram to begin their inner work. Inner work always has the challenge of conscious integration in everyday life, but this book assumes the reader understands its role.

    Nature demonstrates the mystery of oneness through the observable connectedness of a flock of starlings, for example. Their interactive synchronism and impossible communications exceed any understanding or explanation. By the tens of thousands, they gracefully dance through the air, without a leader nor any sign of confusion in their perfectly coordinated maneuvers. Like a dance of desire, it is always a fleeting display, far subtler than any communication theory.

The only possible alternative is simply to keep to the immediate experience that consciousness is a singular of which the plural is unknown; that there is only one thing and that what seems to be a plurality is merely a series of different aspects of this one thing.

Erwin Schrödinger, ***What Is Life?***

Part I described the first three of seven first kinds of self-nature as they relate to awakening from the limitations of our animal ancestry. The entrapment of sense-consciousness, compulsive identification with body, mind, and outcomes of thought are inescapable until we understand the game. This may occur for the narcissist and individual bound up in family security (the first two kinds of self-nature), but it leads to not fitting in (the third kind of self-nature) to existing life patterns. Entering this third stage, recognizing the game is likely, but understanding is rare, except with good teachers.

So far in Part II, we have gone beyond the first three stages of awareness and entered the fourth kind of self-nature: understanding the formlessness of our existence. Maybe grasping Mind-only intellectually or intuitively, as the active nature of our existence, we begin germinating the seeds of non-dual, not-separate. Here synchronicity, as an understanding, may begin, and things begin to pop. As you might guess, this is the birth of what is loosely labeled spiritual. But spirituality is no panacea as we have seen in religious charlatans; the spiritual narcissist is accountable for a myriad of ills.

This is the stage of belief merged with the devotion that started in the second stage of family security. These aspects are the positive attributes as well as the challenges per the ancients, as they dissolve and morph into more intuitive awareness during the growth of a connection with formlessness and the non-dual.

CHAPTER TEN
OUR TRUE SELVES

From this point, we will begin to explore what the *Lanka* describes as our true nature and the revolutionary idea of being not-separate. It is a subtle but very different view of physical reality, which science is discovering in leaps and bounds. Its implications to biological entanglement, though only my speculation, make sense on many levels. So far, we've established a frame of reference that hopefully has allowed you to grasp where we come from as emergent sentient beings and the limits of our natural collection as only perceived reality. The big question remains, "Who do you really think you are?" To be really awake, this is a constant question.

In most moments of life, the answer is we are our thoughts and a collection of memories with a doubtful grasp of complete truth. The challenge is to step slowly beyond just what we think and what we think we know. What works in the world and between us is public, but now we're entering the private world of solitude and secret knowledge within ourselves that others may not understand. This unique space is about inner meanings and new identifications beyond sense-consciousness. So, it may not seem applicable in our world, or at least not until we actualize it within our lives.

> *The Five Aspects of Sentient Beings are the mechanisms*
> *of collection through the habits of memory, thought*
> *and identification with mind as self.*
> *They are only imagined to be good or bad.*
> *Happiness, peace, joy, and awakening come out of accepting*
> *and loving the existing world just as it is,*
> *without struggle.*
> *This is by means of suchness and loving-kindness.*
>
> ***Lanka*, Chapter 6, section LXXXVII**

Natural State of Suchness

The *Lanka* equates Right-understanding with mental health resolved into a sustainable loving awareness as we see in those who inspire us. This shift may occur by recognizing the addictive nature of thought identification, desire, and habitual patterns. But wise men and women come to the state of peaceful joy, each in their unique way, and this is only one viewpoint. As we describe it, progress comes with pausing to listen, connecting with, and trusting one's innate wisdom—also called intuitive mindfulness or the "still quiet voice within."

Sloka 270 described this innate wisdom as the natural state of suchness within a quiet mind. However, we breezed over a vital part of that sloka, which is that suchness, if fully grasped or actualized, gives certitude of Mind-only to the Yogin[8] or practitioner. This connection may sound like fanciful thinking or a metaphor because we've heard certainty of belief but not the absolute inevitability of Mind-only.

In an elementary sense, Mind-only prescribes that reality, as we know it, is a creation of the mind. Not just contributing or even influencing but creating our reality, as negative thoughts attract negative situations. Furthermore, we attract the lifestyle we have chosen, and often it serves some personal growth needed, which requires hard lessons. But this is not the elementary sense of Mind-only. This certitude is the stage change of awareness to Mind-only or direct connection to and awareness of the action of mind on our reality. Certitude in this context has more to do with direct experience than the certainty we associate with thought.

However, experience leads to another view of Mind-only, beyond the elementary, though not imaginary or transcendental. It is a certainty without the need for belief. Assuming we get to the point of being beyond fears and doubts, there is certainty in the experience of oneness. This doubtlessness is the certainty as described. Our mind and its creation activity exist in a peaceful state, resolved to the inevitability of the present moment or "what just is." Mind-only is the intrinsic mechanism of present-moment awareness as suchness, but it is also beyond words. However, the actuality of awareness transposes observed experience into a disposition of openness, without judgment or discrimination. But this actualization is the sixth stage of awareness, as we will see.

---

[8] D.T. Suzuki's use of yogin from Sanskrit indicates practicing yogi..

So, you might ask, "How do we get beyond fear and doubt?"

The yogins meditation of suchness
Falling away of ego, personality
And all illusory identifications.
To recognize life and death
As the veils of imagination.
Grounded in this intuitive self-nature,
Belief, judgment and opinion
Cease to obscure.

***Lanka,* Chapter 2, section XXXVII**

This possibility of disidentification may be a matter of choice and practice, or how we spend our time. The second transcription in this book, from the *Lanka* (Chapter 2, section IV), talked about three modes of consciousness: collecting, doing, and remembering. How much time do we set aside, remembering who we are? But then again, "Who am I anyway, if not these thoughts, feelings, desires, and persona?" As I described previously, per the ancients, we are all, literally, legends in our own minds.

The awakening which flows from absolute truth reveals
that all things may be understood as appearances of personality
and abstraction, enslaved to habitual thinking.
Circumstances from within the illusion, that reality exists separate
from one's own projection, is where false-imagination
creates enumerable flaws, frauds, and misrepresentations.
These appear to be magically created but in truth,
they are the obsessions with the outcomes of thought.

***Lanka,* Chapter 2, section XVI**

This section describes the delusion of the subjective mind, as identified with sense-consciousness, which serves our survival by providing will and discrimination. However, its misplaced power is our obsessive identification with the outcomes of thought, memory, feeling, and imagination. This identification is like the stages of awareness referred to as kinds of self-nature, which cannot be judged as good or bad, greater or lesser. They are not fixed and not-separate, as we access our narcissism or self-interest in the enlightened act of self-care or service to others. The focal point of awakening, is only to break the unconscious infatuation with thought or sleepwalking through life as our dominant state of being. The change is to a whole different level of infatuation with life just as it is, where thought focuses on walking in the moment, fully present.

What the *Lanka* portrays as "not getting caught in the illusion of separateness" may sound like Right-imagination compared to how we've evolved to function in the world. But the *Lanka* also calls our shared delusion false-imagination, or the source of all fear and doubt.

The Buddhist answer is found by looking at who we really are at heart or the first desires of a child. We began looking for succour; the love, care, and acceptance of our parents and later the greater world. But in cultures based on self-interest, we can never be satisfied for long, as belonging is conditional and identity created from outside in. So, fear and doubt have a strong hold on our thought and imagination to catch us in feelings of isolation. But again, the difference is only a choice in our awareness. These cycles are the waves on the ocean which naturally occur and we are not-separate. We are the ocean, contrary to momentary appearances.

Interestingly, we can't replace false-imagination with Right-imagination. Imagination is still imaginary, and the *Lanka*'s prime focus is reality, just-as-it-is, without distortion. According to the *Lanka*, false-imagination includes objectivity when it is a function of fear, doubt, or separateness. This paradox is where certitude comes in over the long haul of spiritual practice, as one develops the eye to witness Mind-only in practical and subtle ways, but it starts with recognizing our primordial desire for love and acceptance.

A finger may not touch itself, an eye may not see itself.

The mind can not grasp its insubstantiality.

We sense differences, only, not sameness and so it is with the mind.

Thinking is your great tool.

Where thinking rarely sees itself, the cloud of unawareness prevails.

Where we define ourselves, our lives, our world

as the outcome of thought, unawareness prevails.

Your great tool created a structure only to assign meaning.

On faulty foundations, in an illusion of differences,

we cling to this changing knowledge.

We hold onto images painted by dust in the wind, trying to restrain the sunset.

We miss life on autopilot and comfort becomes our prison guard.

But Thou art sameness, oneness, unchanging knowledge,

collections emptied, intermingled with all life.

Love and acceptance displaces fear and doubt's imaginary veil.

But its an inside out job.

Thou art the source of Love and acceptance.

Thou art the Buddha.

Seeing clearly

no preferences

no judgment

no rationalization

no differences.

Keep the tool polished and clean until it has a job.

The Central Oxymoron, OWM

Just as F.D. Roosevelt said, "There is nothing to fear but fear itself."

We seem to be fully autonomous individuals, but in practical terms we depend on the world for everything. And dependence is not just physical, because our connection with each other is our strongest desire and greatest risk to mental health. These may seem to be the associated risks with independence but the independent identity is the shortcoming. Disconnection and disappointing others are created fears of isolating ourselves. Fear arises in not accepting our loving interdependent nature and focusing on that in others.

When we consider our survival in the outside world, we can easily understand how interdependent we are. But we don't think about the same interdependence inside our bodies. During the last few decades the promise of DNA resolving the mysteries of existence, has fueled a phenomenal introspection in scientific understanding. Microbiology now reveals interdependent co-arising at the heart of nature in that we are more communities of organisms than individual humans.

Interdependence, as understood in ancient science, is just now being verified with overwhelming importance in health and biology. Per the human biome project, what I call my body includes endless diverse colonies of microscopic organisms. Micro-organisms have been shown to control and influence most of our vital processes inside and outside the human cells. Our lives depend entirely on trillions of interactive life forms, which provide critical functions from digestion to vitamin production. Microbes such as bacteria, fungi, and viruses within us, show that we live in interdependent existences. Microbes account for 90 percent of our life support system and outnumber human cells by 10:1. Our dependency makes them integral to what it means to be human.[9]

Though this story may sound like micro-nothings, small players who only help here and there, our microbes account for about 1.5 kilos in our gut alone, which is a weight equivalent to the liver. That may sound like an exaggeration until you consider that the average human feces are 75 percent dead or dying bacteria. We are obviously more communities than individuals. Though the accepted estimate is that microbes run 90 percent of bodily functions, they also control much of how we feel, perceive,

---

[9] Collen, A. (2015) *10% Human: How Your Body's Microbes Hold the Key to Health and Happiness.* William Collins.

and react. The Human Microbiome Project has interaction studies that reveal an astounding level of control our microbial partners exercise in our development, health, emotions and thinking. But rather than taking something away from the miracle of being human, it has shown the incredible wisdom of our innate intelligence.

Peeling the Layers of Humanness

This relationship may be the most self-evident scientific example of interdependent co-arising. Our not-separateness is obvious in the vehicle we occupy, which has intimate co-dependent relationships and an awareness of trillions of life forms. Communicating and interacting with our human cells, we are a community of organisms acting as one living animal. We and all life have evolved interdependently and synergistically with our microbial partners.

When James Lovelock and Lynn Margulis proposed GAIA, the synergistic relationship between organic and inorganic systems that cool the planet and create an environment to support life, they could have easily been describing sentient life had their focus not been global. A theory that Gaia or earth is a living organism certainly fits with the *Lanka*'s view of science.

Based on size alone, we can say each of us plays host to trillions of microorganisms. But since we can't live without them, who is hosting whom? Our health depends on creating an optimal environment for microbial partners to thrive. It's a co-hosting relationship or a symbiosis between human cells and bacteria, fungi, viruses, and many life forms. The book *10% Human* explores our microbial environment within and without. And where we think about internal microbes, it is harmless to envision single-cell organisms, which aid digestion or absorb excess calcium. But this story has many elements, both on the skin and in what we consume. Whether carried in the air we breathe, or the food we eat, these minuscule lives contribute to our general wellbeing and even communicate such things as sex appeal through pheromones. Stated another way, we are not only this body, and it is not physically separate from anything. Back to our initial statement, we only appear to be independent and autonomous. If I am not this body, called me, then who am I?

99. Like windborne waves and foam continually dancing on the sea;

100. The collective subconscious is stirred by our individuation in an objective world, to dance with awareness in waves of our own choosing.

101. A beautiful multitude of colors, sensations, tastes, sounds, and fragrances,

102. They are different, yet the same, where sense impressions, thought, and memory merely dances on the surface, as waves upon the ocean.

***Lanka,* Chapter 2, section IX**

Here we peel another layer of what it means to be human and begin to tie the waking mind's psychological constructs to the enigmatic subconscious, which the *Lanka* calls Alaya-consciousness.

In writing this book, it was an earnest desire to minimize Sanskrit usage to maximize comprehension. However, there is a critical concept with no translational equivalent. So, I will have to beg your forgiveness and introduce Alaya.

This exchange is the next critical concept in understanding Yogachara psychology. The *Lanka* repeatedly emphasizes that our sense of self is a formless mental abstraction, like foam and waves on subconsciousness which in comparison is the vast ocean. In this analogy, the grandest expression of self exists within the vast subconscious shared with all sentient beings. All but unknown to most individuals, it is the resource of knowledge, thought, experience, and disposition that controls our reactions.

Much like our physical dependence on the microbes' unseen world, the subconscious drives most of our actions based on fragments of memory, feelings, and experience. These subliminal control responses, especially those associated with emotion, can completely derail our lives.

D.T. Suzuki describes the subjective mind as a "two-headed monster."

Simultaneously it looks to the subconscious for the data of opinion, prejudice, and judgment while reading the sense-consciousness for sight, smell, taste, feeling, sound, or the consequence of thought.

The subconscious—both this vast ocean of self with the potential to access the collective knowledge and a container for our demons or shadows—has two aspects per the *Lanka*. The personal (shadow) subconscious is our collection, subject to rapid accumulation and potential change. But the vast collective subconscious hardly changes over our lifetimes, as it contains our species' memory or shared human collections. In subtler ways, it includes or extends to all sentient beings at various levels, such as the reptilian brain stem response of fight or flight.

> *Identifying oneself with the outcomes of thought*
> *the world of things appears as reality.*
> *Through habit and memory, it nourishes a*
> *disturbed subconscious through ego and ownership*
> *to which it clings and on which it reflects.*

Lanka, Chapter 2, section LIII

However, this is the most normal thing, generally outside our control. The sense-consciousness kicks in judgment and opinion. Beliefs formulated or learned are stored within the personal subconscious, whether they agree or not with the unchanging knowledge of inherited ancestral wisdom. These conflicts, concepts, and habits create the disposition we show the world. This distinction of waking beliefs and subconscious dissonance offers opportunities for personal growth.

To control our behaviors is to redirect the links between subconscious provocation and destructive semiconscious reaction. This pause is mindfulness; its image is the discernment of semiconscious reaction. Though we may get it for a moment, we repeatedly slip back into misidentification. To become awake is first severing the delusion that physical reality is all there is. But it culminates in a revolution where beliefs and the subconscious align to ever deeper levels of agreement.

The first chapter of the *Lanka*, which is wholly presented in Part III, begins with the analogy to this kind of awakening into interdependent relationships. In it, the Buddha emerges from the ocean of the collective subconscious, having spent a week accepting, teaching, and embracing his shadows until they follow him singing his praise in the light. He represents the alignment between the subconscious and sense-consciousness that eliminates psychological turbulence. His balance is the model for our mental health and his level of tranquillity is identity without external needs.

Boundless Potential

A problem arises in comprehending our potential as the boundlessness of an ocean. The waking subjective mind or sense-consciousness has spent a lifetime defining boundaries and labels, in part to limit the influence of subconscious reactions. And the imperative or most crucial definition, in these boundary limits, is our persona or who we think we are. But, this subconscious is an extraordinary, inexplicable kind of boundlessness.

To illustrate, let me recount a story from Sadhguru's (Jaggi Vasudev) life and his realization experience while painting a fence. Recognizing unseen subtlety, the analogy is to drag a wet paintbrush along an infinite fence without stopping to get more paint. The subtlety of boundlessness is when there is no trace of stain, wetness, or vapor on the surface? It disappears, becomes immeasurable but is still present long after our sense of it ceases. This boundlessness isn't about an endless container or lack of one. It is the boundlessness of ever subtler aspects or evidence, which goes much farther than we sense, measure, or detect.

Paint on a fence reflects our boundlessness extending into endless subtle aspects of form, phases of matter, frequency, energy, and resonance. But even more so, boundlessness is the ocean, as the shadows and wisdom of all sentient beings intermingling to influence our connection within the subconscious. To align the waking mind or our sense of reality is like the Zen story of the tea ceremony with the master. We must first show up with an empty cup.

As we share this mysterious boundlessness with all living creatures, the *Lanka* states that our subtle aspects overlap with one another, connected into a collective subconscious field. We may envisage its unknown depths, but our typical view of the mind and brain as the container and source of our being begins to feel very insufficient. As you are this subtle subconscious, you're obviously not limited to the mind or the brain.

But the subconscious may be the most elusive container in which we define ourselves as living beings because it lacks all physical parameters and controls. To influence our deepest selves, we can only make peace by aligning waking consciousness with the primordial parts of ourselves. Not-separate waking consciousness is sense perception directed by innate wisdom through active, open listening and intuition.

Here we also begin to circle back onto the question of displacing fear and doubt. In this innate wisdom are the roots of our true self, like that little child seeking love and acceptance or that teenager rebelling for lack of it. Identifying ourselves, in ever deeper ways with love and acceptance, is to realize our higher nature as innate wisdom.

However, this points out a powerful analogy to enlightenment as the stilling of the thought waves of the mind. Here innate wisdom becomes increasingly apparent, throwing out the transactional view or what's in it for me, and doing the next right thing. Without the mental chatter, serenity appears from the depths, and the surface disturbances lose consequence.

This concept is not unique or unusual as it arose about the same time in history as the *Lanka*, in *Patanjali's Yoga Sutras*. It is echoed in the phrase, "stilling of the thought waves of the mind".

But this subconscious connection to innate wisdom is both subtle and poetic. It may express itself as an overwhelming feeling, such as empathy, which breaks our heart when we see strangers suffering in a foreign land. But subtlety conceals its power, as the emotion based on inner truth may include every cell interaction and function of well-being. Innate wisdom arises through life integrated at the subconscious level to realize our Buddha-nature or original nature as beings of love and acceptance.

> *103. As waves are created by wind and current on the high seas, perception, thought and memory create collections from the subconscious patterns to be experienced as awareness.*

Lanka, Chapter 2, section IX

This sloka ties together the Five Aspects of Sentient Beings with the subconscious, as it identifies our created collections, interacting below the level of awareness. We might think the subconscious would develop in the conscious mind, but a reversal appears in this sloka. The subconscious comes first, with sense-consciousness assembled by our subconscious reactions to external events or forces.

> *104. Memory, belief, will, and desires are examined to judge form and significance in sense-consciousness.*
>
> *But no aspect of sense or outcome of thought functions independently.*
>
> *Subjectively linked they support accomplishment, achievement, and ambition.*
>
> *105. As the ocean is not separate from the waves;*
>
> *so to memory is not permanent nor accurate within awareness.*
>
> ***Lanka**,* Chapter 2, section IX

These slokas are incredibly exciting for two reasons. First, the collection aspects, explained as not having independence from one another, function collectively. Second, memory is an impermanent and inaccurate function as it operates in sense-consciousness, proven in psychological studies. Accuracy is one thing, but the ability to have memories altered by others or even reinvented within ourselves, strips naked the fallacy of certainty in what we think, believe or remember.

Famously highlighted in the September 11 attacks on the World Trade Center in New York, the accuracy of people's memory about basics like "how did you find out about 9/11, or who were you with [...] fell to 63 percent in just one year and 57 percent after three years."[10] The study also showed "memories of emotions" was even worse, "accurate only about 40 percent of the time, after a year." Yet, the confidence of their memories

---

[10] Chen, I. (2011, September 6). *How Accurate Are Memories of 9/11?* Scientific American. Retrieved from https://www.scientificamerican.com/article/911-memory-accuracy/#:~:text=We%20then%20went%20back%20to,percent%20accurate%20at%20survey%20three.

remained incredibly high (four out of five) for changing stories among first-hand witnesses. The study proves our memory varies according to outside influences, especially in emotional memories and the repetition of changing details.

Many aspects of memory and its effects on opinion, will, and desire are like shadows lurking behind silhouettes that once existed but have disappeared. Memory recall may easily be flawed and should never be confused with truth. This is the trap in that human psychological bondage is in the attachment to the outcomes of thought, where accuracy is low, and certainty or belief is high. It has even been said that the higher the confidence, the lower the accuracy.

> 106. *Action and consequence are imprinted on the memory,*
> *reflected by thought, and identified in the subjective mind,*
> *according to its identification with ego.*
> *But the physical world is evaluated and interpreted*
> *directly by the five senses.*
>
> ***Lanka*, Chapter 2, section IX**

Sloka 106 vividly describes filtering experience according to memory and self-identity. The subjective mind is one of eight forms of consciousness we will explore. However, this sloka highlights the first steps in defining consciousness.

Per the *Lanka*, the five senses function as an autonomous consciousness that perceives, recognizes, and reacts to the external world, independent of thinking. To grasp this simplicity, acknowledge how we jerk away when feeling pain, and thought doesn't arise until we begin to figure out what happened. The same is true for every survival response. The eye sees a tiger and the body mobilizes to run. We taste or smell something awful and hold our breath or pinch our noses. This concept is crucial as it focuses on the accuracy of direct perception and reaction. It also highlights the subtle function of the senses, which interpret our surroundings to inform each other at the level of concept and response before culminating in sense-consciousness.

Understanding this interplay and its orchestration of response supports survival and safety. But, these concepts subtly move us closer the *Lanka*'s definition of who you are at heart.

There is no way to peace; Peace is the Way.
There is no way to happiness; Happiness is the Way.
There is no way to love; Love is the Way.

Dan Millman, *Sacred Journey of the Peaceful Warrior*

Happiness is the path, or "Happiness is the Way," sounds like a metaphor from the contemporary rational perspective. But it's not. In a similar quote attributed to Gautama Buddha, it is technically the application of a persevering discipline, then a complete perspective shift of who we are. Happiness is a way to express joy in the service of others, especially ourselves. Optimism, enjoyment, and contentment combined are a choice of loving-kindness. So, what creates this loving awareness or intention of happiness as in it becoming a disposition?

We often pigeonhole ourselves as realistic, rational, and logical to justify a sour disposition or habitual negativity. We might also judge others' happiness as childish, silly, or mentally defective. But this self-imposed alienation is specifically the core thesis of separateness as the illusion creating our misery. It is the obsession with ego-identification resulting from faulty perception, which starts with the transactional view or logical view of "What's in it for me?" This false sense of separation poisons our perception of reality because we fail to recognize our vital connectedness as who we are.

What does loving-kindness or loving awareness have to do with recognizing authentic reality, reality just-as-it-is? In literal terms, this idea defines what we all want, more than anything, but may have misled ourselves to distrust or deny. Without knowing one's core desire or reason for being, misery is inevitable.

Our True Nature: Loving-kindness

According to the *Lanka*, loving-kindness is the essence of our true nature because connectedness is being human. We might remember this exquisite connection in those moments, which hold the most profound happiness, such as being hopelessly in love or seeing our newborn child. However, this may make little sense unless we can listen to our quiet center without the discriminating mind's interference.

> *As did the Buddhas plant roots of goodness,*
> *possess faith, avoid discrimination and attachment;*
> *see all men, women, and children*
> *as one's dearest family.*
> *This is the expression of one's true nature.*
> *Wherein lies peace and joy;*
> *to embrace all living beings as our own person,*
> *with affection, as if they were our only child.*
>
> **Lanka, Chapter 8**

In an absolute or unlimited sense, the *Lanka* asserts our true nature is Buddha-nature, where everything is available without discrimination or attachment. In this view, our ever-elusive self-realization is none other than recognizing and actualizing our peace, joy, happiness, and love through everyone and not against anyone. In this image, love, acceptance, and the benefit of the doubt are the operational modes toward every person, which is very different from the transactional variety. We see transactions reflected in many logical statements— such as presumption, righteousness, insult, judgment, or ownership. Here is misery through false identification with the outcomes of thought.

Of course, what the stanza describes isn't the feelings of a happy child. They are the feelings of a self-realized man or woman, knowing where we all come from, what we desire, and what needs to be actualized for peace and joy. It feels so good to get the inherent truth of what makes us happy;

we might be ecstatic for no reason at all. If we dance through the streets singing, we might well be judged by others, but then we aren't responsible for someone else's reaction.

Though we may not immediately understand the joy of connection, our recollection of childlike bliss keeps us searching for something we may only vaguely remember. However, as we remember the happiest times of our lives, some deny even that. We must have the most compassion for others without pretending to be other than we are, in humility for our shared condition and frailty. In coming home to what is genuine, natural, and authentic in ourselves, we may always present to the world loving-kindness as authentic acceptance and caring.

> *The vast subconscious supports you.*
> *The senses guard and protect, you are safe to be in peace.*
> *Without the chatter of mind embrace your greatest desire.*
> *Belong effortlessly by accepting effortlessly.*
> *Without struggling transactions, forget what you're due,*
> *just give and everything will be yours.*
> *Enter the stream of life by witness of its waves and magic,*
> *not separating the bubbles and debris.*
> *Thou art that.*
> *Life is waves of change but thou art most blessed to love.*
> *Some say without loving, you cannot be loved,*
> *but they miss love's enlightenment.*
> *Every child is thine most beloved child be they nine or ninety.*

Life in Balance, OWM

There is an inherent gift in the assumption of our Buddha-nature, if realization stands apart. Taken on faith, it sets a vision, inviting us to arrange our lives for increasing levels of peace, joy, happiness, and love as the expression of ourselves. Rather than identifying ourselves with what we do, what we earn, or possess, this discipline or mindfulness is monumental in its efficacy. Regardless of circumstances, we can teach ourselves to treat ourselves and others with compassion. That is, we can offer helpfulness, acceptance, kindness, or the benefit of the doubt when given the opportunity.

Practice makes it a habit, makes it a disposition[11] to paraphrase Joe Dispenza's logic. In this way, we build new thought patterns. Such behaviors provide a magical attractiveness, which only a few can resist.

Of course, there may always be those that repel us or whom we irritate. Since we see our reflection in others, these relationships may be our most influential teachers. We may observe something which causes discomfort and accept it, just-as-it-is, we give it to contemplation, prayer, or meditation. Letting go of the outcomes is often sufficient.

But there is also a lovely practice called Ho'oponopono, which can magically soothe relationships by reconciling our part. There are marvelous stories about its effects in places of real-world horror. The method fundamentally repeats a mental prayer on behalf of the offended or offending. While not necessarily letting the person in question know what we are doing, one waits to see the healing flow of change.

I'm sorry.

I love you.

Please forgive me.

Thank you.

Ho'oponopono, traditional Hawaiian healing practice

However, depending on the danger, pain, or vulnerability of circumstances, we may need to practice compassion at a distance, as in self-care. Boundaries are also a healthy application of awareness.

In Buddha-nature, we begin to reap the rewards of our formless nature of existence: the fourth stage of awareness, or self-nature. It may start with the idea, then become belief, but actualization is beyond either, as it becomes devotion to higher self. Here holding tightly to my position, personality, and transactions can dissolve and morph into intuitive awareness and fulfilment of my greatest desires.

---

[11] Dispenza, J. (2008, reprint edition). *Evolve Your Brain, The Science of Changing Your Mind,* Health Communications Inc.

CHAPTER ELEVEN
LOVING-KINDNESS

While the *Lanka* doesn't argue our animal instincts, this premise that our true nature is loving-kindness also goes to the next level of species success. Many sociologists and social anthropologists propose homo-sapiens success is derived from our ability to cooperate and coordinate for the group's wellbeing. Per authors such as Yuval Noah Hariri in *Sapiens,* our species succeeded through empathy, consideration, and cooperation as our principal tools, much more than physical strength, fire, metal, and even the wheel. This success recognizes that the strongest and fittest predators, such as lions, tigers, and bears, have been driven to near-extinction by their one-time prey, an intelligent, cooperating, caring group of relatively weak hominids. The sad reality now is, we need to reverse destruction caused by our success as a species.

Understanding that our species' success has anthropologically been the consequence of our cooperation and coordination is also essential in understanding what-lies-ahead. For better or worse, the current stage of natural selection, seen in our species' dominance over the planet, has caused other enormous problems, albeit due to unintended consequences. In an emerging world of affluence, we can seek meaning, purpose, and fulfilment in serving to correct humankind's past and ongoing destruction.

My interpretation of the *Lanka's* solution is a cultivated disposition of happiness or its source of loving-kindness and generosity of spirit. It is a lovely image to consider joy the highest self-expression, living in the flame of life, the spirit, or resonance of being not separate from anyone and anything. This understanding of life begins to show hope in the possibility of achieving our greatest human desire. And in a very Zen-like manner, love is not only the destination; it is the path.

That aspect of Noble Wisdom called self-realization arises as the guileless heart, sees all things In their nonmaterial essence. The less important consequences of life, both suffering and self are seen to be illusory creations of the mind, where delight in the world as it is, becomes the blissful common thread of creative expression.

Lanka, Chapter 2, Section XI(a)

Noble Wisdom

In this stanza, note the quiet introduction of a new term, Noble Wisdom. Since waxing poetic in the previous paragraphs, this stanza matches that poetry with a few critical aspects of the *Lanka*'s message. Noble Wisdom may be seen as an aspiration, as is the full actualization of Buddha Nature. However, Noble Wisdom is not inherent or immediately accessible in the disentangled mind. Noble Wisdom starts from suchness but includes recognizing who we are, which resembles ultimate compassion, and then extends to imagelessness as showing up without agenda, purpose, or opinion. Being this fully present in every moment requires effort, growth, and integration.

D.T. Suzuki also describes the Buddha's love as an expression of suchness, imagelessness, and Right-knowledge. Not being a possessive love, it is above attachment, a difficult concept for our western frame of reference because the Buddha's love expresses itself in the conduct of purposelessness. Not to be confused with worthlessness or someone not doing their part. Here purposelessness is to show up without a purpose, plan, or opinion. This love is being fully present and fully available for another. It is something we all do when we really care.

Ego-less love is a force that needs no object and shows up independent of form. Just as a flower has fragrance, it is what it is and needs no recognition or purpose, whether you smell it or not. This lack of objectification challenges our rational minds, which are essential to interacting without ego. It is a light we feel in others as comfort and congeniality, often without labeling or recognition. This purposelessness introduces imagelessness, which is the unobstructed light of a teacher. Where's the game without a goal?

Thou art that,
curbing the habit from sleepwalking as thought.
Truth is a place beyond your mind, right, wrong, win, lose.
It's all good and insignificant.
Purposelessness is only an appearance of understanding,
full presence in the moment,
for the greatest purpose of all direct experience.
Holding space fully present for another,
intuition and emptiness,
love in the primitive subconscious.
uncovering the self.
Removing layers of separateness looks like
becoming the experience imagelessly.
Right-knowledge is direct experience or
becoming always, in the disguise of being.
Right-knowledge is emptiness of self-obsession,
available to all life not vacant, lacking, or less than.
Emptiness creates the container for becoming,
not separate in seeing oneness,
non-separateness is effortlessly belonging.
Thou art emptiness as fullness and allness.
No greater ambition exists.

***Effortless Belonging,* OWM**

The development, of purposelessness and imagelessness, is also about the journey into what is often confused as non-attachment. It is more complicated than detachment because separation from the world occurs in stillness or mindfulness within perception. From relationships to lifestyle, detachment appears exactly the opposite of what a dictionary might say. As identification with Buddha-nature begins, we become more outgoing and engaged as that allows service as the vehicle of change. Especially in the service of a loving smile. This is karma yoga by another name, and it dissolves the story or collection of who we think we are. In this way, letting go of outcomes and full presence without agenda, becomes actualized awakening within the subconscious.

In some ways, we may seem less attached because many engagements and attitudes, such as a righteous protest or taking sides, are more difficult when given the benefit of the doubt. The complexity is enormous when we would extend compassion to our most beloved child, which must also include Donald Trump and Idi Amin. But then we can also only do our best.

These changes are a perspective shift arising from the quiet mind identifying with loving-kindness, which forms over time and practice. But awareness isn't like opening a door; it is more like tearing down a wall or journeying to a far land. There's no returning to the old story of self once the facade is recognized because the change occurs without conscious choice.

Tasked by the quest for the Right-understanding of not-separate awareness, I have described the key elements to grasp the lofty image yet simple loving acceptance of Buddha-nature. As a cornerstone, it includes self-realization of our greatest desire. It touches on not-separateness from the inside out. However, Noble Wisdom is an outcome, which combines self-realization, the transmission of Right-understanding, and the ultimate letting go or imagelessness. Later we will approach these ideas as development stages because the question is, "What are we letting go of?"

The key to grasping our nature as loving-kindness lies in exhausting the delusion of separateness. We naturally start our awareness in sense-consciousness before developing a comfort zone in the desire for belonging, which is reflected in the first two stages of awareness as driven by narcissism and fear of not belonging or security.

But, here we are well beyond even the third stage of not-belonging and smack in the middle of our formless identity. However, the first desire of belonging has never really been satisfied until we begin to encounter selflessness. This is the place, and Noble Wisdom is loving-kindness as self, wisdom to awaken, and letting go of outcomes for the greatest and highest good.

However, life is always on life's terms. Our desire to belong is also a fierce teacher and harsh taskmaster, where relationships become an all-powerful cause of heaven or hell. But, this trial is grace too. As the drama of our relationships plays out, they are akin to self-paced interactive lessons. We repeat mistakes indefinitely until we fully grasp what we need to learn. Ultimately our awareness frees us from these habitual choices, which cause so much subjection.

The next level of connection, belonging, relationship, and association processes simplify into acceptance and loving-kindness. The key is to see everyone equally as our most beloved. Ram Dass used to tell the story of his Uncle Louie, who was very dear to him, and how he ceased to care about the competition or one-up-man-ship when he discovered everyone was equally as precious as his beloved uncle.[12] This perspective is the most immediate bridge between loving-kindness and Buddha-nature. This is also a prerequisite for effortless belonging, which can occur at these higher levels of awareness.

The *Lanka*'s message is, first and foremost, an honest expression of self. Only where you and I are wholly interconnected, as in regarding each other's Buddha-nature, is there authentic affection and acceptance. By extension, we can never be faithful to ourselves unless we are functioning in this expanded awareness of cherishing everyone devotedly.

You and I become definitions of little consequence in the perspective which says, "I am you cleverly disguised as me."[13] The magic is, once you become identified with everyone as yourself, you experience yourself as loving-kindness. We must rewrite the myths and stories to fit a new context of not-separate awareness.

> *What I do to others, I do to myself.*
>
> *What I do for others, I do for myself.*
>
> *What I do to myself, I do to everyone.*
>
> *What I do for myself, I do for everyone.*

---

[12] Dass, R. (2013). *Being Love*. Ram Dass. Retrieved from https://www.ramdass.org/being-love/

[13] Unknown source

This is the circle thou art.

When you lie, thou art deceived.

When you give, thou receiveth.

When you steal, thou art robbed.

When you love all others, thou lovest thyself.

To love fully the guileless heart, my most dearly beloved child thou art.

A mystery of discernment applied.

Not seeing guile, thou art free of guile.

Not seeing separateness, thou art freely accepted.

Joy is your true expression, loving-kindness your gift of wisdom.

The guileless heart sees the essence, intuitively, reservedly, modestly.

Exhausting the delusion of separateness,

acceptance and loving-kindness replace old identifications.

***None Other Than Self, OWM**

Though I have presented the Buddha-nature statement as a fact unto itself, it would be remiss to assume your prompt acceptance. Therefore, in the following chapters, I'll endeavor to validate this assumption as we approach forces of connection, entanglement, and ubiquitous life in not-separate particle physics.

Like the craftsman dependent on materials and tools,

teaching is a craft of slow change.

Transformation is taught as it plays to the audience's need

and their capacity for understanding.

Its purpose is to provide progress and relief of suffering.

But it is not intended as the whole truth, which words can never contain.

Truth arises in Noble Wisdom blooming from self-realization.

Lanka, Chapter 7, section LXXXIX

Next, we move into the fifth stage of awareness, labeled non-dual rationality. We have circled the formless nature of existence and determined the incredible gifts of our first and greatest desire; to realize we are a unique expression of loving-kindness, just like everyone else. Now we enter our first self-nature as rationality at the level of natural forces, which have no opposite, no discrimination, and no judgment.

CHAPTER TWELVE
IMPERMANENCE

The ancients understood the insubstantiality of matter or form quite accurately, long before we even discovered the earth was round. However, impermanence meant much more than a method to understand the physical world, as we do in quantum physics. Impermanence appears in the physical world as the constant change within the forces of nature. Expressed as all things intermingle in the continual interchange of energy and charge, it links, defines, and presents itself as individuated change when we observe its detail.

> *When completely magnified and analyzed,*
> *the atom has no substance, which can be found.*
> *Though without static actuality, atoms are also not imaginary,*
> *and so only the concept or belief in matter remains.*
> *We cannot determine their existence or non-existence,*
> *as impermanence is true for all things made of atoms.*
> *How then may we argue what is or isn't real?*
> *Because the imagined may be just as real as the stone,*
> *depending on its position in the cycle of impermanence.*
>
> *Lanka,* **Chapter 2, section XII**

Life in Continual Flux

The idea presented here is that no ultimate reality as form or particle exists, only continual change. There is a reality; there is also form, which is not just fantasy, but we only understand it in theory. Your life is your theory of existence, and it is not independent of your mind.

The stanza's validation of imagination is also intriguing, as we might understand the cycle of impermanence to be time, space, location, or the whole variety of change. In this context, your vision is in itself no proof of validity nor reason for doubt of what is or may-be. That fact that you imagine something makes it neither real nor unreal.

In Newtonian physics, we understand the impermanence of the physical world at the gross level. But at the quantum level, there is a vast space in which ever-changing subatomic energy and frequency only appear as matter, depending on the interaction field. Electrons don't jump from one orbit to the next. They disappear at one level and reappear at another. Where matter is energy in constant vibration, it continuously exchanges charge and energy with no energy destroyed or lost. It has no permanent first atom or particle in this mysterious nature of matter, which the ancients somehow understood, long before particle accelerators.

The relevance to the cycle of impermanent life is that it brings us to the *Lanka*'s view of physicality, which we can relate to quantum physics after recent years of scientific development. Impermanence, as a cornerstone of Buddhism, is additionally one of three marks of existence. The other two are suffering and non-self, explored in the next chapter.

> *Rational men focus on what may be observed in existence,*
>
> *such as form, cause, effect, and interactions.*
>
> *Not accounting for space, and seeing it as separate from form,*
>
> *they envision a separate existence.*
>
> *But in truth, space is form, and as space penetrates form, form is space.*
>
> *In defining their characteristics, we grasp the two as separate*
>
> *but as form evolves it is not separate from space*
>
> *as space exists abundantly within form.*
>
> **Lanka, Chapter 2, section XII**

This stanza amazes me because today, any science student would recognize what sounds like a passionate physics teacher waxing lyrical.

Its vastness might well compare the orbital space within an atom with the expanse between the galaxies. For ancient contemplatives, this was incredibly insightful. Through their enlightened means, they understood what we have just theorized in the last one hundred years. But what does space mean to impermanence and not-separateness?

The best example of non-separate physicality is space itself. Indeed, if you can consider space as the physical separation between all forms, it is also the one singularity extending within the atom and throughout the universe. It is a bit counter-intuitive since it lacks structure, except for what it contains. But the *Lanka* would agree "Space is Form." Like the oceans, where we can't distinguish the Indian Ocean from the Atlantic Ocean at Cape Agulhas. Space is entirely one and interconnected across the universe and into the subatomic realm. In this not-separate oneness, the expanse within me is no different from the same spaciousness that exists within you. Impermanence is energy and vibration moving in fields of attraction, repulsion, and constant change, commingling perpetually.

> *Impermanence exists in actuality and fantasy,*
>
> *is seen in those things made of elements,*
>
> *which exist only in a constant flow of change and recombination.*
>
> *They have no substantiality one may possess,*
>
> *while the elements themselves never change.*

Lanka, Chapter 2, section LXXIX

In this description, impermanence is reminiscent of thermodynamics' principles, such as conservation-of-energy. But this stanza barely fits our materialistic viewpoint. Rather than a limiting principal, impermanence predicts physical behaviors of boundless change. The confusion is our relativistic need for tools. Per the next two stanzas, the *Lanka* goes even further into impermanence as a non-dual force, seen in nature, theorized in understanding but beyond touch or measurement.

Impermanence is incorrectly understood by the learned man in eight dualistic terms. They are:

(1) creation and destruction

(2) growth and evolution

(3) youth and old age

(4) fresh and decomposed

(5) objective and subjective

(6) life and death

(7) temporary and permanent

(8) light and darkness

Lanka, Chapter 2, section LXXIX

These terms are observed effects in time or space, not impermanence itself. We may do battle to define impermanence in the rational mind. As shown in word pairs, we understand differences in our attempts to discriminate this from that. We highlight these distinctions, but what is unique in understanding impermanence? We can never be sure of understanding's truth, as our view is only a moment in time within the constant flow of change. In the moment of time a diamond seems permanent but in enough time everything is temporary. Similarly with all these effects in time or space. This puzzle requires an attempt to define non-dual, which will be useful later as well.

For something to be non-dual, it has no subject, object, opposite, or other. Gravity may seem non-dual, in that anti-gravity is the stuff of science fiction so far. Still, any engineering student uses gravity as an acceleration to predict static and dynamic behavior. Forces oppose gravity, like lift or buoyancy, but they are not anti-gravity. We can only know many natural phenomena by their effect on other things. This paradox is the problem pointed out in the stanza above. Impermanence is only known by its effect, as an aspect of the non-dual.

Our relative terms, such as gravity and most natural forces, only have measurable effects with opposing but different forces. Their non-dual aspects exist beyond definition in terms useful to us. So duality is just a perspective of observed appearance. Impermanence expresses these non-dual characteristics of nature. Like the subconscious beyond our control, they contain unimaginable energy.

We may understand the forces of nature as laws of impermanence. As the fabric of the universe, we may adapt to nature's laws, but no adaptation can influence the impermanence of all things.

> *Impermanence is the cycle of life.*
>
> *Time is our measure of the day.*
>
> *But time is the wheel, impermanence the water turning it.*
>
> *Life appears to be death, death appears to be life, not just connected,*
>
> *they are one continuous cycle.*
>
> *With each breath you kill.*
>
> *With each breath you create.*
>
> *Life consumes life and death, while dying continuously.*
>
> *Non-dual and relative, embracing death only,*
>
> *may you embrace life's impermanence; denying death, you deny life.*
>
> *Confusing death with the loss of energy, the loss of resonance*
>
> *the will to command a form, you are afraid.*
>
> *Today is a good day to die.*
>
> *Life is in order.*
>
> *No regrets go unresolved.*
>
> *No harms go unrighted.*
>
> *No love goes unexpressed.*

One with it all in nightly sleep, thou neither collects nor relates.

There we merge each night without individuality as boundaries vanish.

Where will you go?

Thou art everywhere

Life Consumes Life, OWM

In the cognitive sphere, the non-dual exists without discrimination. Laws of nature make no judgment and have no preference. They create change itself. We subject them to names and forms. As the prime mover behind nature's laws, impermanence demonstrates agency, as the cause of effects . That's as much subtlety as my mind can explore, trying to understand terms beyond reason or logic.

As you might guess, impermanence also gets much subtler as we consider the nature of human existence. Beyond the physical manifestations, we must engage in non-physical human nature with its emotions, feelings, thoughts, and ideas. The Latin root of the word "subtle" originally meant "finely woven" like a fabric. This idea was many threads to make a fabric, which provides an image of the non-dual as a departure from conventional rationality. Like the fabric of the cosmos, direct experience is so slight that only observation is available from which theories are derived.

As to the meaning of non-duality, it means that all terms of opposites are relative in nature and do not exist independently from one another.

There is no darkness without light to define it.

There is no short without long to define it.

There is no hell without heaven to define it.

Therefore the wise understand all things as non-dual.

This is to realize the emptiness of things,

No-birth, non-duality, and no-self-nature.

Lanka, Chapter 2, Section XXVII

Like the earlier analogy of a brush full of paint, dragged along an infinite fence, it keeps on going long after we can sense or measure it. This dispersion is the progression into the non-dual; it is not only like space or the cosmos; the non-dual is space. In terms of the paintbrush or our existence; the non-dual is the agency, the force, the channel, the influence, the instrumentality, the mechanism, and the vehicle of our lives, but you can't see it, smell it, taste it, touch it or hear it. It is humbling in its ethereal nature, as it defies explanation.

> *As we search out failures and defects, the basis is not found.*
> *Even the mind fails to serve as dualism is mere appearance;*
> *non-duality is itself suchness.*
>
> **Lanka, Sagathakam, sloka 675**

Here we meet the enigmatic Zen challenge of the rational mind, which is approached with koan study and practice, to penetrate the essence or the absolute. The fifth stage of awareness or the fifth self-nature is seen in reflection entering this doorway, where definitions are not clear and boundaries disappear. Such practice as koan study and immersion in the non-dual suchness, is not only to see beyond the mind, it is to alter its wavelength to the essence appearing from suchness. My favorite vehicles in approaching these spaces are the *I-Ching* and the *Hsin Hsin Ming* as translated by Richard Wilhelm and Richard B. Clarke, respectively. I find opportunity and surprise in books not fully understood.

To the scientific materialist, who has made it thus far, this may sound like a lot of hooey, but there is a very pertinent reason for perception beyond duality. Shamanic paths, mindfulness, and especially intuitive penetration make available an aspect of ourselves lost in domestication. We start with only the primordial inheritance of our animal natures and something more. This perception into the emptiness of things reconnects us with repressed and denied aspects of our psyche. This connection in turn removes blinders, inhibitions and prejudice to open the door to greater excitement and fulfilment in life.

Inquiring further into *Yogachara*, several concepts lack clear dualistic expression because of their similar agency within dualistic concepts.

Non-dual forces include the collective subconscious and Mind-only. Like impermanence, known only by its consequences, the non-dual leads to a massive dilemma for the thinking mind. To be known by results leaves a concept only understood by effects to dualistic terms, which cannot and will not ever define it. It's like the reflection in a mirror, seen as an image but never seen in actuality. This relationship is significant for the physics of reality within the *Lanka*, but these concepts don't remain as unattainable images.

Non-dual impermanence says that everything, whether physical (form) or mental (formlessness), is a co-mingling of constant change, including all life types, all minerals, and even all thoughts. Of course, where form and formlessness are interconnected is the space between matter. The connection itself must be elemental to the structure, which means communications start within vibration and resonance.

If we look for an analogy in modern life, we know that wireless networks are capable of communicating vast amounts of information globally. But most of us know the technology only by its affects, like impermanence, the subconscious and Mind-only. As this concept is expanded within the Lanka, you will be presented the possibility, that we not only live among wireless networks; we also function in much the same way. To grasp this possibility, impermanence and the non-dual are foundational.

CHAPTER THIRTEEN
THREE MARKS OF EXISTENCE

Impermanence, as the first mark of existence, is the mechanism of all-natural forces at work. So, if we exist, we are subject to the natural effects of impermanence.

> *Impermanence equates to a non-dual force of nature.*
>
> *The atom is just an idea and form itself is only change which seems to exist statically.*
>
> *This is that which is not seen, unborn, beyond modification, but constantly fluctuating with thought.*
>
> *The ever-changing dependence on thought is the most important limitation of impermanence to perceive the non-dual.*
>
> ***Lanka*, Chapter 2, section lXXIX**

Encountering, experiencing, and perceiving the non-dual is the object of practice per the *Lanka*, which may be apparent to the Zen or Vajrayana student as the essence of suchness. But this requires a shift in awareness, which we will pursue as one of many significant streams, feeding the central theme of Mind-only. However, of huge significance in this transliteration is the connection between and dependence on thought, which links back to our early discussions. It shows the intermingling of causal effects, to realize thought alone is the learned response which limits access to the non-dual, but simultaneously causes unconscious effects.

This idea, handed down for thousands of years, is the first glimmer of where we are going. In quantum mechanics, we will attempt to integrate the observer effect into the overall thesis of not-separate.

But for now we will discuss the second mark of existence, suffering. In common terms, it is the opposite of pleasure or happiness. The first Noble Truth, that sentient beings will suffer, may be more accurate in saying that beings live in stages of dissatisfaction and stress.

The second noble truth says the cause of our suffering is desire, greed, craving or obsession with filling life's sense of lack. This links with holding onto things as permanent and real, not accepting impermanence. The original meaning of suffering infers craving, which is addiction of the mind. Beginning in the childish response to not getting what we want, at the dawn of sense-consciousness, other common characteristics include unpleasant circumstances, disturbing our ease, or things that are uncomfortable, challenging, all causing pain or sadness.

The third noble truth is that suffering, manageable with detachment or proper identification of self, ceases in stilling of the mind's waves of thought. This is the natural quiescent nature of the mind, as thoughts step from center stage to allow intuitive penetration of what is.

The fourth noble truth that there is a path leading to fulfilment, peace, purpose and a quiet state of bliss. Suffering can be mitigated by the eightfold path which presents separate aspects to address every arena of life. Included are right view, intention, speech, action, livelihood, effort, concentration, and mindfulness. All this is available within authentic schools of thought. Their epicenter is suchness, your own quiescent nature. This is the Lanka's thesis also.

The confusion comes in the idea of detachment, which can be interpreted as only available by stepping out of life's joys, sorrows and experience. This is our slight difference and focus on misplaced identification, so as to not exclude humanity at large. Suffering at the extreme of craving is the addiction to thought-outcomes caused by living life compulsively. Waking up to our imprisonment, in the form of habit and compulsion, is where my adamancy comes from. Pushing the basic envelope beyond mental identification repeatedly, dissatisfaction may become a gift and tool to a whole new world.

> *Finally, some holy men and women define suffering as emotion itself?*
> *Highest soul, those afraid of life and death sufferings seek nirvana,*
> *not realizing the inseparability of pain and bliss,*
> *nor the unreality of discrimination.*
> *They imagine the annihilation of senses and circumstance,*

> *not realizing nirvana is the radical shift in one's subconscious fabric as revulsion to the delusion and compulsion of sense identification.*
>
> *This subconscious shift in perception we call self-realization.*
>
> ***Lanka,* Chapter 2, section XVIII**

The *Lanka*'s approach is that suffering is no more real than what we make it, but this statement that "nirvana is the radical shift in one's subconscious fabric as revulsion to the delusion and compulsion of sense identification" is revolutionary in my understanding. This idea of foundational change will lead us to another esoteric concept, "the Great Turning Back". However, the ideal viewpoint may cause an internal reaction, as we often feel justified in our pain, infirmities, and tragedies, but it's not intended to be hurtful; it is only the extension of Mind-only. Much like Dr. Wayne Dyer said, "As you think, so shall you be." In this context the pain, infirmities and tragedies of life are hard-love gifts leading us to nirvana.

> *What is the mother of all beings?*
>
> *Desire procreates commingling joy and anger, nurtured through motherliness.*
>
> *But ignorant indifference is the father.*
>
> *His seed guides his children into the six realms of pleasure and suffering.*
>
> ***Lanka,* Chapter 2, section LVIII**

The Function of Misery

Some texts label desire as the cause of suffering, the *Lanka* is clear that misery is the function of two aspects—ignorance and compulsive craving. It raises a critical question for an old-householder like me. What is the outcome of desire if we manage to live in Right-understanding?

From a psychological view, suffering often motivates the incredible potential we see in human development. In the *Lanka*, suffering, seen as a creation of the mind, may also indicate opportunities or gifts when embraced. Society has recognized a learning difficulty called dyslexia as related to superior math skills and abstract thinking in recent years. The limitation of inconsistently arranging characters in words causes the brain to develop other perceptual skills in abstraction and calculation. When seen from another perspective, hurdles or suffering often prepare us for abilities and even greater fulfilment. In this light, we can embrace challenges and limitations by accepting "what is" with gratitude, as challenge creates abilities and perception, which is otherwise unavailable.

According to the *Lanka*, suffering is the function of misplaced focus.

As one destroys the notion of externality with realization of Mind-only's creation; form, sensation, thought, disposition, consciousness, appearances, ego, and subjective reality loose their hold and lift their veils, to reveal an insight into reality just as it is.

Students, at this stage of concentration, step beyond suffering and gain Right-understanding while still working on habitual life and their own cycles of transformation.

Lanka, Chapter 2, section XVI

In another sense, suffering is the conditional friction or abrasion necessary in the experience of life. All life is dependent on its evolution, decay, and elimination. The second mark of existence is a natural outcome of resistance to change or impermanence. In the life lived compulsively, suffering arises in the notion of externality or the belief that one's life results from circumstances beyond our control. This idea of gaining Right-understanding to facilitate working on compulsion and misidentification with externals, is incredibly powerful because it recognizes pain, challenges and difficulty as the teachers leading to freedom.

Suffering ends when discrimination of form, desire, and thought, ceases to be the identification of self.

This is an end to ignorance and craving, masked as accomplishment and achievement.

The objective world, like a dream, is seen created by one's mind.

Lanka, Chapter 2, section VI

To label suffering an illusion may offend unnecessarily. This conceptual detachment readily creates disagreement because grief is genuinely experienced. Usually, it is fiercely defended as an outcome of uncontrollable external conditions. But this is precisely the opportunity of freedom, in that only when one grasps full accountability is alleviating our craving, pain, or sorrow possible.

But that is also the whole idea of Mind-only, destroying the notion of externality or blame by engaging total accountability. Though suffering is different for everyone, it may guide self-determination as an avenue of healing through a change of awareness, habits, and disposition. As implied earlier this real change begins to occur mentally but the ultimate change is a revolution within the subconscious or the origin of perception.

> *Thou art alive, the only constant change, as thou art born, you begin to die.*
>
> *As love blossoms with passion, it begins to fade.*
>
> *Everything thou hast is fleeting, but suffering happens as you choose it.*
>
> *The choice is the choice of story; no story, no suffering.*
>
> *Thinking makes it so.*
>
> *Relaxing makes it go.*
>
> *A resonate chord there is, a chord of all souls.*
>
> *Thou art our most beloved and innocent child, if you choose only to see.*
>
> *Loving completely and letting go completely, thou art free.*
>
> ***No Story: No Suffering*, OWM**

Non-self

The third mark of existence is non-self, no-ego-soul, or, said another way, not-separate. At this point, we might as well face the elephant in the room on a subject often forbidden in circles of objective reasoning. The controversy arises around reincarnation, an ongoing debate, which often misunderstands whether there is a soul or not, per Buddhism.

First, the rationalist may say that objective reasoning finds no proof of soul or reincarnation. This argument labels the two constructs as superstitious religious tools to justify beliefs and religion's place in the world. Another discussion, not unrelated, is between Buddhism and the rest of religious philosophy. Similar to non-theist objectivity, Buddha is said to have found no proof of a continuation of personality and selfhood, as generally understood to be one's soul. This question surrounds what is permanent versus transitory in the ancient Buddhist text.

Seven sense channels of consciousness are thought, attached mind, and the five senses which are characterized by their temporary and vacillating nature.

As they arise from habitual patterns, they are destitute of suchness and their collections do not pass beyond the mortal existence.

Lanka, Chapter 7, section LXXXIX

This stanza describes seven out of the eight doorways of consciousness. The seven impermanent structures we generally lump together are the objective and subjective mind, sight, hearing, taste, touch, and smell. The eighth form of consciousness is the subconscious. According to this ancient text, what continues or reincarnates is the subtlest level only. We leave impressions in the subconscious field or collective subconscious through actions, thought, and desires. Memory as we know it disappears, and most of what we call self or personality, is a temporary fabrication to get along in this life.

These soul images, or that which transmigrates, are more similar to our disposition, inclinations, or tendencies than an individual personality. Lacking memory, judgment, and attachment, this soul represents the non-dual aspect of self.

Additionally, the stanza is about reincarnation or transmigration of the no-ego-soul, as defined within the *Lanka*. But it only says what doesn't pass beyond life (all the collections of sense-consciousness). Like a good game of Monopoly, no matter what the result, all the pieces end up back in the box, at the end. The *Lanka* also doesn't argue "soul or no soul," as do my Buddhist and Hindu friends. It only claims that the soul is beyond sense-consciousness.

According to the ancients, our mental constructs and sensory impressions cease to exist when we die. Furthermore, attachment to who we think we are, may be the most transitory, vacillating continually and compulsively. These misidentifications are the smallest and most fleeting foam on the subconscious ocean.

This foam and waves are the perfect analogy for the ego-sense-of-self. As we naturally fear the ocean depths, we also find it unimaginable to let go of our definition of self, in which we have nothing invested, except the habit of preferences. Otherwise, who would we be, and what about our reason for being? The question appears always to be, "Am I conscious in this moment, or is it just compulsive habit?" *Be-Here-Now* comes to mind, as the reflection of moment-by-moment presence.

> *If you do not do what you cannot do, that's no problem.*
> *But if you do not do what you can do, you are a tragedy.*
>
> **Sadhguru,** *Mystic's Teachings*

This statement has been taped to my monitor for several years to remind me there is work I can do, but most important has been realizing the game is rigged and all that I have to offer is sneaking awareness of the trap.

However, the subconscious and letting go of our ideas of self were not so foreboding with the introduction of meditation. When Maharishi Mahesh Yogi introduced Transcendental Meditation to the west in the 1970s, his student-teachers introduced the practice. By sitting quietly and saying a mantra, and observing the breath, the student was directed to see the experience without expectations, as gently and naturally diving below the surface awareness to encounter the transcendental. In this way, meditation is a lot like learning to swim safely. Though Maharishi didn't argue about the existence or non-existence of souls, he extraordinarily influenced my generation to experience the subtle aspect of self which exists without identity.

Unlike conventional Buddhism, the *Lanka* doesn't argue no-soul

Three Marks of Existence

consistently. Despite contesting the relevance of ego-soul or attachment to personality, the *Lanka* defines the non-dual aspect of self as so ethereal as to be energy itself. Transmigration is a fact, per the *Lanka*, because it occurs naturally, like energy, never destroyed, but without most of what we call personality, memory, and individuality.

> *762. Before enlightenment, one cannot find the essence of things in both permanence and emptiness, caught as they are in the identification with form, sensation, thought, disposition, and consciousness.*
>
> *763. However, without the ego-soul, we have no purpose in stages of development, self-mastery, clairvoyance, attainments, or the bliss of meditative consciousness.*
>
> *764. When the inquisitor comes to say, "Show me this ego-self, if it exists," the sage shall respond, "Show me your own discrimination."*
>
> **Lanka, Sagathakam**

These slokas demonstrate what I love about the *Lanka* and its place in history. It confronts the questions of relative and absolute in the classical Zen challenge. It asks, "who experiences?" Where there is no-self or other-than-self, everything "just is." In talking about Sagathakam slokas 762–4, D.T. Suzuki also expressed confusion. In the conflicting idea of no-ego-soul as contradictory to consciousness, he saw this part of the *Lanka*, as violating the traditional Buddhist doctrine of Non-atman.

In a relative sense, the idea of soul minus ego gives new meaning and purpose to our practice of compassion and loving-kindness. We all fundamentally want acceptance, happiness, and peace while simultaneously having been fooled by nature. No-ego-self as empty, may be precisely what we need to understand existence.

However, it cannot be known just as the atom. Self lacks substantiality in form and formlessness. I can have a sense of self, or concept but I only experience it beyond the senses, in reflection and intuition.

Thich Nhat Hanh describes flowers as made of countless dissimilar parts. None of which is a flower. None of which has the full essence of flower in it.[14] Flowers, made of minerals, water, fields, energy, and vibration, harmonize as life to become something that only exists in their mutuality. Like looking in the mirror, their image returns an understanding which is transcendental because it transcends discernment and requires acceptance.

> *Impermanence is emptiness in terms of time*
> *Non-self is emptiness in terms of space.*

Thich Nhat Hanh, *Peace Is Every Step*

The *Lanka* also tells us that by understanding our existence as impermanent but connected, we influence the abrasion of suffering from the power of our awareness. So, without the illusion, we are an interconnected, interdependent commingling of life, which only appears to be many individuals. My preference is to focus on interdependent co-arising because it conveys a sense of visceral mutuality.

> *The nature of all things, like a vision, dream, illusion or reflection has nothing to do with birth and death; eternality, or extinction.*

***Lanka*, Chapter 2, section XXVI**

The *Lanka* takes this image to the next level by examining impermanence through the lens of suchness.

Without each other and empathic social cooperation, none of us would survive long. To be interdependent is to be entirely dependent on the planetary ecosystem: plants, animals, and especially microbes. We are born as a part of a system, we live by consuming living things and feed others in one continuous cycle. In this cycle of impermanence, food eaten becomes you, and in respiring, defecating, and dying, you become food for another life form.

Impermanence and not separateness may be "marks of existence," but these concepts are by nature, beyond fully understanding.

---

[14] Hanh, T. (1991). *Peace Is Every Step*. Bantam Doubleday Dell Publishing Group.

The grand trinity of masterhood,
the self-realization of no-self and no other than self.
The power of the Buddha's dharma teachings,
Right-knowledge and the understanding of being fully human.
Then a mystery beyond knowledge… imagelessness?
The emptiness of self and the fullness of all life,
in each moment without agenda.
Thou art that, tat twam asi.

Noble Wisdom, OWM

CHAPTER FOURTEEN
THE CYCLE OF LIFE

We don't usually recognize the fragility of life because we take it for granted. But, without the sun, all life disappears in seconds. Without air, it's a matter of minutes. No water and we have a few days; food maybe weeks. Furthermore, we don't know how long our bodies were designed to last if we could protect them from disease, injury, and natural decay. At seventy years old, I can't count the times I would have died without natural or modern medicine, and some plumbing in my chest.

However, through this same advancement in medical science, we have also created our most significant environmental problem: overpopulation. Around the time the *Lanka* appeared, world population estimates were less than the USA in 2019, less than 350 million or representing approximately 4.7 percent of the current world population. At our current rates, some people say we may be looking for other planets to support us by the year 3000. This trend may not be a surprise, but it took about two hundred thousand years of population growth to reach one billion and only a few years more to reach six billion. A quick online search says we've grown by 67,000,000 this year alone.[15]

However, the advancement of scientific materialism has created the first opportunity in humankind's history for large-scale enlightenment or an evolutionary tipping point. This trend isn't just because we live much longer, though we can expect to live about six years longer than our grandparents. The opportunity is created in the time to contemplate, study, and develop because our lives, in many parts of the world, are no longer spent struggling to survive.

To better understand this fragile life cycle, reconsider our interdependence upon an unseen world. The Human Microbiome Project,

---

[15] Hartley-Parkinson, R. (2019, October June 26). *UK Population Rises to 66,436,000 and Migration Is Biggest Factor*. Metro. Retrieved from https://metro.co.uk/2019/06/26/uk-population-rises-66436000-migration-biggest-factor-10074103/

referenced in *10% Human* by Dr. Alanna Collen, revealed the human body as the symbiosis of billions of life forms[16] (see Chapter 10). Furthermore, these are predominantly symbiotic relationships. We can't live without our bacteria, viruses, fungi, and archaea. They have evolved right along with us, and our microbial makeup is as unique as our fingerprint. Our bodies are the perfect definition of interdependent co-arising.

> *This groundbreaking guide reveals how our personal colony of microbes run 90 per cent of our bodies, challenging how we view diet, modern disease and medicine. Microbes influence our gut, weight, immune system, mental health and even our choice of partner.... As biologist and zoologist Dr. Alanna Collen argues, these conditions are rooted in our lack of care for our microbes, and this is the indispensable study, life – and becoming a healthy human – is impossible without them.*
>
> Dr. Alanna Collen, ***10% Human***

The Human Biome

Since our estimated hundred trillion human cells are inhabited by and in symbiotic relationships with some quadrillion microbes, "How much is us and how much is them" isn't the most exciting question relative to the *Lanka*. In a not-separate thesis it is "How do we understand and communicate with our host of life partners?" Fluid transfer and chemical reactions are plausible for many cellular interactions. But that is a slow process considering the whole-body response to impending danger in less than 300 milliseconds with trillions of near-simultaneous interactions. How can microbes communicate sense perceptions that become desires holistically, controlling the mind, as with pheromones. How do we understand their huge variety of unconscious sense awareness?

Since microbes can tell the body what to crave, what else are microbes

---

[16] Collen, A. (2015) *10% Human: How Your Body's Microbes Hold the Key to Health and Happiness.* William Collins.

telling us that we understand in microbe-balese?[17] Intuition is too broad a term, as the autonomic nervous system taught in grade school is too simplistic. The mechanism is unclear, but there is a conscious, nearly instantaneous interaction, among cells, below sense-consciousness everywhere in the body. A sour stomach can undoubtedly cross that line, as can sexual attraction based on bacteria growth. But the list of interactive dependencies could fill a library. Here we can recognize pervasive innate communications, which connects our human cells to our microbial partners as ordinary and everyday experience and yet beyond our understanding.

> *Consciousness itself is only known in its agency,*
>
> *through its reaction to or interaction with the physical world.*
>
> *Consciousness is simply to perceive, discern,*
>
> *or judge without necessarily having the ability to show response.*

Lanka, Chapter 2, section IV

Here the *Lanka* distinguishes sense-consciousness by its effect on the objective world. This agency is also how we can recognize our dependence on a commonwealth of life forms. But has science uncovered the most exciting question of simultaneous communications?

Unconscious influences from symbiotic organisms often control awareness; our perceiving, discerning, and judging. We could say microbes inspire our awareness, lacking distinct agency like the five senses. But a bad stomach can be an overpowering force of nature. But mostly the influence can be attributed to what we've labeled instinct or even intuition.

This innate relationship of awareness, knowledge, and communication is fundamental to all life. But it's not the whole story. Progressive science has recently begun to identify neurological networks throughout the body, which have the directive ability to initiate reactions, feelings, and awareness. These discoveries relate to the simplistic definition of consciousness, which the *Lanka* expounds.

---

[17] This is the language of microbes.

Interdependent co-arising thou art.
A small environment of all life is your body.
Composed of trillions, yours is worlds within a world.

No electron or atom is uniquely yours, flowing to and fro,
they resonate, attach, then leave.
You are one with all life as aspects, tendencies, and expressions only.

Thou art the resonance, waves of energy and particles.
You move through space leaving a trail of atoms, energy and vibration.
Gathering equally you collect, absorb and embody.

This impermanent form has no beginning or end fully determined in space.
It exists in the unseen commingling with all others.
Infinitely small and infinitely large, just the same.

So being, thou art part of everything and everything is part of you, boundaries vanish.
Thou art boundless.

Boundless, OWM

The gut and heart connection to the brain, once understood as purely sensing, is now recognized as bi-directional communications and control. So, a gut feeling or heartfelt moment may more accurately be described as consciousness, which may perceive, discern, and independently direct our actions, overriding the brain. With this independence from our mind, we recognize intelligent sensory organs.

We used to think that neurons were concentrated exclusively in our brain and spinal cord. Now we know that they are also concentrated in our heart and in our gut. The fields of neurocardiology and neurogastroenterology study the interactions of the brain and whole body, with the "second brain" in the heart and the "third brain" in the gut.

Terry Patten, *A New Republic of the Heart*

The concept of co-processing within the body resolves how we perceive beyond the five senses. It links primary sensory centers in a more comprehensive network, though it still doesn't answer the holistic questions of cell-microbe communications. Co-processing leads us to question what senses are activated in a gut reaction or a heartfelt moment and what is discounted as intuition? Like tears in a movie, a truth response may be a composite of tears, slight choking, and even a runny nose. The particular correlation is uniquely our own.

On a more subtle level, a gut reaction is the feeling that something isn't quite right, which we often discount as intuition. Without recognizing neurological interdependence or the influence of symbiotic life partners, we make judgments with a small part of the information available. This idea also questions whether the gut might be a composite processor of unconscious inputs such as smell, body language, vibrational changes, subtle auditory clues, temperature variations, etc. Maybe autonomic senses, of bacterial smells, communicate sexual attraction based on best breeding choices? Though it may seem far out, experimentation, at Berne University [18], has proven highly sophisticated innate judgments, in just such a scenario.

Consciousness, as a higher function of life, only means: to discern, comprehend and possibly react.

So, in seeing, we distinguish a red apple or white cloth, which is eye-consciousness.

Sound, smell, taste, feeling, and thought are experienced similarly.

---

[18] Lobmaier, J. (2018, September 12). The Scent of a Woman: What Makes It Attractive. Bern University. Retrieved from https://www.unibe.ch/news/media_news/media_relations_e/media_releases/2018/medienmitteilungen_2018/scent_of_a_woman_what_makes_it_attractive/index_eng.html

> *Each consciousness has the ability to perceive and react independently.*
>
> *Through these five forms of sense consciousness and thought consciousness, we comprehend the world externally and internally.*
>
> **D.T. Suzuki, *Lanka: Introduction, Psychology***

The *Lanka*'s description of the senses as independent fits our experience. We ordinarily associate gut feelings with likes, dislikes, or maybe intuition, making these more than desires. You don't have to think about removing your hand from a hot stove! Subconscious choice, maybe including a heart or gut sense, directs immediate reaction without the conscious mind's interaction. Simple examples are clear enough, but there is so much more going on.

Eight Doorways of Consciousness

Also, I must clarify that the paraphrased section of D.T. Suzuki's explanation was only about cognitive consciousness. This section only identified the function of consciousness in its interactive or waking forms. According to the *Lanka*, there are eight forms of consciousness, with thought separated into objective and subjective, as described here.

> *What is judged good and bad is only due to the eight channels of consciousness.*
>
> *They are the subconscious, the mind of objective thought,*
>
> *the attached mind of subjective will and discrimination,*
>
> *and the five senses of sight, hearing, smell, taste, and touch.*
>
> ***Lanka*, Chapter 6, section LXXXVI**

Besides laying out the structure, the Buddha's statement establishes a priority or proportion. As, our consciousness arises from the subconscious, proceeds to thought, then subjective will and discrimination. The senses inform the mind and stand ready to discern and react of their own volition.

However, besides functionality the *Lanka* puts major emphasis of grasping the subtle awarenesses we have lumped into intuition.

> *There are those Buddhas of other paths recognized in their truth response.*
>
> *When feeling the insights of solitude, selflessness, and worldly detachment,*
>
> *they will shed tears or the hair of their body may stand on end.*
>
> *These Buddhas of other paths may develop powers of transformation*
>
> *to the extent they are true to their path.*
>
> **Lanka, Chapter 2, section XX**

When I start talking about intuition it includes the possibility of psychic powers, and people begin to get uncomfortable. But in the *Lanka*, psychic phenomena are mostly anecdotal references. However, within this passage, the transformation powers relate to personal growth and human potential within us common folk. It describes a test by which we see ourselves. This is very exciting because it's talking about listening to our intuition or our full senses and being true to its message. From the ancient's perspective, allowing for parapsychology is also only the natural outcome of accepting its physics. So, we open the question of what is normal? What is going on that we may or may not be aware of?

First, what is this thick air we breathe made of, besides nitrogen, oxygen, and argon? The atmosphere is alive with living microbes, carried mostly in water vapor, but not only. The earth's atmosphere is between 0.4 percent to 1 percent water vapor but may approach 5 percent in tropical conditions. What we exhale can easily reach 50 percent humidity and is typically full of living organisms. Every breath includes microbes, charged particles, along with someone else's exhalation. But what do we sense without knowing it?

As mentioned, the respiratory system is more of an atmospheric environment than a mechanical air exchange system. With each breath, we sense smell, taste, temperature, alkalinity, and acidity while we consume micro-organisms. You could calculate that in a lifetime, we inhale about

300,000 kilograms of air or about six hundred elephants in weight. Luckily, we exhale approximately the same volume as outstanding carbon dioxide providers and frugal oxygen consumers. But that's a lot of air.

Consider the constant interchange of just micro-organisms, which communicate at levels beyond our waking sense-perception. They freely cruise into one's lungs, making themselves at home. We often associate germs and contagion with our shared air, but today microbial science indicates a great deal more is going on. We receive a huge variety of subtle communications, similar to our sense of pheromones. The population differences of microbes communicate our physical individuality and provide for a profound, subtle awareness.

We may have no awareness of how smell contributes to sexual attraction, whether pleasant or not. We only feel the tingling urge of desire, not necessarily its actual source. So, in a primal sense, sexual attraction begins beneath conscious awareness, as odorless pheromones communicate a woman's fertility or a male's potency. Science has uncovered these microbial differences are hundreds of times more complex than the apparent good or bad smells. We sense complicated health relationships and respond before discriminating, without noticing on most occasions.

The subtler influences of subconscious perceptions and their subsequent effect have been investigated experimentally at the University of Berne.[19] Young female college students rated their attraction to natural male scents, independent of other input or identification. The young men's pajamas captured their pheromone-laden odor. This way, each young woman's intuitive appreciation could be quantified and analyzed against a broad spectrum of physiology. It provided a unique window into our subconscious sense-perception. The researchers were overwhelmingly surprised.

One of the critical issues was the health profile of each participant. Comparing immunological characteristics indicated that the male who ranked highest for each female's choice repeatedly had the most dissimilar immune system profile relative to their own. This surprising result, scientists theorized, indicated a very sophisticated, innate, intuitive, or instinctive judgment by the females. Their choices consistently provided

---

[19] Collen, A. (2015) *10% Human: How Your Body's Microbes Hold the Key to Health and Happiness.* William Collins.

potential offspring with the best biological advantage: the most diversified and, therefore, most robust immune system.

The complexity of this innate judgment can't be over-emphasized. Sexual attraction or revulsion are consequences of microbial population, as in pheromones. That we, as a species, instinctively make non-rational judgments to focus on long-term species health, leaves the door open to infinite possibilities. What about emotions or other judgments, attractions, repulsions, and desires, perceived through sight, smell, taste, touch, hearing, or even intuition? How often are the mechanisms of intuition really subconscious sense awareness or microbial feedback?

With each moment, a million stimuli
rush the eyes, nose, ears, taste, and touch.

Only in quietude may you perceive
one-one hundredth of their meaning.

But in that perception echoes
the combined wisdom of every ancestor.

It is yours to deduce and bring to consciousness
for thou art the combined wisdom of every ancestor.

Thou art that.

Your Hidden Power, OWM

CHAPTER FIFTEEN

INTUITION

Today, progressive science is beginning to accept the gut and heart minds as active centers of non-cognitive discernment. Labeled intuitive awareness but differentiating between subtle observation, cognitive, or innate functions, it may be confused and misunderstood. We generally accept gut instinct, and heart intelligence theories are under research by folks like the Heart Math Institute, researching the heart's role in directly processing and decoding intuitive information.

We often perceive another's comfort, tension, anger, fear, or resentment without thinking about it. Our perceptions have associated indicators such as tone of voice, body language, etc. Still, as we get caught up in thinking, these external clues become suppressed. But we sense many things innately, and our instinctive perceptions are rarely side-tracked, though we choose to ignore them.

Intuition often gets an undeserved bad name. The confusion is in the two stages of intuition, labeled visionary and universal. The problem is trusting the often misunderstood and sometimes misused visionary aspect of intuition. ESP or psychic perceptions are from the outside-in, as seen in a fortune-teller. This aspect isn't of interest in a psychological thesis.

So, our references to intuition are limited to those surrounding personal awareness only. The universal label is applied because we all have similar experiences related to non-logical knowing, which may actually be subtle sense perception as with the girls in the Berne experiment. Excitement comes from mindful reflection, getting in touch from the inside out, connecting with innate wisdom, the still quiet voice, or one's intuitive vision. Professor Brene' Brown says it beautifully,

> *Intuition is not a single way of knowing. It's our ability to hold space for uncertainty and our willingness to trust the many ways we've developed knowledge and insight, including instinct, experience, faith, and reason.*

Brene Brown, *Cultivating Intuition and Trusting Faith*

Intuition vs. Imagination

The *Lanka* emphasizes intuition without derogatory labels and takes it one step forward as an active state of awareness. It does, however, differentiate intuition from imagination, which common use sometimes intermingle. As mentioned before, much of our feelings and subtle awareness are likely the processing of subconscious predispositions. In this sense, intuition is non-cognitive, non-judging, sensory perception which doesn't easily lend itself to simple verification. There are also other levels of intuition, which should never be discounted at the inspirational and provocative edges of awareness.

> *Meditative consciousness and the correct acquisition of truth*
>
> *can be understood as synonymous.*
>
> *They refer to a singularity of mind, concentrated and focused thought*
>
> *in the receptive state of intuition, rather than the active state of thinking.*
>
> **D.T. Suzuki, *Lanka:* Chapter 2, section IX,**

This paraphrased note indicates intuition as a single-minded discipline or a disidentification practice with doing and thinking. It includes the receptivity, Professor Brown pointed out, which is the attitude of acceptance that makes listening possible. The *Lanka* brings intuition away from broad metaphysical terms and back to stages of awareness like suchness, solitude, and eventually Right-knowledge.

Two crucial facts appear. One is the correlation of meditative consciousness (Samadhi or suchness) as prerequisite to Right-knowledge. The second idea is the sympathetic nature of intuition, which is receptive, able to discern a situation's truth, and available only in peaceful awareness.

From a biological perspective, the threshold between intuition and innate intelligence is hardly discernible. Related to subconscious communications, innate intelligence interacts continuously with our cells, organs, and systems. As seen when massive stress causes chronic health problems. Only when it crosses the threshold into conscious awareness, do we call it intuition. It again begs the question of communications methods and relationships. How might this interchange of information be possible in rational terms? That's where we are going.

Recognizing our electrical functions while acknowledging that most perception is below cognitive awareness, why shouldn't our senses hear, feel, taste, smell, and see subtle variations in the electro-magnetic field? Our senses perceive stimuli from a gentle touch to a cool breeze without any difficulty. What about the hair that stands up with a static charge or acrid smells associated with high voltage? Then there is the mirage in the desert attributed to heat waves. How much more do we perceive but not discern?

Like our communications through micro-organisms, internally and externally, we function predominantly on a subconscious level. Here the vast majority of received data is at the formless margins of mind, as they influence and stimulate various responses.

That which is unique to the individual, exists only in the formlessness of mind.

Lanka, Chapter 2, section LII

This concept is also another way of saying thinking is a secondary reaction to life processes such as feelings, senses, fear, appetite, and a host of subtle sensory insights. It has been more widely understood in recent years, inspired by the psychological approach pioneered by Dr. Carl Jung, who identified four modes of orientation:

1. Thinking—conscious thought and reasoning
2. Sensation—any conscious perception through the senses
3. Feeling—process of emotional or subjective evaluation, distinct from the intellect and sense perception.
4. Intuition—the process of unconscious or non-cognitive perception, an understanding or insight without conscious reasoning.

Dr. Jung separated sensation from intuition at the boundary of conscious awareness. However, the famous experiment at the University of Berne demonstrated a subtle and highly evolved subconscious discrimination.[20] Intuitive, for lack of a better term, it demonstrates an inherited judgment or the collective wisdom, we all share but don't recognize.

When the young ladies in Berne chose a nice smelling pajama shirt, their likes or dislikes correlated sense inputs with a hither-to-unknown breeding intelligence. Labeling this discernment as merely breeding instinct diminishes its exceptional accuracy for an entire cross-section of young women. If we can grasp the power of such natural awareness and bring it to light, we can expand the potential of human consciousness. In a larger sense, the experiment in Berne highlights our extra-ordinary powers of perception, which go unnoticed, often ignored to our detriment. This perception is no less than miraculous in the context of scientific materialism. That's one example among hundreds of thousands of choices and sense perceptions we all make routinely.

Intuition in this context is accessible use of the subconscious. It makes sense as we've related to sensory input, tied together with the understanding of Mind-only. Whether we call it a gut feeling or following our heart, with a high level of certainty, intuition from a calm mind determines what feels right, with a high level of accuracy.

We have a spectrum of semiconscious states identified as unconscious in modern psychology. Our thesis distinguishes that they are often subconscious rather than unconscious as they have direct effects or agency, operating just below sense-consciousness. In this ancient science, the subconscious is key in its active support of awareness, which will become clearer as we introduce the *Lanka's* field concepts.

The *Lanka*'s use of the term unconscious applies to unaware behaviors like childish acting out or instinctive response. It is where the individual is reacting compulsively and completely unaware. It is the shadow behavior taking hold and one step removed from semi-consciousness or not fully awake. To be unconscious in these terms, is to operate in blind instinctive reaction.

As an example of what this means, I can look to my own behaviors.

---

[20] Lobmaier, J. (2018, September 12). The Scent of a Woman: What Makes It Attractive. Bern University. Retrieved from https://www.unibe.ch/news/media_news/media_relations_e/media_releases/2018/medienmitteilungen_2018/scent_of_a_woman_what_makes_it_attractive/index_eng.html

In the past my unconscious reaction has been conspicuous when I felt physically threatened, such as a time when teenagers drove between me and my small children on a Texas beach. My mind almost shut off and my reactions became primal, putting myself between the truck and my children on a return trip. It was like a blind rage but without anger or violence, my body reacted quicker than my thought could catch up. My fixated awareness took control and a reaction was determined subconsciously. But, these are just word choices attempting clarity; the distinction appears in the *Lanka's* structure of consciousness.

> *As the subjective mind wills and discriminates, it is a double-headed monster.*
>
> *One face peers into the subconscious; without awareness the other scans the sense-consciousness, to see countless things and hold them as real.*
>
> *Clinging to this outcome of thought, he or she is caught in circumstance.*
>
> *Here we can say desire is the mother of compulsion and ignorance the father.*
>
> **D.T. Suzuki, *Lanka:* Introduction**

The Repository of the Waking Mind

The subconscious is vital to the *Lanka*'s psychology as the cornerstone of ancient wisdom. As the eighth channel of consciousness, it is a vast repository below the waking mind. It accepts whatever it receives without judgment or comparison. As the beginning of awareness and the starting point of sense-consciousness, it records everything we experience, including perceptions below our awareness. It continuously supports the mind, organizing overwhelming amounts of data according to countless associations such as sense memory, images, and ideas. However, it is not an independent consciousness, unlike the other seven forms of consciousness.

From immeasurable sense perceptions, memory, feeling, emotion, and experience, it extracts our reference points in every moment. It establishes our frame of reference from which preferences are reconstructed per the circumstance. In literal terms, the *Lanka* defines the subconscious as a non-dual awareness and repository or database of all individuated knowledge, experience, and perceptions.

> *The Buddha discards addictive habit from which false-imaginations arise.*
>
> *In this suchness, the external world is seen in the reality of Mind-only,*
>
> *where intuition of mutuality reveals the realm of unimaginable surprise.*
>
> *As the subconscious unencumbered, it creates a world of effortless belonging.*

***Lanka,* Chapter 2, section XIV**

This section from the *Lanka* pulls together many streams of psychology. And although it may sound mystical, pointing to a realm of unimaginable surprise. This just means learning at a whole new level, being inclusive of the fourth through sixth stages of awareness. Within this purview is the knowledge of our formless nature, non-dual rationality, and a new one which is certitude.

The sixth stage of awareness is where doubts have vanished, and direct experience is frequent. This is a life lived in synchrony or harmony within the flow of the universe. Synchronicity becomes every day. Like our daughter in Australia calling last night, laughing about a car we drove on my first trip, about nine years ago. And us laughing about our private conversation, the day before, about the same car door. The incredible becomes frequent.

The text also describes the practical functionality of suchness to eliminate false-imagination in the connected awareness of Mind-only, the intuition of mutuality, and the co-creation of an unencumbered subconscious. Where we started with our ego-creation story, mindfulness, and suchness, the increasing awareness of mutuality reveals the spiraling aspect of not-separate awareness. What may seem fanciful is the potential we are all born to.

One intriguing practice that addresses the possibility of subconscious self-alignment is Pema Chodron's observation of Shenpa. These are the shadows or left over pain points that can derail our mindfulness.[21] She makes a good case for self-observation and a practice based on an intuition of internal conflict. It is recognizing subconscious triggers to unconscious behaviors, which rise uncontrollably. This is like I described my own threat response. Grasping this fluid perception of reality, one pauses to recognize the trigger and investigate its origin. In this way, we may repeatedly align with the subconscious, awakening into various awarenesses. Taught by Chogyam Trungpa Rimpoche, she teaches holding a special awareness to our triggers, bringing it into the light, to illuminate an unconscious reaction and remove its power.

Intuition doesn't seem mysterious or weird if we recognize it is part of ordinary life to which we are generally unaware. Correlating a host of subtle sense perceptions, the senses read the air around us, receiving thousands of subliminal messages. Though we can't process every sensory input, nonetheless, it is all correlated and fed back as intuitions below the radar of thought, and that information, essential to our survival, may also be a valuable asset to our well-being.

Just as young women can sense the most beneficial biological partner by smell, haven't we mislabelled such non-cognitive judgment as extra-sensory? It is beyond sensory perception only in our underestimating our natural abilities and it points out we are only scratching the surface of human potential.

Often we develop an indirect, non-logical sense of others through visual and verbal clues. But through the Bern experiments,[22] we recognize that scent is extremely powerful as a conduit of intuition. In my own experience, I had been a yogi for about five years when I lived in New York City. On several occasions, I sensed an acrid odor and saw a gray-green hue around people who were angry to the point of violence.

Though it may sound crazy, our sense awareness is a highly developed connection into the source of sense consciousness, our subconscious mind.

We know that most of our action and reaction starts subconsciously. But the subtle perceptions are more rarefied in occurrence and recognition. I learned to stay away from angry people as a young man in New York.

---

[21] Chodron, P. (2004). *Getting Unstuck.* Sounds True Inc
[22] Collen, A. (2015) *10% Human: How Your Body's Microbes Hold the Key to Health and Happiness.* William Collins.

However, the certainty of intuitive sense perceptions is a matter of individual verification, requiring development and refinement.

This idea of sense-consciousness is a structure to understand neurological responses and the construction of psychology, as laid out by the *Lanka*. It says that the five senses of sight, smell, taste, feeling, and hearing are independent consciousness while dependent on one another to grasp multiple inputs to the whole situation. They can discern, comprehend, and direct our reactions, independently and instinctively, before thought. But they are mutually integrated at the subconscious level to construct the multiple aspects of perception. At the level of reacting to a tiger in the jungle or blinking to avoid dirt in the eye, the importance of this immediate physical control is glaringly apparent.

The *Lanka* makes a separate science of intuition, as a specific and distinct doorway of awareness. A scale of advancing perception, it indicates our attunement to a subtle, subliminal, and subconscious understanding of reality. The *Lanka* presents this awareness as grasping the suchness of all things. These development states, which employ the full gamut of observable phenomena, are not limited by our perception, only our mind. Our inability to find verification or a label hinders acceptance. The integration of intuition isn't explicitly metaphysical or, from my perspective, not predominantly mystical. It is merely looking for the extreme subtlety in life, like Sat Guru's paint-on-a-fence analogy. The essence or suchness of a situation exists way beyond a point where there is any physical trace of paint, color, oil, or smell.

> *If you continue this simple practice every day, you will obtain some wonderful power. Before you attain it, it is something wonderful, but after you attain it, it is nothing special.*

Shunryo Suzuki Roshi, *Zen Mind, Beginner's Mind*

In this case, the simple practice refers to Zazen or formal sitting practice and a "ceremonial way of life." Additionally, this description sounds a lot like intuitive integration. Intuition is nothing special, though it is beyond critical thinking. Like peripheral vision, it informs and correlates what is otherwise too much information. However, the *Lanka* allows that intuition, like everything else, is what we make of it as a personal and individual choice.

> *Buddha-nature each recognized equally as*
> *thou most beloved child.*
>
> *Loving intuition free from circumstance,*
> *judgment and opinion.*
>
> *Habit sits aside inconsequential thought and*
> *Mind-only reality.*
>
> *The subconscious undisturbed teaches, informs, and creates.*
>
> *A life worthy of effortless belonging perceives no-other-than-self.*
>
> *Step-wise progress begins the transformation.*
> *Find your most beloved child, then another…*
>
> *Thou art becoming.*
>
> ***Self-realization,* OWM**

So far, we have looked at what it means to be not-separate. We have examined our shared characteristics and the nature of our existence, the construction of sense-consciousness, and what it means to awaken. We've considered our true selves from several angles, and life's basis in impermanence. Next, we opened the box into scientific materialism, looking into recent microbiome advances, pondering innate biological communications. Then based on a marvelous behavioral study, we pulled these dispersed concepts together into a healthy and useful understanding of intuition. As the integrator of subliminal sense perception rather than a psychic phenomenon, it becomes a great asset. Now we go a step farther. We will examine quantum mechanics related to being not-separate.

Though we have considered many positive aspects of interdependent co-arising, we have only resolved part of the communications mystery.

Biology and microbiology have proven co-evolution, along with innate connections between our cells and our microbial life partners. But where science, focusing on verification, examines the details of transmitters, receptors, and observable mechanisms, I am interested in how subtle communications might function holistically and instantaneously throughout every cell in the body and with every microorganism. This is what it truly means to be not-separate.

Next, I will address reasonable speculations around two cornerstone discoveries of quantum mechanics, which explain, to my satisfaction, what the *Lanka* presents as our physical reality of being not-separate. My intention isn't to argue a view of physics. It is only to present plausible support for the *Lanka's* thesis of not-separate. I've tried to be accurate to my education level, but this is beyond electrical engineering and field theory. My only wish is that it inspires you as it has me. So my speculation is just what it is.

CHAPTER SIXTEEN
THE OBSERVER EFFECT

First, you might ask why are we leaving a philosophical space of Mind-only, awakening, suchness, and loving-kindness to discuss physics? As I've tried to serve the *Lanka* by presenting its roots, origin, message, and personal impact, I've also wanted to offer the complete story it has revealed to me. Since I am of both the scientific and the spiritual communities, it is my offering to those like me with unanswered questions in both arenas. It is a viewpoint in recognizing our modern science for validating ancient science and recognizing both for going beyond mere brilliance. For me, the ancient ideas hold gifts as relevant today, as they were when they were written. It feels true to our evolving potential. As we, humanity, seek meaning, purpose, and truth in our complex world.

Physics starts with the basic idea of quanta, or the smallest particle, by which we can distinguish the subtlest characteristics of matter. We begin with the premise that what's valid for the particle is true for all matter. However, biology has struggled to be incorporated into physics as it expanded beyond relativity into quantum mechanics. Few scientists can easily entertain anything which is not available to specific and repeatable measurement.

Where physics reduces experimentation to elemental components and verifiable results, an application to biology requires broad generalizations across trillions of organisms in each living organism. However, in its material composition, the relationship between biology and physics is incontrovertible, and logic requires simplification to approach what the ancients had tried to tell.

Two unusual results in quantum mechanics have challenged scientific open-mindedness for several decades. The controversy surrounds the interpretation of the observer effect and quantum entanglement. Though the jump from matter to living organisms is difficult, both particle physics and biology share a dependency on electro-magnetic measurability, which spans the gap.

Observer Effect

Scientists verified a behavior called the "observer effect" when an electron beam showed an unusual response when being monitored. In the dual-split experiment, the stream of electrons typically creates a wave pattern, as predicted by the Schrödinger equation. However, when tracking the beam with sensors, the resulting pattern changed from wave to particle.[23] The observer effect, demonstrated conclusively by the Weizmann Institute in 1998, exhibited what the Lanka might judge as an awareness and reaction as the electron beam shifted interference patterns from a wave to particle function. These experimental results provide the tantalizing notion that electrons may exhibit the *Lanka's* simplistic definition of consciousness.

> *127. The macroscopic and subatomic are bound together in mutual interchange. Where life is determined, it is among elemental particles and where elemental particles are seen there is also life.*
>
> ***Lanka, Sagathakam,*** **sloka 127**

The discussion and experimentation go back to the early 19th century when Thomas Young presented wave theories for sound and light.[24] Later, scientists scattered an electron beam through two slits in a card to create patterns on an energy-sensitive surface, expecting to validate

---

[23] Weizmann Institute of Science (1998, February 27). *Quantum Theory Demonstrated: Observation Affects Reality.* Science Daily. Retrieved from https://www.sciencedaily.com/releases/1998/02/980227055013.htm

[24] Einstein, A. Podolsky, B. Rosen, N. (1935). *Can Quantum-Mechanical Description of Physical Reality Be Considered Complete? Phys. Rev.* **47** (10): 777–780. Retrieved from https://journals.aps.org/pr/pdf/10.1103/PhysRev.47.777

the Schrödinger equation.[25] The normal wave-like distribution was verified until they added instruments to provide positioning information. Introducing electronic beam detection, the particle's behavior changed. This controversial observation was argued and retested many times until the Weizmann institute ruled out all forms of interference and imprecise methods to see their results as consistently repeatable.

But then another surprising thing happened. The monitoring device sensitivity also affected the level of change from wave to particle patterns. The interference patterns became more and more particle-like as they increased the monitor device sensitivity.

Of course, the metaphysical community went wild and sometimes misinterpreted what the results might mean. What are the implications when an electron beam can sense, observe, and react to outside observation?

> *Consciousness itself is only known in its agency,*
>
> *through its reaction to or interaction with the physical world.*
>
> *However, consciousness is essentially*
>
> *to perceive, discern, distinguish or judge*
>
> *without necessarily having the need to show response.*
>
> ***Lanka*, Chapter 2, section IV**

This section, repeated here for clarity, says that primary consciousness is a simple function. Simple and straightforward; it's the ability to perceive and discriminate. After discerning is the ability to react or respond, but only in this way can we identify the consciousness of things. Awareness is not limited by our ability to see it. Does that mean an electron beam or the electron itself is conscious? Per the *Lanka*'s not-separate premise, it does. But people also disagree about what consciousness means.

The electrons demonstrated reaction to observation, although many will argue it is not consciousness because we can't verify self-awareness of the electron. But we can't confirm they don't have self-awareness either, and the reaction itself is the most rudimentary self-awareness.

---

[25] Bell, J.S. (2004, 2nd edition) *Speakable and Unspeakable in Quantum Mechanics.* Cambridge University Press.

We should all agree that plants have a natural, though simple, apprehension of light as they turn toward the sun, not arguing whether they like being talked to or have preferences for a particular Bach concerto. As a gardener, I don't doubt any of it. But doesn't reaction indicate an innate awareness?

However, even the *Lanka*'s description expands on the mind of sentient beings. But the common denominator should hold from particle to matter, which appears to be the case with the *Lanka*'s visceral connection between senses and reality.

In a peculiar way, this experiment creates an analogy for our awareness. Like an electron beam's interference patterns going from wave to particle being observed, we might also recognize our perception going from wave-like suchness to particles or thought-outcomes with our observation.

> *The educated man says, "When discrimination of the objective world ceases,*
>
> *consciousness stops; and when the consciousness has ceased,*
>
> *there is no further awareness of change."*
>
> *However, they fail to understand that eye-consciousness occurs*
>
> *from the simple interaction of form and light.*
>
> *They assume a first cause for each sense consciousness,*
>
> *such as spirit, soul, God, time, or the atom.*
>
> **Lanka, Chapter 2, section IV**

This transcription is obscure and interesting because it separates the conscious observer from the senses as autonomous. The observer experiments showed that the first particle, an electron, can sense and react. By fundamental consciousness, the electron beam demonstrated a basic awareness through reacting. This lends a shadow of meaning to the obscurity of autonomous senses because as the electron is conscious, why not the form and light? Form and light being conscious may sound stupid, but how else could we understand what the ancients were saying.

By extension, if the idea holds true, only those parts of matter without electrons or photons fall into the non-conscious category. The only matter which may fit this criterion is theorized as dark matter.[26]

Electrons are the most conspicuous particles within visible matter, elemental to all known atoms and molecules. So, verifying that electrons can react, we can conclude that their consciousness is only indiscernible with our limited perception. Could that mean the stones are alive and aware? What elements compose a sentient being, and when do they change from inorganic minerals to living cells?

> *When completely magnified and analyzed,*
> *the atom has no substance, which can be found.*
> *Though without static actuality, atoms are also not imaginary,*
> *and so only the concept or belief, in matter, remains.*
> *We cannot determine their existence or non-existence,*
> *as impermanence is true for all things made of atoms.*
> *How then may we argue what is or isn't real,*
> *because the imagined may be just as real as the stone,*
> *depending on its position in the cycle of impermanence.*

Lanka, Chapter 2, section XII

I like the questions and assume they can only be proven depending on our ability to perceive and verify. There's the rub. This stanza questions even the reality of imagination, which, seen in the vastness of time, maybe the energy of what was or will be. Its poetry, as well as its mind-bending thought, captivates me because it presents the non-dual in the shadow of imagination and the ethereal nature of matter. I like to just sit with it a while.

This is the choice of mindfulness or suchness as fully developed. To understand that there is an awareness and knowledge beyond our

---

[26] Lee, C. (2017, May 22). *Diving Deep into the World of Emergent Gravity*. Ars Technica. Retrieved from https://arstechnica.com/features/2017/05/emergent-gravity-and-dark-matter-explained-by-excited-universe/

rational limits or our ability to conceive. This isn't magic or even weird once grasped; it is experienced. Also, the fact that the *Lanka* summarized a key aspect of quantum theory at least sixteen centuries before our academic understanding is very significant to what else they may have decerned.

> *Energy observed, straightened his tie, combed his hair.*
>
> *Thou art the life observed, living in the flow or reacting with thought.*
>
> *Your waves within waves, rise and fall without distinction, caught in swell and foam.*
>
> *But observed you lose sight, missing the horizon clinging to driftwood or supertanker.*
>
> *Circumstance and detail develop particles as thoughts, bouncing on waves, fleeting and changing, they hold no permanence and questionable value.*
>
> *Thou art a particle observed, but thou art a wave in solitude.*
>
> *Dive to the quiet within each moment being fully present to what is.*
>
> *Thou art life itself, expressed uniquely!*
>
> *Just like everybody else.*
>
> **Thou Art Life, OWM**

It may seem like I've gone beyond all sanity and rational limits, trying to argue the consciousness of an electron, given only pattern recognition differences. But that would miss the point of discussion. The observer effect though interesting in particle physics, is also a cornerstone in human potential, in the *Lanka's* terms. It says we are alive in a living reality, where independent existence is the illusion, and we are only a small part of its continuous movement and change. However, I do understand the *Lanka* to say explicitly that life exists at the most elemental level and would therefore comprise a ubiquitous reality, such as described by Jesus around the same time. Also, if this seems farfetched, then you will have a very good laugh at my conjecture to communications theory, as proposed by this thesis that all things are not separate.

Anyway, I have sought surprise all along, as that is the only indication of real learning and it means an openness which brings scientific speculation into question. But, we still have a very long way to go, as the nature of existence is and may always be, well beyond what we think.

CHAPTER SEVENTEEN
UBIQUITOUS LIFE

The *Lanka*'s explanation, from awareness to reaction, is arguably consciousness at the most basic level, comparable to all life. Therefore, the observer effect could validate a theory for subatomic awareness and reaction but not life in our current organic biological definition. Our definition of life is limited to observable organic characteristics, not including the *Lanka*'s elemental consciousness.

> *LIFE: The condition that distinguishes organisms from inorganic objects and dead organisms, being manifested by growth through metabolism, reproduction, and the power of adaptation to environment through changes originating internally.*[27]

This definition, chosen for its inclusiveness and holistic perspective, still distinguishes something living as a process from metabolism to adaptation. It excludes elemental life as functions of only perception and response. Perhaps the *Lanka* is talking about life-force instead of life form? But what is life-force if not an immeasurable electromagnetic resonance? At least, that is what we can measure when we look at the electro-chemical relationships of organic matter. If matter is made of energy and vibration, elemental life seems to be even more subtle because inorganic matter doesn't demonstrate growth or reproduction that we know of. Perhaps this life or life-force is the dance among living particles? But how?

We might guess, inorganic matter moves more slowly. We might not recognize either the catalyst or a stone's reaction in a lifetime. Such provocation as gravitational shifts or solar radiation swings might seem apparent in retrospect, but our few centuries of scientific observation are more like a photo than a movie. Also, we may not be looking to find life-force where we assume it doesn't exist. It is true, however, that we can only

---

[27] Dictionary.com. Retrieved from https://www.dictionary.com/browse/life

perceive matter because it all shares an appearance on our electromagnetic spectrum. Is that its' lifeforce? There is some poetry from *Hsin Hsin Ming* which puts time in the context of a non-dual nature and not-separate awareness in its' description of "not two."

> *No matter when or where,*
>
> *enlightenment means entering this truth.*
>
> *And this truth is beyond extension or*
>
> *diminution in time or space;*
>
> *in it a single thought is ten thousand years.*
>
> **Richard B. Clarke, *Hsin Hsin Ming***

Of course, that doesn't validate an argument for universal life, but it does lend itself to reimagining life-force without a beginning or end, such as the nature of electrons in our universe. We've talked about space, as in size, and time as to the perceptibility of response, but can we reimagine what the bounds of life-force might be?

Interdependent co-arising makes sense if matter itself is alive and aware at an elemental level. When particle interaction responds, as seen in the observer effect, it makes perfect sense that the same fundamental laws of attraction and repulsion activate each other from an undiscovered awareness, resembling consciousness. From the *Lanka*'s standpoint, the boundary between organic and inorganic is only a carbon-based circumstance of discrimination. Though many things have a limited ability to respond in our awareness, it leaves us with intriguing questions.

> *128. Looking into the heart of an atom there is no form which can be judged as this or that.*
>
> *What is confirmed is the truth of conscious projection or Mind-only, which cannot be grasped with ordinary thinking.*
>
> ***Lanka, Sagathakam*, sloka 128**

Here the *Lanka* relates life and elemental particles as undefinable, leading to this thesis of universal energy. But it also speaks volumes about our inabilities in ordinary understanding. It is then reminiscent of a famous quote from Albert Einstein about "problems not being solved with the same thinking that created them." But the most exciting part of these slokas relates to the living nature of everything, as it not only provides the modality for the mind to produce a projection of consciousness; it also alludes to the influences of the mind in the field of attractive and repulsive forces.

Things get inspiring for Schrödinger's and D.T. Suzuki's disciples when we see a connection between measurable energy and consciousness, as in the electron beam. Of course, this goes toward my persistent question of the communication among cells and microbes. If everything is alive at a particle level, information exchange could efficiently occur outside our observation range. It implies that life-force is only beyond our instrumentation. This means communications may be at an energy level or frequency bandwidth; we can't easily observe. But like infrared rays, the effect is still there and can burn the skin regardless.

The Living Nature of Everything

In the behavior of electrons, Schrödinger's wave model[28] presents the electromagnetic principle used *ad infinitum* in the evolution of modern telecommunications. This function appears because particles exhibit harmonic resonance with other particles. They demonstrate an affinity by vibrating together, creating waves, which we modulate, digitize, amplify, codify and interpolate.

Like echoes in an alpine valley, the electron's resonance may be reflected and propagated in a chamber of sorts to sustain and amplify propagation. This is an oscillator, which is the origin of all electronic communications. Physically it is an energized crystalline structure, tuned

---

[28] Schrödinger, E. (1926). *An Undulatory Theory of the Mechanics of Atoms and Molecules* (PDF). Physical Review. 28 (6): 1049–1070. Retrieved from https://journals.aps.org/pr/abstract/10.1103/PhysRev.28.1049

by a biasing network, which provides the heartbeat in every computer or cell phone and, without which no communication happens.

The tuning for this resonance effect may be a model for life energy at the subatomic level. Its extension into organic matter has at least the image of life-force and the obvious presentation as a heartbeat. That being said, it seems that life is always here and only waiting for a viable opportunity to appear and evolve.

Reimagine the heartbeat of life
alive and aware,
living nature life-force filled.

Observe the wave become particle
waveness dissolves to space,
energy and vibration
boundless,
immeasurable.

Observe the mind
the wave of intuitive understanding
becomes the particle of
rational thought.

Life, gone in an instant.
It comes from emptiness.
It returns to emptiness.

Emptiness is the wave as
awareness and reaction.
The field of interconnection as

interdependent co-arising,

mutual support,

linked in infinite dependencies.

Thou art everything alive.
Thou art Gaia's corpuscle.

The Awareness of an Electron, OWM

In this realm of living energy, the world is a vast space, and the electrons as particles of life create a constant field, much like a soup. The charged, oscillating behavior of particles may lead us to the *Lanka*'s ultimate surprise. Still, we need to look at an even broader picture of what quantum effects, say about the magic of life.

The ancients' study to understand the creation mechanisms didn't stop with grasping universal life; it only began there. If indeed, there's another way to understand, it is a perspective shift. Like shining a laser on a holographic plate from various angles to see all the dimensions of my baby's smile. But then "not-separate," as a thesis, is similar to "connected" at a basic level. Not-two is a step beyond "connected" because duality is the basis of two connected things, whereas being "not-separate" is non-dual, no observer-no observed.

Hobbling fear, wondering desire
or discipline understood,
all thought is prayer,
All prayer is answered.

I call my soul's desire in
quiet moments.
I call other things
unaware.

Secret Koans, OWM

From the *Lanka*'s point of view, the obvious conclusion is that in all this energetic sensitivity, everything is alive, commingling, and reacting with everything else to create, dissolve, and recreate. From this perspective, we are aspects of a living planet, operating in fields of whirling electrons and elemental matter. Attracted by gravity, they become teeming molecules that react with each other to evolve into living things. The record of all these energetic developments, estimated to go back about four billion years, has had some time to co-arise interdependently.

It follows that we should acknowledge all creation stories, which often supposed that everything is alive and all life is sacred. However, scientific supposition is also useful in this context; everything has a cause and may ultimately be understood if we are open to surprise. This shift in perspective allows some separation from metaphysics, which may still get very far-fetched and imaginative. This search for objective meaning most closely relates to the *Lanka*'s ego creation story and its underlying science of a metaphysical reality. But, this re-creation or story we tell ourselves of "what is," blinds us to objective reality and retards our potential to an animal existence.

To see that science, we must thoroughly investigate the possibility that everything lives in a continual interaction of one living thing, not many.

Next, we'll consider the possibility of entangled life, which sounds like it may be the problem and the solution from a Zen perspective. It is the entanglement of being not-separate, which explains communication between cells, microbes, and even electrons.

As we approach another precipice, I'll reach for a new postulation to push the envelope. In this minor deviation into quantum physics, I hope to share a possibility that, for me, explains the mechanism of synchrony and a living intelligence. It's not just the communication between cells and microbes which are up for question. In my simplistic conjecture is a vision of true not-separateness.

CHAPTER EIGHTEEN
QUANTUM ENTANGLEMENT

Per the *Lanka's* science of not-separate reality, the observer effect[29] is overshadowed by particle behaviors discovered some decades earlier. No matter how astounding the idea of an electron's consciousness is, quantum entanglement takes the ancient hypothesis of elemental life-force to the next level. These discoveries of quantum mechanics are the definitives of not-separate physics; as they demonstrate the mechanism of dual appearance between particles but do not explain the mechanism. I am talking about a synchronicity in space and time, so a change in one particle's state, simultaneously and irrespective of distance, changes the other.

Though they came along many years before the Weizmann experiments, the two discoveries together went beyond the limits of logic and rational understanding. In 1935 or thereabouts, Albert Einstein is said to have called quantum entanglement "spooky action at a distance."

This next level came from extensive experimentation, where photons split through a polarizing crystal, demonstrated entangled quantum states. Said another way, photons split into horizontal and vertical polarities, demonstrating a relationship where they both responded to changes as if they were still one particle. Their synchronized interdependence broke the boundaries of space-time propagation and so defied the conventional view of physical reality.

Coming from the same photon were two quanta; identical in every measurable respect, except polarization. The polarizing crystal isolated their orientation into horizontal or vertical, much like a pair of polarized glasses. These almost duplicate twins were entangled to link their quantum states. What affected one interdependently changed both instantaneously demonstrating an unknown cause of mutuality. So, by altering one photon's

---

[29] Weizmann Institute of Science (1998, February 27). *Quantum Theory Demonstrated: Observation Affects Reality*. Science Daily. Retrieved from https://www.sciencedaily.com/releases/1998/02/980227055013.htm

spin, both reacted accordingly, synchronistically, or simultaneously and identically. But synchronicity is not a term we hear about in physics. Carl Jung coined the term with a slightly more metaphysical meaning.[30]

> Synchronicity: "to describe circumstances that appear meaningfully related yet lack a causal connection."
>
> **Kerr, Laura K.** *Synchronicity*

My usage of synchronicity is simultaneous sameness from the word structure. But it is not a coincidence of circumstance, as it has a measurable causal connection in quantum entanglement. It is only the mechanism or cause of quantum entanglement that is still a mystery.

I correlate this relatedness to the missing, unverifiable life-force, which connects everything in the *Lanka*. Entanglement of living energy as tuning forks on the rungs of DNA, account for the mutuality of experience in this body. Synchronicity in Jungian terms, rather than coincidence, is accounted for as a living intelligence, when everything experiences mutuality. But we haven't closed the net and connected the dots by defining the field, as the Lanka does.

But, as the scientists altered one of the entangled pairs, both particles changed identically and simultaneously, regardless of the distance between them. So, one particle could be in England and another in California, and as one turned, so did the other, with no time delay. Rigorous control experimentation disqualified electromagnetic interactions and known field effects, not to mention a hundred possibilities I could never conceive.

Though we may assume "spooky action at a distance" is unrelated to organic mitosis, it is difficult to ignore the similarity of DNA duplication and then separation to create two identical daughter cells. And just because we can't measure a thing doesn't mean it doesn't exist, as every natural force is measured purely by effect.

Additionally, quantum research looked beyond subatomic particles that demonstrated synchronised entanglement to larger, more complex molecules. The quantum entanglement experiments successfully established that photons, neutrinos, electrons, molecules, and even small diamonds

---

[30] Kerr, Laura K. (2013). *Synchronicity. In Teo, T. (ed.). Encyclopedia of Critical Psychology.* Berlin, Heidelberg: Springer-Verlag.

could be split and entangled in various ways.[31] These results confirmed a broad-spectrum possibility that many things, if not all things, could be interconnected in this way, though beyond our current knowledge base.

Entangled particles have been demonstrated under precise control, but the possibility of entangled energy seems like the logical cause, since both electrons and photons are constructs for energy. Again we don't know what we don't know and my purpose is to support the *Lanka's* thesis.

So, this open interpretation of quantum entanglement as a subtle aspect of everything, validates the *Lanka*'s foundational precepts of interdependent co-arising and not-separate reality. It is at a level of possibility rarely considered. Extensible to elements, molecules, and, notably, life, as a speculative field theory, entanglement defines a causal source of synchronicity in both senses and more importantly a living intelligence.

The implications reflect the potential between closely related particles, especially complex living organisms that grow and live through cell division. In the sphere of biology, it seems overwhelmingly straight forward that each cell has levels of entangled energy or particles which don't communicate as such, because their experience of a single stimuli is simultaneous. Along with trillions of sister cells and microbial partners, one can consider a resonant mechanism of communications for sentient beings.

In direct experience, I'm reminded of the splinter in my hand. The injury may be too small to see and impossible to remove, but my whole body knows it and whatever else is going on, such as a sore back, takes second place in sense priority. All I can focus on is the splinter and every cell of me knows it.

Entanglement in this inclusive speculation, is like all of natural forces, essentially non-dual. We may not yet have the means to verify entangled relationships outside laboratory creation, but the mutuality of living cells' might easily explain the mystery of cellular and microbial communications. It's difficult not to consider, that natural entanglement could explain a huge array of interdependent life mechanisms.

Importantly, my speculation is just a possibility with no proof. But the similarity, between splitting particles or DNA in the process of mitosis,

---

[31] Lee, K. C. et al. (2011, December 2). *Entangling Microscopic Diamonds at Room Temperature.* Science. Retrieved from https://www.science.org/doi/10.1126/science.1211914

is overwhelmingly apparent. However, the analogy at an energetic level could mean there are thousands of associated entanglements with each cell division. So, what one cell experiences all experience relative to specific aspects of DNA. Per instance, one entanglement might specifically relate to the flight or fight sense, so when one cell is injured, they all perceive it. This could be why that bloody splinter can give me such grief. However, for the Lanka, entanglement is elemental life-force and it's all-inclusive field of resonance, as we will see.

Entanglement experiments also demonstrate interdependence as a natural aspect of energy among particles, assumed to be otherwise non-living. So, as life occurs at the elemental level per the *Lanka*, so the stone lives, though at a noticeably slower rate of change.

Also, we might need to consider that we and our hosts of symbiotic microbes operate somewhat like a wireless network, where entangled communications has naturally evolved between species. It is clearly beyond my comprehension, except in its working similarity.

This theory of particle, energy or elemental entanglement answers my question sufficiently. Communication between the same organism's cells requires no interaction as they experience change simultaneously through trillions of entangled elemental and energetic relationships. This mirror-like embodiment explains the instantaneous levels of communications or mutuality, which biology leaves unanswered but on which, the *Lanka* makes literal rather than figurative sense.

> *Nature's entangled particles by the trillions shift, swirl, and dance in the semblance of waves ...until observed.*
>
> *We see form, particles, and DNA, where energy and vibration only exists.*
>
> *It is the not-separate connecting us, within ourselves and among ourselves; unchanging knowledge, effortless belonging, one thing in many places.*
>
> *What is it, to react in mutuality?*
>
> *Our access into all there is, if we can but listen.*
>
> *How far from reality is synchrony?*

The starling's ephemeral dance, murmurings of millions in the sky.

Or the timing of migrations, by the destination's weather, month's ahead and thousands of miles away.

More mysterious yet, this vehicle I call man, creating balance within trillions of cells and vastness of symbiosis, one being.

No obstruction of space and time; one thing, one life-force in many places.

Thou art the wave of trillions upon trillions of entanglements.

Thou art energy entangled with all energy.

Thou art oneness and allness.

The Wave, OWM

Quantum entanglement, independent of distance and simultaneous, expands the probability that physicists observed the first principle of life and living communications, though not the whole story. It's mind-boggling to consider the possibility of aware, entangled particles influencing scientific observations without a mechanistic cause. Much of progressive science comes into rational plausibility, and pseudoscience, as such, needs reconsideration. We might also need to consider the type of music played in the particle accelerator's control room relative to boson perturbations. Fermions might prefer Haydn!

However, joking aside, the hypothesis and suppositions are beyond a provable, repeatable, and/or a priori defence. Lacking scientific rigor, as I do, my argument can't account for layers of possible misinterpretation. But from ancient science to glimmers of modern science, the questions are intriguing. And though no conclusive evidence is available nor implied, my speculative theory of entangled interdependence applies to a huge variety of issues. Common, normal, and poorly understood mechanisms within organic life's communications can be modelled to the concept, but experimental proof is not available, that I have found.

My distant intention is to provide a logical bridge to the *Lanka's* field theory integration of subconscious connection, which is the next farfetched correlation I will attempt to wrestle publicly.

No judgment of right or wrong, no thought of good or bad, the tiger kills the deer to feed the cub.

Thou art the tiger, the deer and the cub.

The non-dual is caring for the whole of life.

It is loving beyond identification with me, mine, or who I think I am.

Thou art life without limits.

Life is devoted to life and death is comingling impermanence.

Thou art that.

Thou Art All Life, OWM

Quantum entanglement is synonymous with synchronicity in an energetically living creation. The image it creates is diversity of life, and life forms intermingling without distinction, which is largely what the human biome project revealed. Perception of this as a physical reality is the "not-separate" essence of Mind-only, which brings all the concepts together.

Demonstrations of quantum entanglement in the early 20th century inspired new approaches in every field of science. Subtle field theories were also the next logical step from a biological point of view. Biologists focused on self-organizing morphogenetic fields, coined by A. G. Gurwitsch.[32] Also, Erwin Schrödinger, father of wave mechanics, postulated "negative entropy effects," or non-chaotic particle relationships or fields, as self-organizing systems of life.[33] But science and even Schrödinger tended to avoid what cannot be seen or measured. In this immeasurability lies the continuing difficulty with organic field theories, which extend beyond the cell to define the organ and then the body. However, the problem is not just measurability but the awareness that only sees the physical existence and only believes in outcomes of thought.

Quantum science may seem to be unrelated diversions from

---

[32] Beloussov,,L.V. (1997) *Life of Alexander G. Gurwitsch and His Relevant Contribution to the Theory of Morphogenetic Field.* International Journal of Developmental Biology (PDF). Retrieved from https://works.swarthmore.edu/cgi/viewcontent.cgi?article=1182&context=fac-biology

[33] Margulis, L. & Sagan, D. (1995), *What is Life?* Univ. of California Press

understanding the *Lanka*, but actually, it is necessary to grasp the deeper levels in this science of consciousness. Only by realizing your buoyancy can you let go and float or swim. Only by realizing your interdependent connection and support of life itself can you trust to let go of the subjective mind or at least begin to question its control.

CHAPTER NINETEEN
OBSERVER SYNCHRONICITY

The most immediate literary descendant of the *Lanka* was a poem by the Third Chinese Patriarch of Zen. It became central to my practice as a young man. I found it included in the album: *Love, Serve, Remember;* by Ram Dass and friends. It was a poetic reading by Ram Dass, which stimulated my curiosity through my inability to understand it.

It simply blew my mind as it started with the line. "The Great way is not difficult for those who have no preferences." As a good friend said when introduced to the poem, "All I am and everything I understand myself to be, are preferences."

I began writing out the poem longhand and giving away copies in my early twenties. In fifty years, it has never lost importance as a source of awakening, in small surprises. Its Chinese name is the *Hsin Hsin Ming*, loosely translated as *Faith Mind Verses*. Believed to have been written by the Third Chinese Patriarch of Zen, Jianzhi Sengcan (Sozan), it is my feeling that as a Taoist scribe, he took very good notes from Bodhidharma and Huike the previous patriarchs. My favorite translation is the first one by my late friend, Richard B. Clarke, created in 1972.

> *To live in this realization*
>
> *is to be without anxiety about non-perfection.*
>
> *To live in this faith is the road to non-duality,*
>
> *because the non-dual is one with the trusting mind.*
>
> **Richard B. Clarke, *Hsin Hsin Ming***

Though many parts of *Faith Mind Verses* chipped away at my old grasp of reality, this last line brought it all home based on suchness, as the natural quiescent mind, the trusting mind. From the perspective of quantum physics, the *Lanka* presents the fabric of reality as conscious particles with elemental entanglement. No matter how unprecedented, this theory of naturally occurring phenomena, marks an open playing field for science and expanded reality.

However, it must be asked, "What about the life-force exchange the *Lanka* noted on conception?" Might life-force be the consequence of entanglement, or might entanglement be the consequence of life-force? Or are they just the same thing?

The challenge has always been defining a function of nature that is non-dual in dualistic terms. We haven't figured out how to observe the scope of entanglement beyond a few particles at a time. But the *Lanka* says the same thing about our lack of understanding of form and formlessness.

> *If form is to be found in the oneness of formlessness, it is not visible.*
> *Its apparent non-existence contradicts the truth,*
> *though there is neither mechanism nor operator.*

Lanka, Sagathakam, sloka 732

This sloka is one of my favorites, first because of my fascination to understand: what could possibly be one in the universe as we understand it. Only space is uninterrupted, as I concluded earlier. But this question of no cause takes a creation story to answer. However, answering it, the *Lanka* presents concepts so incredible that only entanglement provides a mechanism in a natural sense, which is also the reason for the unpeeling, or spiraling logic of this book.

Energy exists invisibly till vibration appears and form materializes. Where did it come from? Like the phase change of gas to liquid, it talks about the boundlessness of subtlety, like the paintbrush in reverse. Form appears from emptiness with no known source. Just sit with it a while, and the word or sound at the beginning of creation may come to mind. The yogis call it "AUM," leading to a science of energy called "prana." Another creation story and biblical quotation would lead me to say science found God acting in "spooky action at a distance." So, I guess I must admit my experience as the beloved child of an intelligent creation.

Anyway, ubiquitous life and elemental entanglement, also without a mechanism or operator, explain this interdependent co-arising of form from emptiness. A particle of entangled energy has vibration induced by its twin. The poetry, as well as its mind-bending questions, captivates me, presenting the non-dual in the shadow of imagination and the ethereal first cause.

D.T. Suzuki alluded to this obscurity of form and appearance in an understanding of Mind-only, which points us to the next step. Rather than describing mind and reality as an interaction, Mind-only is a stage of being or awareness that brings us to the experience of synchrony. He said that the mind appears in the highest possible sense as Mind-only, not limited to thinking or knowledge. Nor is it narrowing one's perception with sense-consciousness.

Identified with the subconscious via intuitive awareness, Mind-only is connected to the intelligence of a cumulative life-force. This connection without "mechanism nor operator" provides direct experience of absolute or Right-knowledge.

This is the boundary of my thesis, as method and its community is the realm of practice where I will always be just the student. Zen, Chan, Vajrayana, and Classic Yoga are the best teachers in my experience. However, as an experience, you might also think of direct experience as certitude, unchanging knowledge, or knowing without rational context and doubt. This is the sixth stage of awareness or sixth self-nature, as you will understand.

This stage of awareness, Mind-only, becomes available as we cross the threshold of awakening, away from our comfortable subjective mind, losing only compulsiveness. In a state of receptive intuition, we experience a shift in perceived reality by recognizing synchronicity within the flow of our life. This awareness requires diligence and the fundamentals I've laid out, especially disempowering identification with the outcomes of thought. And of course its logical next step is recognizing our essential nature, loving-kindness, which is also the most fundamental desire for every infant striving to belong.

As synchronicity was the Holy Grail for my hippy generation, the *Lanka* describes conscious evolution not as godlike omniscience but as an ever-increasing experience of oneness, mutuality, or a life connected to the intelligence of one living entity. This is ultimate effortless belonging. Of course, it's a long way from one among billions of separate animals. This is the next step along that journey.

Next, we enter the realm of field theory, modeled on a simple principle; life loves life. After being dragged through two principles of quantum mechanics, your reaction may have been, "Oh no! there he goes again." I understand, but we aren't done yet. The struggle to climb a mountain can often seem impossible, but it is the view from the summit which takes our breath away.

Field theory is necessary to understand a concept that was probably just taken for granted at the time of Yogachara. But I will avoid derivation of abstract terms and show you a trick, which is to reverse engineer from solution to knowns using units of measure rather than zero balance algebra. Sorry, that's a joke unless you're a young engineering student, in which case it makes many problems easier. But if you are a student of any sort, try working as hard as you can, then meditating, listening, and the answer will just arise. See how often it works and you might gain certitude.

Before we get to the Seven stages of Awareness, we need to cross through Alaya-consciousness and sudden awakening. And if you've followed me thus far, you might still expect a surprise or two.

CHAPTER TWENTY

FIELD THEORY

In the early 20th century, a great deal of interest arose in field theory, which extended into the realm of biology for several decades. The morphogenetic field was researched extensively in biological science, primarily between WWI and WWII. A few free-thinkers began experimentation and initially arrived at some fascinating hypotheses.

In 1910 A. G. Gurwitsch with a colleague, Ross Harrison, introduced the concept of morphogenetic fields.[34] Together, they put forth experimental support for their premise, and for many years scientists such as Nobel prize winner Hans Spemann and National Medal of Science recipient Paul Weiss further developed theories.[35] They discussed and experimented with field concepts in parallel with the quantum physics discoveries of the day, such as entanglement. The primary problem for a biological study focused on the blueprint or the self-organizing structures of organic life. Though field study got an early start, it was rapidly overtaken as genetic research claimed center stage.

The problem these ideas address in modern science is the disconnect between biology, physics, and chemistry. Erwin Schrödinger pointed this out, even while standing as a bastion of what can be proved or verified empirically. Schrödinger was aware of the problem but also presented the aperiodic crystal theory of genetics, predicting the human chromosome discovery, which changed the focus away from morphogenetic, self-organizing fields.

In the absence of immediate practical applications, biological field

---

[34] Beloussov,,L.V. (1997). *Life of Alexander G. Gurwitsch and His Relevant Contribution to the Theory of Morphogenetic Field.* International Journal of Developmental Biology (PDF). Retrieved from https://works.swarthmore.edu/cgi/viewcontent.cgi?article=1182&context=fac-biology

[35] Gilbert, S.F., Opitz, J.M., Raff, R.A. (1996). *Resynthesizing Evolutionary Developmental Biology.* Dev. Biol: 173. DOI: 10.1006/dbio.1996.0032. Retrieved from https://pubmed.ncbi.nlm.nih.gov/8605997/

theories quickly lost popularity to antibiotic break throughs, and the considerable medical developments motivated by two world wars.

Today the notion of biological fields is often shunned by the scientific community like a superstition. However, the notion of fields is only common sense and the only area for question are it's affects and potentials. Because every form of matter is a function of energy and vibration, where there is vibration there is resonance. Resonance is a field effect, not easily measured but always experienced. And, then consider the electro-chemical exchange throughout the body which is very measurable in the nervous system. We create electro-magnetic radiation. The doubt of biological fields is illogical prejudice and field study provides a vast resource of unexplored potentiality.

Our Ocean of Existence

What the *Lanka* understood long ago was a functional model for the interconnectedness of life wrapped up in the living field as a metaphysical entity. Based on the limitations of science at that time, they identified its origin as possibly organic and perceived as metaphysical the characteristics of entanglement, we've only recently demonstrated. The metaphysical aspects may easily be attributed to entanglement as in the mutuality of energetic perception within life.

Coming from life, Alaya must also be at the highest concentration within the brain and body, as this field component exists within each living cell and organ. It could easily extend the model of a morphogenetic theory of self-organizing organs. In this theory, a stem cell created in the bone marrow can differentiate into any body structure. Arriving in the heart and influenced by body chemistry and the localized morphogenetic field, the cell understands to become heart muscle rather than a hair follicle. At least for a layman like myself, this makes more sense than other descriptions because it offers an idea of the mechanism for concepts such as body memory, microbiome communications, heart or gut intelligence, and autonomic functions below the nervous system. These idea's were also specifically considered by the original pioneers of morphogenetic fields.

However, the field called Alaya is synonymous with the ocean of existence, the collective subconscious and the all conserving mind. But it is not a consciousness as it holds no judgement, or discrimination, only accumulating patterns of energy which resonate from the karma and consequence of all life.

Said another way, the view of a telecommunications engineer is that Alaya is like a cloud storage device, where we and all living things exhale, respire and radiate entangled energy. But this energy doesn't travel ten feet and die, because energy can't be destroyed. It commingles with all entangled energy creating new relationships through resonance. The attractive energies coalesce and a living atmosphere is the result. So we feel what's in the air and sense the energy of those around us consciously, subconsciously, intuitively and spontaneously. We may perceive the unchanging knowledge and karma of our ancestors or just our own noise. As such, Alaya-consciousness or the subconscious mind may be a stable resource or our own rubbish, which we access in every thought.

But Alaya is not a living intelligence per D.T., which runs aground my desire to label it so. The little boy in me, who's always had a higher power connection, was a bit disappointed. But, because of metaphysical synchronicity or more honestly my experience of amazing grace, understanding the living intelligence or what we have called God, I wanted an object or higher power to worship.

However, my higher power is not Alaya per the *Lanka* and the closest I get in my loose understanding, is that the living intelligence accounting for the miracles and synchronicity of my life, is an entangled living energy which functions as a mutuality or collective resonance within the field of Alaya, much like our wifi. But in fact there are far too many levels of conjecture to describe what is beyond my comprehension. The Buddha is said to have called it, the Infinite Unknowable.

But, the *Lanka* describes Alaya as the field supporting existence, as the continual subconscious resource for every aspect of life. With the concept of organic origin, it would also be synonymous with the atmosphere surrounding our planet. It has two primary aspects, the collective or all conserving mind and our individuated collection or subconscious mind.

The all conserving mind is the resonance of existence, and predominantly the function of what we call life. That is to say the living intelligence is the resonance of existence or all life, inanimate forms, and fields of energy beyond the spectrum's vernier, above, below or within.

What we call life is the dominant field interaction. This is mostly due to our familiarity but the field is not limited to what we call life. As the natural effect of vibration and energy, an entire spectrum of resonance is available. In most cases perceiving it is limited by one's receptivity which requires complete stillness in a practice of clarity, or it may be touched upon without full integration through mind altering drugs. Of course, the practice of clarity would be the case with a great yogi or mystic. I only comment in recognition of mere glimpses.

Per the *Lanka*, as we live and die, so does our individuated collection or subconscious mind. This is where the argument of soul or no soul comes in. And I would suppose in this mechanistic view, it follows that without life, its resonance would cease, in which case only the resonance of matter remains.

This resonance of form and existence is much more subtle than an audio resonance or high frequency sound breaking a crystal glass. This resonance is non-dual and its vibration includes what we can measure as form, motion, attraction, and repulsion which merge into formless energy. Being non-dual, it is measured and seen, not in itself but only in its effects. We see extreme examples of partially explained resonant behavior at the leading edge of material science, where superconductors capable of suspended gravity create frictionless bearings.

What is life giving air, around us?

Without which we die in minutes.

How delicious on a cool summer morning

In it I feel your pleasure, love and desire

Though senses perceive, the reaction is a humming glow.

And what is it that makes you so special to me?

The list of requirements had no room in our lives

Before love was known, we knew oneness

Before our lives merged, we knew it must be.

The resonance of our thoughts
The effortlessness of belonging
The effortlessness of accepting
The harmony of togetherness
Thou art the living air I breathe.

The Living Air, OWM

Back to the original point, the ancient mystics argued their positions and agreed that the subconscious we call memory, experience and inherited dispositions dies with the organism. But not all of it dies and not the collective field itself, sustained by the continuity of life. The soul itself is an interesting topic as I've addressed, but as grandpa would say, I don't really have a dog in that hunt.

However, Alaya is also described as the collective subconscious called the "all-conserving mind." The ancient theory is that we live in constant connection within an energy environment, which provides our inspiration, ideas, and even memory. This connection is commonly called the subconscious mind and given little thought. But it is the essence of who we are, controlling us from data points of experience, long since forgotten.

Not unlike the wireless network communications to which we have become accustomed in the 21st century. In this analogy, we are seen as receivers and processors in a field of mutuality, which exists within every living cell, be it human or otherwise. But Alaya is not just an alternative means of insight or data. In this context, it is a library of all existence in us, around us, and between us, though we are predominantly infatuated with thought, experience or collection.

As the subconscious mind shares a mutual experience in every thought, it is our direct and continuous connection with all life. Not just when you are asleep or hypnotized, the subconscious is our non-separate essence and primary resource of life experience and collective wisdom on a moment to moment basis.

Normally we regard the subconscious as only brain cell recordings. Below the level of direct awareness, the structure of the brain is understood, like never before. But in the *Lanka's* science, its more about the subtlety we don't understand, like the paint brush on an infinite wall, limited only by our ability to perceive.

Of course, our brain or visceral form dominates in field energy, at a quadrillion to one ratio over an external aspect. But that doesn't denigrate the field within the body mind integration nor consider resonant aspects more inclined to radiation. Where the overlap of external fields is interesting, it is marginal compared to species entanglement or morphic resonance as studied by Dr. Rupert Sheldrake. The compelling evidence is in the field sense of smell, as seen in the intuition of college girls at Berne University.

It's the field of mutuality, I find most captivating. Electromagnetic for sure, acoustic to gamma rays but now a new dimension of not-separate entangled interdependence. The Lanka also describes various relationships between our sentient awareness and Alaya consciousness.

> *When sense-consciousness differs from the subconscious, their dissonance is not caused by the collective subconscious.*
>
> *When sense-consciousness does not differ from the subconscious, shutting down of the sense-consciousness and the subconscious occurs simultaneously, but the collective subconscious does not cease its operation.*
>
> *It is only the sense-consciousness, which experiences change or dissonance. What ceases to function is not the original subconscious but only the agitated augmentation of shallow identification.*
>
> *However, when the self-form dies, there will be an end, also of the subconscious.*
>
> **Lanka, Chapter 2, section IV**

This section from the *Lanka* speaks of an organic connection between life and a subconscious field with a clear link between life and death. Another exciting part is in the second stanza when waking consciousness doesn't differ from the subconscious. This idea may be a critical clue as to what conscious evolution, awareness, or enlightenment meant for the ancients. In Zen, this alignment is related to meditation and mindfulness.

Aligning the subconscious with our waking consciousness has long been understood as the key to tranquilization. But there's the problem, it has been confused with detachment and developed into extremes of self-mortification. The Buddha's middle way addressed the same problem, but is rarely translated to the common man and woman. In the tranquilization mentioned, the waking consciousness is observed to be beyond the limits of sense-consciousness, where it no longer identifies with the body, mind, or outcomes of thought as self. This is our next subject, sudden awakening or the Great Turning Back.

Understanding Alaya, much like the *Lanka*, is like peeling an onion. It has many layers, and if you peel too many at a time, your eyes will water. So, we have to go slowly. First, the living field of non-separate mutuality is just a function of life. It has an actuality we only perceive by its' agency, effect, or the reflections we call layers of memory, knowledge, inspiration, and intuition. Your body is the clearest example of how many parts and many organisms can share a mutual experience. But as a storehouse of knowledge, it can be fantasized as something other than a natural aspect of life.

However, the alignment of the waking mind and subconscious awareness has long been the question of great scientists like Dr. Carl Jung. His research was interested in the subconscious mind influences within the waking and sleeping consciousness. Recently his paintings and descriptions have been published in the *Red Book*.[36]

However, in the *Lanka*, field theory connecting the life-force is essential to understanding existence. The entangled experience and elemental consciousness of particles as synchronistic systems anticipates an intelligence within the field. In this field relationship, species entanglement or morphic resonance may present the particle and wave versions of life-force, respectively.

With a little optimism, envision a more interesting science of the future; one predicted by Schrödinger in the gulf he recognized between biology and the reductive approaches in physics.

---

[36] C.G. Jung, Sonu Shamdasani (2009), *The Red Book*, Foundation of the Works of C.G. Jung

> *... living matter, while not eluding the "laws of physics" as established up to date, is likely to involve "other laws of physics" hitherto unknown, which however, once they have been revealed, will form just as integral a part of science as the former.*
>
> **Erwin Schrödinger, *What Is Life?***

Schrödinger acknowledged the limits of physics regarding the fabric of life. He understood that limiting ourselves to classical and even quantum physics leaves a void in a holistic mechanism for living matter. The same is likely true for the other sciences, but they all have a great deal of knowledge invested in systems, the way they are.

The blueprint and networking aspect of morphogenesis appeared in Dr. Rupert Sheldrake's *Morphic Resonance Theory* (1988). Dr. Sheldrake built on the previous science surrounding individuation fields but with the next logical development. He presented the hypothesis that morphic resonances of the field define form, construction, operation, shared characteristics, and individuation across a species.

The *Lanka* appears to support Dr. Sheldrake's morphic resonance theory in the field of Alaya, accessing an individuated and collective resonance for form and life. One can also recognize that the field would include the blueprint aspect and species consciousness as proposed by Sheldrake. But the biological aspect of Alaya, is literally the tip of the iceberg, relative to its psychological and metaphysical characteristics.

The concept of Alaya goes much further than my simple life-force definition of entanglement, saying memory and all knowledge also exist in the formless space around us and within us. This concept of field intelligence resembles Sheldrake's morphic resonance, and where his experimentation shows amazing evidence of validity,[37] it is substantiated in a not-separate model of field interaction.

Though the *Lanka* paints the picture of a universal field of energy, it looks like a an ethereal non-dual database and metaphysical transmitter at first. That is, until we consider the mutuality or energetic entanglement as the metaphysical communications link. What we measure as electrochemical reactions miss the wave function of mutuality. So, what

---

[37] Sheldrake, R. (2011). *The Presence of the Past.* Icon Books.

looks like discrete particle interactions to the scientist may actually be wave functions of entanglement the ancients observed as metaphysical, lacking our discoveries. But they understood the source to be physical.

> *217. Alaya, the subconscious field, comes from our own bodies.*
> *Then the individual will claim a reality based on imprinted messages,*
> *according to likes and dislikes.*
> *The subjective mind mistakenly interprets this as objective reality*
> *coming from the outside in; without understanding,*
> *this reality is only what we ourselves have created.*
>
> **Lanka, Sagathakam, sloka 217**

Considered as the non-dual source of life and consciousness, Alaya accounts for what we termed the subconscious and life-force in previous discussions. But here, it gets interesting because the sloka specifically says it comes from life, which resembles the sciences of today rather than metaphysics and religion.

This logic leads me to a presumption that Alaya is the subtlest aspect or resonance of organic life, which is supported and sustained much like the atmosphere, as a consequence of life on earth. When particle consciousness and mutuality are intwined, it is only rationally understood on a small scale, as the causal effect within living organisms. As said before, the interpretation substantiates the *Lanka's* thesis of a not-separate reality and all that may imply.

Alaya-consciousness refers to the individual subconscious, which I have used consistently to understand the *Lanka*. Though D.T.'s description and many orthodox Buddhists may disagree, holding to a view of Alaya as a purely metaphysical, non-dual entity.

In several places within the *Lanka*, the visceral relationship is described, as in the *Sagathakam*, sloka 217 above, where it says that the Alaya has an organic origin and cohabitation, sustained by life. Subtler aspects do focus on the metaphysical which might also be understood in the Akash, the prana, or the vital principle. But for my purposes, I prefer the western rationalizations such as morphogenetic fields and my speculation of mutuality or entanglement within life. Transliterating my terms to D.T, Suzuki's understanding, his statements become as follows.

> *The Alaya is not a consciousness; it does not discern, judge, comprehend, or react.*
>
> *As the collective subconscious, it is a neutral or a non-dual force within nature, which imprints and stores the resonance of action, consequence, experience, thought, and instinct for every life form within and outside their bodies.*

D.T. Suzuki, *Lanka: Introduction*

Here, neither judging nor discriminating, the subconscious Alaya stores details from life for future reference. Its energy is relatively faint outside the body, with trillions to one concentration difference. But this mist of external life-force has also been called the aura or energetic body, which yogis and clairvoyants are sometimes credited with observing. It is described as an external field, usually about ten feet beyond the body. Some say, it may be a hundred feet or more, for the most dynamic, energetic beings. Arguably, the overlap of energy bodies and the collective subconscious, account for metaphysical potentials among those interested in more subtle aspects.

Alaya is also the combination of all living fields, so like picking out the human face in a crowd of animals, we attract and are attracted to that which we are. So Alaya is like a radio spectrum full of stations in the particle model, where we pick up or tune into only the aspects or frequencies relevant to human life. However, in the wave model, preference and perception relate to parameters of resonance. So, when the old hippy said, "feel the vibe," he wasn't wrong. He was perceiving the nature of an entangled field. As different as it may seem, this ancient observation, of not-separate reality, in no way discounts the relevance of genome studies or allopathic medicine.

It should be clear in this field theory; all life exists in reliance on its interconnection and resonance from our usual perspective and from an entangled mutuality in the other. It is also the air we breathe and the thoughts we think, shaping our lives.

However, Alaya moves well beyond western belief and measurable verification. So from here on, I will describe its characteristics and functions assuming the view of holistic acceptance of subatomic living energy and entanglement. With this idea in mind, we may consider the soup aspect of our existence and what the *Lanka* says about conscious evolution. Though, like fish, we may never quite see the water in which we swim, nor realize we are not separate from the current.

We know that we are fundamentally energy, like all matter, and that our body/mind function integrates electrochemical processes. In light of the physics, the Alaya makes sense with a subtle consciousness at the electron level and entangled cells' interaction. This theory gives us some building blocks to model our communications and interaction with the collective field. But it falls far short of practical understanding, and useful application is rare unless applied to continuing human potential, such as conscious awareness of synchrony.

> *The subconscious field of life is one,*
>
> *though without independent significance of its own,*
>
> *only as experienced in the perception of the observer,*
>
> *as the non-dual source of the innate does it gain significance.*
>
> **D.T. Suzuki, *Lanka: Introduction***

One Field

The above transcription from D.T.'s introduction seems to agree with the historic understanding of a living field. "The field is one," reflects the fifth element in Hindu cosmology as well as the mutuality of entangled energy.

However, the most far-reaching and exciting potential for evolution of the human species relates to the field's wave effect on species evolution, where the consciousness of one effects many if not all. The possibility of collective species learning, as expounded by Rupert Sheldrake in *The Presence of the Past*, leads us to reconsider the importance of our individual conscious development.

Thou art energy and vibration only, feeling in mutuality the elemental life of every particle.

Organic energetic brew radiates from your body to copious entanglements.

The formless soup of existence communicating, sustaining, and creating.

Following the tides, carried by currents, dancing in waveness upon the ocean of existence.

Thou art the wave.

Soup, OWM

My romantic sense is that our powerlessness to influence humanity as individuals is limited thinking. More than we can imagine, what each of us does to expand our conscious awareness affects us all through field propagation and entanglement as a particle aspect of morphic resonance. This idea of holistic species learning; leads one to envision connecting through the collective subconscious, species entanglement, or morphic resonance to affect a broad simultaneous evolution.

Consider first that what you actualize is picked up by those with whom you have the most energetic resonance, such as like minds. Your personal growth makes it easier for everyone you connect with, as seen in normal cultural awareness, such as equal rights and every advancement since the caves.

Though one person may seem to be a small signal, that is linear or particle thinking, where more significant numbers are required to affect a tipping point. But in this theory, awareness is cumulative depending on wave characteristics. Of course, there are linear tipping points, such as the social conscience, as we've seen around slavery and later the equal rights of women, races and sexual preferences. They are effective by sharing our awareness and concepts with like-minded people, so we can amplify the effects of our influence on the whole population. But what about a shift in consciousness which may occur coincidentally across the planet at the same time.

When we include the wave characteristics of mutuality, this function takes on a whole new aspect as we reach a tipping point. In scientific terms, wave mechanics are dependent on time, proximity, spin, momentum, frequency, and energy. But the inclusion of entangled mutuality means the parameters of proximity and time no longer limit the effective change. So many more people, if not all, at some level, may instantly and regardless of distance get a consciousness upgrade given sufficient energy, frequency, momentum and spin. It sounds a bit like a Public Relations (PR) presentation but this has been seen before in the evolution of consciousness.

In historical golden ages, such as when the Buddha, Christ, Confucius and Lao Tsu, lived within a few hundred years, they influenced the world dramatically and in very similar ways. My point would be, that these teachers were in-tuned to a resonant tipping point in human consciousness and they experience the mutuality of inspiration. They contributed sufficient frequency and spin, which developed the energy and momentum to amplify the consciousness of compassion across the globe. It allowed their wisdom to be heard, where before it fell on the ears of a purely war like mentality, which feared and rejected introspection.

However, for our next steps, we must reach new tipping points. Through Schrödinger's equation, we can describe wave behavior, which implies that the tipping point is not just a case of more significant numbers. Certain frequencies, spins, and momentum have inordinately large effects on the whole. So evolution is also about establishing the optimum frequency, holding a space, and providing energy to help others. Of course, this can all be correlated as the right message at the right time.

From a field of all-conserving mind to a mechanism of entanglement such as morphic resonance, species' consciousness has demonstrated shifts many times throughout history. During certain windows of time, worldwide consciousness went beyond feudal systems, women became cherished partners rather than chattel, and slavery became culturally unthinkable. These worldwide synchronicities are available in various documentary studies.

However, the Alaya is where the *Lanka* most dramatically deviates from the popular understanding of biology, physics, and psychology. Traditional ideas that all memory, thoughts, and knowledge are a function of only the brain, maintained and managed through the senses and thought alone, are progressively being refined by growing evidence and unanswered questions. The Alaya field concept does deviate from the basic premise of design and health information held exclusively in genetic physical mechanisms. But without discounting existing progress, it adds a premonition of potentials to explore. Modern epigenetics is similar to the ancient view of outside influences and their environmental consequences. It may well evolve a modern scientific conception of the morphogenetic field.

Per D.T. Suzuki, Alaya or the collective subconscious shouldn't be confused as a mystical, magical superconsciousness. He says it is a transcendental entity beyond psychology because we may not find it limited to body, mind, or ever having form or malleability. D.T. also says that the subjective mind backed by the Alaya is the seat of desire, karma, and ignorance. As such, it is equally responsible for the subjective chaos of willing and discrimination. Rather than a metaphysical, spiritual anomaly, maybe it is a naturally occurring subtle, possibly organic, aspect of life we have yet to understand?

D.T. shares a feeling of constraint in the assumption of ethereal metaphysics. He points out that Alaya is known only in its consequence and has no significance except in relationship to the expressions of life. As the subconscious is mostly unconscious, Alaya is like a fabric behind the mind or more accurately a resonance of the mind, body and intention.

From a technological perspective, this formless resonant field of life seems incredibly relevant and entirely normal, just misunderstood.

However, this is also what my new-age brothers and sisters approach as the Akashic Record and give great esteem, which I would never reproach. In that light, the Akash, Alaya or the collective subconscious is what you make of it. Based fundamentally on Mind-only, its value and nature are self-determined, and fall into that vast arena, where I can only respect another's path.

Though D.T. and I share a similar love of the *Lanka*, my interest is more related to scientific abstractions. It seems obvious that the *Lanka* talks about unknown aspects of science yet to be fully explored. In this, Alaya is central as the great database of life, which we have related to as the subconscious, at least individually. It doesn't make out the field to be a vague far-fetched concept either. It is resonant, energy-based, and dependent on an organism. There is much more to it when we explore its defining characteristics and phases.

This idea of the subconscious as a vast resource is the *Lanka*'s linchpin, connecting the quietude of mind or suchness, to the repository of wisdom and intuitive knowledge. However, as D.T. says, these infatuations with thought and what we create in thinking, make intuitive penetration of the undisturbed subconscious impossible. In turn the disconnection leaves us uncoordinated with our true selves, rendering authentic life beyond our grasp.

Alaya is more than life-force according to the *Lanka*; it is a living database recorded for future use. Memories and images of thought, action, and emotion create and update our running thought-images as they continuously frame the next idea. Next, we'll explore Alaya-consciousness as more than a field concept with limitations and practicalities.

CHAPTER TWENTY-ONE
ALAYA-CONSCIOUSNESS

In psychological terms, Alaya-consciousness is both the problem and the potential solution per ancient science. The problem is similar to cognitive dissonance but at a level far below the misalignment of behaviors and beliefs. Subconscious dissonance has no handles to be grasped, metrics to be measured, or behaviors to correct.

Alaya-consciousness along with the five senses, subjective and objective mind, convey everything we experience as sentient beings. As such, the subconscious is the eighth channel of consciousness in the human model but also the key to a connected life.

Many have understood that the subconscious is the unseen engine that runs almost every aspect of thinking without discernment, consciousness, or self-control. Generally seen as the dark shadows of the mind, which collects all the minuscule data and input that rationality can't handle. It was also understood to be intrinsically important by the ancients as the gateway to tranquillity, effortless belonging and enlightenment.

But the subconscious mind isn't sinister or disruptive unless we make it so, through unconscious abuse. Because we made it, we can influence its content and potential for disruption. Our collection can be influenced by a variety of personal development techniques. Several thousand years of human potential science exist within Yoga, Zen, Chan, Vajrayana, Buddhism, and many other paths, both east and west.

The challenge for an everyday guy, like myself, is finding the solitude of my own innate knowledge. My rational mind says the subconscious is available via intuition and self-observation but requires holding habitual, compulsive thinking at arm's length and under constant scrutiny. This surveillance observes my natural reactions, not being caught up in the drama or especially ego identification. But these concepts are stress focused thinking, which intrude on intuition and miss the point of quietude.

It is important in my own practice, to remember how life works best and not over analyse. My most basic experience is also *Lanka's* magic key, to escape the cage of cognitive problem solving by letting go of outcomes. When I step beyond just thinking uncontrollably, solutions appear naturally in every situation, every time and without fail. This "letting go" is freeing myself from a self-created cage and tapping into my innate wisdom, the gift of subconscious penetration. But what the *Lanka* offers is a method of approaching the subconscious which works magic. What seems like a paradox is the pathway to non-dual rationality, the fifth self-nature or stage of consciousness.

To understand this point, the *Lanka's* statement, of not separate delusion, says that through our perceptions and relationships with what appears as "other," we create heaven or hell. This is very different from our rational idea of healthy and not healthy thinking, because underlying "other" as delusion, is that thinking itself may be the problem, whether good, bad or indifferent.

You may have heard it said, that the good is often the worst enemy of the best. The famous phrase, "As you think, so you become," attributed to everyone from Buddha to Bruce Lee, goes only so far. We often use it to empower our thinking to do better, which sounds pretty good. However in the search for our own innate knowledge, it is often counterproductive to hearing that small quiet voice. But it is not a panacea in any case, though it resembles Mind-only as a very useful perspective.

There is also another fundamental idea, which hinders intuitive penetration in the most simple way. We attract difficulties and disagreeable people from negative attitudes; conversely, we engage happy relationships and inspiration from positive thoughts. And though that may sound sufficient, it doesn't protect us from the compulsion of desires, taking offense unnecessarily and placing the responsibility for our state of mind, outside ourselves and our control. Many great ideas, in one sense, miss the point in another.

However, inherited wisdom, unchanging knowledge, inspirations, and intuitions also wait for our use, but they are needles in the haystack. It takes quietude and intuition to understand the non-dual reservoir of our own deep memory, much less the inherited influences and wisdom of our ancestors. But all that was just words, until I learned to set an intention and let go of the outcomes. This is where my acceptance mantra comes in handy, "all according to plan, just not my plan."

As a melding of indistinct characteristics, the subconscious isn't merely information and the collection is more like a movie than an inventory of information. It's like a library with no books, index or card catalogue. The aspects of the subconscious are indistinct, where everything recorded is self-organized. Composed and associated with sequential experiences, reactions are not always as much about the stimuli as they are about subconscious associations, influencing our thinking and reactions in unseen ways. This awareness is an opportunity to recognize the source of compulsive reaction and exercise an objective choice.

Understanding these terms, we can see that a specific stimuli or emotional memory is generally associated with the whole experience and a variety of circumstances. So a terrible fight, that resulted in a serious injury to one's self-image, may cause irrational responses when stimulated by a similar situation, phrase or even a smell. At another time we may physically hurt or get ill, when subjected to certain feelings of remembered betrayal, anger, pain or disappointment.

At various times, it is a normal struggle to control the non-rational with the rational will. Associated with stress in many forms, there are various moments in everyone's life, we don't admit or choose not to remember. Continual control of the non-discriminating subconscious awareness is an impossibility through sense-consciousness alone. Often, the best we can do is admit irrational reactions and note the triggers. This kind of observation practice, mentioned earlier, is part of Tibetan practice applied through the teachings of Chogyam Trungpa Rinpoche, by Pema Chodron in observing one's shenpas or trigger sensations.

Additionally the subconscious isn't limited to mind or brain, which is reflected in physical ailments that present themselves based on psychological trauma. Body memory can be affected by physical therapy, healing distortions in the psyche and improving health. A physical release through Hatha Yoga, Qi Gong, Pranayama and many forms of physical therapy, may relax a muscle memory to ease a psychological trauma long since suppressed and forgotten.

As you may notice, everything about approaching subconscious access, integration and tranquilization has to do with letting go. Letting go of outcomes, observing-letting go subconscious reactions, and letting go of physical stresses by taking care of ourselves, accounts for a lifestyle change for many of us. And where our grandparents might of said, "having faith" is the path, the subconscious isn't separate and doesn't want adoration or worship. It is your non-dual self and doesn't have the capacity to care.

Diminishing faith in something outside of oneself, may seem to be a great loss. But as we evolve, certainty as an experience within suchness, replaces faith. It occurs as we fully recognise that in stepping beyond cascading thought, or into the quiet space between thoughts, solutions appear naturally in every situation, every time and without fail.

However, the *Lanka* points out, this challenging aspect of nature, Alaya consciousness, also gives access to our most profound awareness and greatest potential within the Womb of Buddha, another name for the subconscious.

> *Oneness gives birth to the highest bliss; diving into the womb of enlightenment, the subconscious, Alaya.*
>
> *Here lies the realm of imagelessness, transmission, and self-realization.*
>
> ***Lanka*, Chapter 1**

The Gateway to Human Potential

This transliteration refers to meditation symbolically as diving into the transcendental or non-dual aspect of the subconscious mind. As our gateway into our highest human potential, it presents the characteristics of a fully accomplished consciousness, which reflect a wisdom of tranquility, where effortless belonging is possible.

Imagelessness, transmission and self-realization are the attributes of Noble Wisdom, which fully evolve in the Womb of Buddha or the individual's subconscious. The first thing is that understanding isn't enough. These characteristics are changes within the fabric of who you are, which is barely affected by cascading thought flitting from here to there.

The Lanka does say that acting 'as if' for long enough, does facilitate progress, through a gentle means. However the means of getting there, change going beyond mind is a Great Turning Back, which is not usually gentle. The opportunity for greater awareness starts with dissonance, as my cognitive mind often functions in disregard to the subconscious. Living without "peace of mind" is ordinary and often tragic. The opportunity this understanding offers is that peace is beyond the mind's cognitive ability. Peace, to be more than a mental construct, requires a realignment in our subconscious whereby thinking has a new reference. The difficulty is this isn't just a near-death experience. It is a death to an illusion we have come to love as our own creation. The Great Turning Back initially occurs as a mental doubt, but experience in the primordial subconscious, creates change, culminating in a tipping point. This is the point of practice, to push beyond the limits of self, embracing no-other-than self.

From understanding the potentials and limitations of a rational approach, the *Lanka* expects us to realize that cognitive-subconscious dissonance may be the most common and fundamental mental disorder, given humanity's disconnection from themselves and nature. But this diagnosis means almost everyone is suffering primarily from misidentification, exacerbated by grasping, craving, and delusion.

What we really are and what we must align with, is our own primordial consciousness which includes the beast, the demon, the angel and the god. Then you may roar like the lion or lioness you are, and love like the sage of wisdom and peace. This connection is visceral and all the domestication of the last millennium has no use.

Noble Wisdom, as the gateway of human potential, can be summed up in Right-knowledge and the revulsion of everything we thought we knew at the subconscious level. It is a complete reset, an encounter with the absolute and the wrenching of our delusions, usually by means of a hugely traumatic experience. The near-death existential experience is probably the most conclusive shift, where one's world view is instantaneously ripped away. But a window can be created through shamanism, trance, and hallucinogenic drugs. The primordial can be experienced as the momentary result of an altered state of consciousness, but stability and sustainability requires much further work in my experience.

My limited grasp of Noble Wisdom is first that the "no-other-than-self" realization is ultimately to realize and actualize our most essential human desire, the need to love and be loved unconditionally. This self-realization was described as our inherent Buddha-nature or transcendent compassion, such that everyone is embraced as a most beloved child. This is a level of inclusiveness few have experienced or understand.

But in a practical sense and most relevant to humans in general, the path of compassion and acceptance leads to relationships approaching effortless belonging. For this reason, it is the most important message of Buddhism and the vindication of religious practice.

Transmission refers to the power of Buddha, which for me is primarily through practice and right-understanding via books such as the *Hsin Hsin Ming, I Ching* and others I have mentioned. Schools of Buddhism often can be heard to say such a self-directed path is very dangerous, but I do check in with various teachers. At this advanced stage of life, my wife and I have a ceremonial practice following Jaggi Vasudev Sadhguru. Anyway, having known a few great teachers, my clay feet or humanness meant the path was there to support my life, not the other way round.

The next major aspect of Noble Wisdom is imagelessness which may look like the falling away of personality and worldly identification. But it is actually the disintegration of who we thought we were, not because it was wrong but because it isn't useful and has become the limiting factor. Revulsion is D.T.'s term for the beginning of imagelessness or falling away, as it must occur in the subconscious to be authentic.

This revulsion is in the core of our being, beyond the mind itself. For a few years I kept my distance from the term revulsion, as it condemns a life for which most people hold an extreme infatuation. But in reflection, I realized my great turning back began with returning from overseas, completely disenchanted with the culture I had grown up in. The Viet Nam War, our cultural revolution and minor psychedelic experience contributed. But I was mostly revulsed by the way everyone walked through life asleep to our effect on the greater world. I had been so asleep as to be a pawn for the US industrial-military complex. Then I observed first hand, the lies by which we weaponised other cultures to sell our Gross Domestic Product. I had been the dupe of miracles, mystery and authority but under the guise of culture and freedom, rather than religion.

But I was young and relapse was inevitable. My turning back took hold to set a direction, to no longer be tricked; first by culture, then politics, separatist thinking and ultimately the internal cause, my own ego construction. My slow awakening occurred as life destroyed my delusions and only quietude never disappointed. It was solitude and practice which provided direction, as I began to see the reflection of entrapment by sense-consciousness. The hardest thing is still, not to get caught up in the outcomes of thought as reality itself. It comes from just living in the world.

> *The subconscious is known as the womb of awakening; archive of all things good and bad, pure and defiled; but who's original nature is itself immaculate.*
>
> *It becomes soiled in life experience, as it indiscriminately collects sensation, thought, concept and awareness.*
>
> *Though this collection is the normal sentient experience, it can make intuitive insight impossible.*
>
> *Blocking this innate knowledge, we follow imagination, superstition, a creator or the ego-self.*
>
> *This choice leaves us to experience the six realms of existence, sometimes called hells.*
>
> *However, intuitive piercing of one's primitive subconscious purity creates a revolution at all levels of consciousness.*
>
> *Except for this puzzling concoction of pure and unclean, good and evil, this climatic transformation would be impossible in stepping beyond our sentient existence.*
>
> **D.T. Suzuki, *Lanka: Introduction***

This idea is where the *Lanka*'s practical magic and psychological wisdom become most apparent. This transformation called sudden awakening, or the Great Turning Back, is possibly shamanic, ceremonial, a near-death experience, or altered consciousness by any number of means. The *Lanka* refers to this climax of transformation as a revolution at the depths of the subconscious, which means the implosion of personality as having any meaning at all. As my wife joked yesterday, "I have never been so certain of nothing at all." The hole is filled with fully present awareness, loving-kindness, non-judgment, and the presence of peace.

But how do we grasp the connection and take control of our lives, happiness, and wellbeing? It is the mindful awareness I have described from the beginning. Suchness ultimately takes hold as the subconscious disengages thinking identification. We are free from the addictions of mind, but most importantly, free of thought as self. What sounds so easy and simple from within can seem amazing and impossible from without. Because this is a self-determined awareness, it is to be awake beyond the focus of outside effects and the narrow influence of environment.

In the womb of awakening, reaction, interpretation, and self-nurture optimize the gifts of our inherited nature. Otherwise would be madness, returning to addictive compulsion and the mental illness of being controlled by happenstance. Still, the necessity of subconscious awakening establishes the gravity of our choices on the path. If you want to be happy, first and foremost, you must choose happiness every day.

Uncovering the Deepest Layer of Self

Paradoxically, our growth opportunity is at the deepest level of the subconscious rather than at any level of doing. There are no handles to grasp it or tools to find it, but it begins with recognition; the choice only starts with conscious awareness. This challenge, addressed in the science of Yoga for many thousands of years, is one of exercise, re-education, and unlearning our conditioned domestication.

> *Turning back is the inner revulsion from unconscious, habitual, mundane life and its suffering.*
>
> *Usually occurring mentally, it is mostly temporary and shallow.*
>
> *So, to become effective, turning back must be grasped directly, experienced intimately, and penetrated intuitively.*
>
> *The Noble Wisdom occurs within the all-conserving subconscious.*
>
> *This subconscious, Alaya defies psychological analysis because it is only known by its consequence behind the fallible relative mind.*
>
> *But Alaya exists also at an untainted level, which may be reached in suchness.*

Turning back is, therefore, a purification of one's subconscious access by ceasing the obsession with the collection of sensory experience, things, and thoughts.

This quietude allows the perception of our oneness and allness.

D.T. Suzuki, *Lanka: Introduction, Turning Back*

Two points are vital from the above transcription. First is to note that the revulsion or turning back isn't from life or the world itself. It's disgust for a compulsive existence, being bounced around by circumstance, emotion, and useless stories. The method of turning back is the purification of access to our deeper selves with a perspective change in quietude of mind or suchness, which recognizes the compulsive nature of ego-identification.

As with my generation of flower children and baby boomers, many people experienced a wide variety of experiences, including psychotropic drugs, to encounter the primitive purity of the subconscious. But the lucid moments didn't last. Life comes back, and the collection process of sensation, concept, and sense-consciousness identification quickly rebuilds the walls of separateness. But each day is a new chance to tune in.

This combination of ideas brings us an understanding that defines life as a formless reflection of experience, randomly recorded to support brain, body, and field connections. These are primary concepts to understand the *Lanka*'s biological theory and its relation to psychological science.

Dance in the moonlight however you may.

Howl, chant, sing till compulsion is exhausted,

in the ceremony of being free.

Shun the routine, destroy the habit, explore the unknown.

Connect in solitude to your first joy, to your first love, to your primitive emptiness.

Turning back, tuning in, turning off the noise, free yourself from compulsive existence.

Thou art master of the seas.

***Never Surrender*, OWM**

Once occurring at a subconscious level, the finality of revulsion has no means of returning because the old definitions have lost all foundation. But even if temporary, as was my initial recognition, it may become a practice, which over time becomes a slow transfiguration rather than a revolution. In my case, clarity looks like loving awareness, which might seem like nothing but when combined with quietude, is the greatest gift worth striving for.

Thought as in judgment, opinion, discrimination, and especially beliefs, are battling against our tranquility until we loosen their grip. Gautama Buddha recommended a monastic path. The more complicated way was my choice and it is that of a householder's normal life, which is to follow our highest potential within life's joys and difficulties. This requires creating another kind of sanctuary, a solitude of mind, from which worldly interaction is observed and directed.

> *Like windborne waves and foam continually dancing on the sea; the subconscious is stirred by the winds of life's form. To dance with sense-consciousness in a field of choice are a multitude of colors, sensations, tastes, sounds, fragrances, and sunlight. They are different and the same as ocean and waves, so to with sense-consciousness and subjective mind.*
>
> *As waves are stirred on the high seas, the subconsciousness is stirred to create consciousness. Subjective mind, will, belief, discrimination, and the senses consider the significance of each form in life, but no part functions separately, as they lack independent character.*
>
> *As the ocean is not separate from the waves, so too subjective mind does not change consciousness. Action and consequence are recorded in the subjective mind, recognized in will and discrimination. From this perspective, the physical world is evaluated directly by the five senses. Perception is colored with all the variety of imagination.*
>
> *How are these colors like waves on the ocean? No such colors exist in formless consciousness; it is for simplicity that mind is described as altered by form.*
>
> *Subjective mind does not collect or change in itself, which is unknowable. There is comprehension only where there is another to understand, as with the waves and the ocean. The subjective mind cannot see itself and the apparent world is assumed as such by*

sense-consciousness. Memory itself only appears to change, as do the waves. The ocean is seen dancing in waveness.

How is its collection, in the subconscious, not recognized by the intellect?

How is the ocean of self, confused with the waves of mind?

Lanka, Chapter 2, section IV, slokas 99-111

In these slokas, memory, understanding, will and discrimination, are wave-like appearances of mind, but not effective change agents for subconscious tranquilization. They are unable to see themselves or their distinctions as functions within a captive awareness. This captivity is what it means to be subjective or caught in the experience of life, identified with will and discrimination. Going back to Part One, this is what it means to be awake, to see beyond the cage of sense-consciousness. It is to recognize the entrapment of defining ourselves by what we think.

What smooths access to the Womb of Buddha, is living in harmony, recognizing this trap of subjectivity and disengaging, by letting go to hear one's intuitive voice. This trick is learning to see one's ocean-ness and observe the waves without being fooled. In this idea, one can understand statements like "There is no path to happiness. Happiness is the path."

The process of letting go has a few basic steps by which progress is challenged and recognized. Where sense-consciousness provides our frame of reference in this world, it can also be used to loosen the bars of our cage and remove obstructions in a basic sense.

There are lessons of development, which I label freedoms, as they have been incremental steps in fifty years of practice and essential in my developing awareness. They may not be the great awakenings of Noble Wisdom or the overwhelming emergence in the absolute, but they show a path of understanding and common sense once you understand the goal. The freedoms are small steps or tools which put sensation, preference, judgment, opinion, and habit in a healthier context. They also follow the stages of consciousness referred to as the first self-natures.

Each freedom is an aspect of recognizing being trapped in thought. The potential, of loosening our grip on the outcomes of thought, is huge but its reflection is modestly just acceptance of what is, as it is, with no need to control. The basis for the freedoms are to grasp the not-separate reality that we are not the doer. As part of one life the totality of Alaya on this planet is such that, to become one with it, is only a matter of getting out of your own way. Perceiving life as self-created lessons, we embrace the grace of sudden awakening, whether a cool breeze or a train wreck. In this mindfulness, is the next step toward effortless belonging, learning just to be.

As an indiscriminate feedback system, the subconscious can be the source of mental disturbance as it reacts to our habits of thought. Many disturbances in life, go well beyond a conflict of actions and beliefs. Where psychology may try to fix the behaviors or beliefs, the *Lanka's* focus is still behaviors but beyond beliefs, where it seeks to influence subconscious harmony with waking consciousness. Where we normally analyse thinking, this opportunity is within Alaya-consciousness or the individual's subconscious mind.

Our subconscious supports sense-consciousness beneath or behind the mind, operating within everything we think. Where in modern usage it is hardly given a sound bite, it is our path to happiness and acceptance, which is ultimately consciousness.

> *Understood collection and accumulation, the physical world evolves.*
>
> *Revealing plainly the significant, the lesser, and the average; corrupt and pure, good and bad equally.*
>
> *But evolution is also effortlessly one where intention or prayer, empty of collection, become seeds of change.*
>
> *Creating effortless circumstance, called luck and coincidence, in a synchronistic creation.*
>
> *Consistent in alignment and resonance are thine, empty, loving, suchness.*
>
> *Thou art the channel of all life.*

Seeds of Change, OWM

As our collection grows, the resources of memory, knowledge, emotion, and experience formulate more and more concepts, judgments, and self-UN-awareness. Of course, it's all built on concepts and ideas which must be incorrect in those parts of life that don't work. But what about the parts that do work, like being a productive human being? That part of life goes to unimaginable new levels.

But this is the grand opportunity. Waking up starts with fully understanding our construction and how its components fight to maintain their creation of ego identity. Only when we reach a level of dissatisfaction, pain, or disillusion does it make any sense to face facts. But, when the pain, trauma, or potential loss gets bad enough, something breaks the mirror we created, and only broken shards remain. This is sudden awakening, but it also points to another possibility: the direct experience of the non-dual. This is where we go next.

My wife likes to say, "We are all solar-powered vehicles." I may have added, we are interconnected using wireless technology to access a cloud storage facility, which we ourselves create.

> *Thou art cause and effect in this eternal space.*
>
> *Everyone thou meets you know, before you know.*
>
> *Dimly seen past life or prophetic future love, all are family.*
>
> *Brother, lover, friend, thou sees within their eyes, what has been or what will be.*
>
> *Homeless beggar, entitled pretender, giving—taking all the same.*
>
> *Every shop girl, once your mother, later your child.*
>
> *She broke your heart.*
>
> *She made thou whole.*
>
> *Energy moves in familiar streams to its favorite ocean depth.*
>
> *Thou art energy made form by love.*
>
> *Your little stream has only familiars.*
>
> *When thou art willing to look inside, your wants, the sincere smile, the friendly word, going beyond judgment, you change the world.*
>
> *Listening purely is effortless belonging; the vision that all just is.*
>
> *Expressions of the one as everything speaks thine name.*
>
> *Thou art that.*
>
> ***Listening Thou Art*, OWM**

CHAPTER TWENTY-TWO
SUDDEN AWAKENING

People talk about sudden awakening as the master's power to deliver the experience of the absolute. But that is not my experience. So, the story of Ravana's awakening is included in this book as the example of what I know. It contains the best description of the shock and awe which happens in ego implosion. Because I recognize it in my own experience, it expresses the nature of my path.

Like lapidary, where stones with sharp edges are tumbled together, my ego refinement is in smoothing the edges within life as direct experience of what is. My implosion experience or sudden awakening was much less profound than Ravana's. But there was an unforgettable moment of lucidity and an irreversible shift in awareness, where the ego's megalomania was exposed to the light then collapsed on itself. Since then it has continued to be revealed and smoothed in everyday practice. It is the plain, methodical awakening, I'm mostly interested in, reinforced daily as a life style. This path leads to freedoms of awareness to see the world in new perspectives.

Sudden awakening maybe confused as transmission, salvation or as a magic power instilled by the spiritual awakening of a great master. But I am inclined to believe the view leads to an illusory reliance and likely disappointment, as Dostoyevsky pointed out in the *Grand Inquisitor*. In the Lanka's view it is a misunderstanding, recognized in two doctrinal disagreements, mentioned earlier, where doing good works doesn't achieve non-dual awareness nor can greater awareness be given by another, no matter how enlightened. Spiritual awakening or actualization of non-dual awareness is the *Lanka's* single purpose for spiritual practice. But that is not to say doing good is of little value or that the field of a master cannot influence in amazing and magical ways.

To understand my own awakening, I find it useful to look at my own experience and concentrate on four aspects. First, the living intelligence, that we are all part of, has been nurturing and coaxing me along, always.

Second, as I'm able to focus on this mindful connection, my lessons or the questions in life are answered by teachers, who can be anyone or anything. This builds my connection as well as providing direction because I perceive others and everything as expressions of one thing, the living intelligence. As it's expression other sentient beings often communicate separateness based on the limits of sense consciousness. So, I empathize but only embrace that part which is not-separate. This recognition requires suchness or a mind empty of agenda. However, all the rest of nature, doesn't have the limitations of self-awareness and so can be directly instrumental in perceiving oneness.

> *Gardening is a spiritual retreat and*
> *my greatest opportunity to play god.*
> *Serving nature's path to create something more,*
> *the chaos or abundance is mine.*
> *Part of the organic cycles, interacting with care*
> *emulating nature's ways.*
> *I plan and consider past lessons, inevitably letting go.*
> *Non-dual nature regards no greater, lesser, weed or fruit.*
> *Without emotion for the tender abundance,*
> *I prune, tie and discard what does not serve.*
> *Though not the creator, there is art and love in my choices.*
> *Preparing, planting and letting go of outcomes,*
> *I can accept the bounty and loss as lessons of craft and messages of spirit.*
> *Today I read a sad corn crop as unfulfilled potential and missed harvest.*
> *The drying ears of corn remind me of impermanence, imperfection and its unquantifiable beauty.*
> *Each cob a unique and diverse creation, beyond our greatest knowledge, wisdom and awareness.*

Life comes from life and we can only observe, nurture and marvel.

Though no longer sweet corn on the cob it will become delicious corn meal.

Realizing the bounty of every experiment, I try to learn its lessons.

Today the corn teaches me pollination is nature's purview alone

as nature rejected my experimentation.

Also playing god with squash breaks its spirit.

Shrinking with pruning, it must be free to find its own way.

So it is with me, beyond my best buy date,

old friends teach new lessons.

I am nature, I am corn, squash and far to often beans.

But, I can joyfully await next years experiments,

dreams of permaculture and biodynamics.

Gardening, OWM

The third aspect is that ordinary experience of life is self-creation as collections, patterns and habit. But the practices to gain mastery are a continual choice, a discipline which must be sustained. Here teachers and the various paths create the mixing of concept and experience to step beyond the ordinary.

The fourth and final aspect is that I try to accept all lessons with equal gratitude. Moments of clarity and major trials contribute equally. The challenge in clarity is not taking it for granted, through generosity and gratitude, realizing this also will pass. The challenge for trials is maintaining the detachment not to get sucked in. To observe the long wave, we see how the pain or disappointment led to the greatest good. Providing steps to strengthen and ascend, life goes on naturally with the work of being more present, aware, and loving.

As I mentioned, sudden awakening happened many times in my life but one instance was closest to Ravana's, as described in the *Lanka*. It was a moment of shock and awe, rather than my normal, aha moment. It occurred when Swami Satchidananda (Swamiji) named me Gurudas.

With his hand on my head, the ego instantly expanded like a giant balloon to hear Guru. I heard it like a title. My ego said, "he recognizes my greatness!" But then my bubble burst just as suddenly, as I understood, das meant servant. I was the Guru's servant. There was a visceral thwack and it was several days before I functioned normally.

Many of the feelings described by Ravana's sudden awakening, where also mine. I was completely caught out, exposed in my fantasy and ashamed of self-aggrandizement.

However, where there have been many points of awakening in my life, it has been repeated flashes of comprehension and the continuity of life lessons, that effected permanent change. There have been far too many climatic turning points for me to share. So, I'll try to point out major signposts, in hopes you can relate.

In this chapter, I will try to share the freedoms of awakening which demonstrate an environment where effortless belonging is available. This includes several key aspects pointed out already, which act as stepping stones. I use them to gauge how I'm doing in my awareness, they are similar to recognizing the subconscious shadows of shenpa in a practical and understandable way.

Freedoms

The freedoms begin in an understanding that quietude of mind is where suchness exists. Between every two thoughts there is an opportunity for pure awareness and it's not alien, it's every beings most natural state. Thinking is a distraction and all the layers of collection are useful but often unnecessary baggage. Awakening to this self-image is to not be defined by things, accomplishments, or relationships. It is the first doorway to freedom as our basic identity with quiet awareness, listening.

The second freedom comes in understanding the servitude of our desires. As ego was constructed, our preferences evolved before concepts and together they created a sense-consciousness, capable of survival. But we can easily recognize the childishness and immaturity of being led by preference alone. Every child says, I don't like it, but later learns that very thing may be their favorite. For me it was pineapple.

Holding preferences at a distance is the second freedom. It creates the space to enjoy new experience and find marvelous surprises in life. Letting go of preferences, keeping life's door open, especially keen in maturity, is a pure gift to ourselves.

A great example of freedoms was presented by Don Miguel Ruiz in *The Four Agreements,* as noted earlier. From the ancestral wisdom of his tribal heritage, he describes four agreements with self. They can be summarized as an impeccability of word, not taking anything personally, not making assumptions, and finally doing one's best.

These agreements give freedom in several ways, as well as paving the way for the *Lanka's* vast concepts. First, impeccability of word includes doing no harm and speaking one's truth. Like Grandpa said, "If you only have one story it's much easier to keep track of," and life is simplified. And like Grandma said, "If you don't have something nice to say, say nothing at all." Life in this way is peaceful. It teaches me to distance myself from gossip and avoid stirring the pot, especially someone else's. This is also what it means, to be true to myself by being true to others.

The second agreement is related to a huge lesson for me, as I slowly learned, it's rarely about me. Grasping, not to take things personally, was the beginning of a larger liberation. It is the childish response, we all went through or in many cases, are still going through. But the power came in at deeper level for me, when I understood that to take offense was my choice and my fault. It came in the guise of justified defensiveness, opinion and the need to be right. Eventually, I understood it was a sign of my insecure self-identity. It revealed that I was still caught up with labels, things, circumstances; in other words, sense-consciousness and its collections.

This other side of self-control, was learning to withhold the response internally. To pause and observe, waiting long enough to look for misinterpretation, unintentional slips, or just someone else's stuff.

Recognizing being offended as a bad choice, is a very powerful freedom, which came to me originally through the *Hsin Hsin Ming,* mentioned earlier. It is also observance of Mind-only, to see that taking offense, is my choice in that moment of compulsive reaction. And as such, the consequences as in damaged relationships or hurt feelings, are my own creation and responsibility. Though I can't be responsible for what others do, I am always responsible for how I react, both internally and externally. But it all starts with not taking things personally.

The third agreement of Don Miguel Ruiz, starts going into the deeper levels of the Lanka's cosmology as he talks about not projecting what will be or even what is. My wife was so inspired by "not taking things personally and don't make assumptions," she has said it changed her whole life. In not making assumptions, she focused on observing that others don't know our wants and it takes courage to ask.

This is a classical problem in many marriages, where a woman might assume her guy fails in his love for her, because he should have seen her need or desire. For our relationship, clarity and honesty is crucial, as I'm generally in my own world and often clueless to common sense. But she's right, that we all can put a test out there for someone else to fail. Not wanting to look foolish or the fear of being judged, can set us up for a trap. Pretending to be cool, not happy and not communicating what we really want, is expecting the other to be psychic and prove their love. It's a recipe for failure. Freedom is avoiding the trap.

The fourth agreement is to always do my best; stop the self-flagellation and try to do better. These are little freedoms or awakenings, we use in everyday life. They lead to greater freedoms which escape the chaos almost entirely and for me are activated in the Lanka's adamancy in letting go of outcomes.

Letting go of outcomes is my personal flag to wave as it is central to the Lanka's message and directly relates to my understanding of wave theory and the observer effect. Nature, including it's metaphysical aspect of entanglement, function as waves of mutuality, which we disturb in trying to control and manipulate. Not that we shouldn't interact but we should do it consciously.

Of course most people don't have the luxury of retirement and my life of contemplative choice. But the model might be helpful. For me setting an intention and following a path is all I need, to apply my preferences. From this stand point, I set preferences aside and look for the organic path, allowing for changes and outcomes which were unexpected. This is where my mantra comes to remind me, all according to plan just not my plan. It applies easily to my daily life, because I rarely have to deal with expectations, other than my wife's. Then my mantra is especially useful anytime we face a disappointment or challenge to a direction.

In this mode of living, our lives are full of synchronicities because we allow room for them. Not to say it's all comfort and ease, but life in this way, backed up with daily practice, is far beyond anything either of us ever knew before. For our daily life, this is generally enough but for the *Lanka*, it only indicates the beginning of the path of conscious evolution. What is unique, in its view, is that the evolution of awareness means stages of effortless belonging which aren't bound to a master's magic wand or sudden awakening. These stages can be applied and developed by everyday people like us.

Not the Doer

D.T. Suzuki would say that no one awakens except by the irrational means of non-dual direct experience. Therefore awakening requires transcendence by intuitively penetrating the unchanging primordial subconscious.

Transcendence is a simple shift in perspective, usually associated with meditation and mindfulness. It is the culmination of all the freedoms where one realizes, no matter how busy and active I may be, life is happening around me and I am not the doer. The cause in life is life itself.

One way to understand transcendence is by observing how the autonomic body functions. The heart beats and our breath happens without our conscious recognition. The body transcends the mind, as in independent operation. If you try to control either for too long, like holding the breath, the body retakes control and returns to normal. We can accelerate the heart or breath for a short time as we can appear to control life. But after a short time we naturally return to a wavelike function of habitual thought. Transcendence is first seeing our interdependence and impermanence.

Transcending mind is freedom from defending the collection of sense consciousness, how we have defined self and what we call personality. When the big I doesn't need defending or reinforcement, we can relax. This is the key note of effortless belonging.

Another way of looking at transcendence is to realize that in the freedoms of mindfulness, minimal preferences, circumspect words, not taking things personally, avoidance of being offended and letting go of outcomes, we may transcend the sense-consciousness and live in greater harmony with our higher selves. The Buddha is a primary example of this, but on a whole different level.

> *Buddha,*
>
> *"My highest reality it the eternal-unthinkable, conforming to the idea of cause beyond actuality and imagination.*
>
> *It is the self-realization of no-other-than-self as the highest reality.*
>
> *It is causation where there is no doer.*
>
> *Classed with non-dual space, nirvana and the end to discrimination, it is eternal.*
>
> *Different from the eternal-unthinkable spoken in philosophy.*
>
> *It is thatness or suchness, realized by noble wisdom within oneself".*
>
> **Lanka, Chapter 2, section xvii**

The Buddha's description of the eternal-unthinkable alludes more to real magic than down-to-earth, relatable advice on our attitudes. Unless you look closely back to the freedoms, it may be confusing.

Beginning with cause as beyond actuality and imagination, he is talking about the entanglement of our living intelligence, the ultimate cause in every moment. This is where our worship has evolved to separate us from the sacredness of life itself. Falling for the miracle, mystery and authority, we have missed the point. For me, this is always and only about awakening from compulsion to go beyond my animal limitations.

Though our experience is usually bouncing off of this non-dual cause with will and discrimination, we might just see the light in old terms such as "letting go and letting God." The living intelligence or the eternal unthinkable are terms of recognition that something other than our own will and discrimination are at work. Where the mind tries to construct our lives with struggle and suffering, getting out of the way allows the subconscious to create the connection with source. This effortless penetration is the essential link to freedom from sleep walking through life.

The usable key is right in the middle, "where there is no doer." This no-doer isn't stagnant, inert, or passive. Through it the Buddha is calling everything into creation through entangled mutuality, where the force of intention, patience, and quiet observation attract resonant energy which manifest as synchronicity. This is also the seventh stage of awareness, the seventh kind of self-nature, which is completion or perfection. In it, the world arises, as the pure land of life's innate intelligence. It is our ultimate destination, seen as a distant dream. Finally, the verse goes on to say that this awareness is a closed loop from the eternal unthinkable to effortless suchness. The magic awaits between each two thoughts. It is apparent as freedoms of mind, which progressively recognize ourselves as the non-doer. This has been called detachment in many schools but in understanding freedoms, one can see the benefit and mechanism.

Previously I referred to "letting go of outcomes" as the productive mental attitude going into any situation. It's staying open to change which flows into a synchronicity of life. So, setting an intention, doing the next right thing, thinking of others, and being grateful for whatever comes, reveals the next step, on a continuous path. This is how we create a resonance with the non-dual, but it's still broad brush ideals without clear understanding why it works.

Nirvana

Synchrony appears as nirvana, where waves within the entangled energy field, unfold the experience of effortlessness. Though the discipline to observe its dance may be confused with complacency, nothing could be further from the truth. This is an active practice of awareness and a continual discipline, pursuing the moment-to-moment truth of "what is," not what I think it is.

The Lanka is clear that is analogy is also not to say fatalism, nihilism, or atheism are being promoted. The Buddha describes a level of completion that incorporates Noble Wisdom or the realization of no-other-than-self, full knowledge of existence, and, importantly, imagelessness.

Imagelessness sounds like an letting go of personality but in fact it is the discipline to embrace the magic of acceptance and synchrony. From this place of connected compassion, one can let go and ride the waves of the non-doer, master of suchness, thatness, and nothing at all.

However, as high flying as this may seem, it points to a rationale for the thinking person. The man or woman who needs some help may find greater certainty through observation and experience. The exercise is one of learning to trust life, one step at a time and actively seek out the freedoms. Doing it perfect, is not going to happen the first or even fiftieth time. Progress is found opening and trusting in this moment, allowing the expression of living intelligence, where judgment is by nature, missing the point.

Generosity

If I can experience the world through gratitude, loosening control, and a suspended judgment, I gradually develop awareness of synchronicity. Gratitude is the prerequisite which is often just lip service, in my experience. Acknowledging what brought me here and being thankful, is confused to be gratitude. But, it's not nearly enough. Generosity in all things, is the active side of magic and the only way to develop the humility of true gratitude, otherwise ego simply has a new mask.

This discipline is different from simple material generosity as its true reflection is generosity of spirit. Gratitude is its outcome where one cannot be truly grateful while supporting the separation of judgment, opinion and discrimination. This discipline, of holding the path is rigorous acceptance, but it reveals the patterns of life's entangled field to become increasingly real in experience. It is the Buddha's expression of no other than self, one's most beloved child or oneness with all life. A new plateau arises, first as the practice and then the certainty of experience.

A step closer to the common man are the highly evolved, who's experience is called embodied goodness and truth.

> *As selfless ones experience peace and tranquility, their love and sympathy cultivate their character in service to others.*
>
> *Their path unfolds in certainty and faith, whereby all means to their work are provided through vows of devotion and surrender.*

Nirvana ceases as a goal because their life, without the agitation of discrimination, judgment, and opinion, is the experience of Nirvana itself.

Here loss and gain are seen equally as nothing to grasp and no one grasping.

The world is observed as mind itself, and belief is suspended.

***Lanka,* Chapter 4, section LXXX**

In this stanza, selfless ones are enlightened Bodhisattvas, and their relationship with the world demonstrates life in the synchronicity described by Jung, but at another level. As the caveat or expression of not-separate-reality, it isn't only what defines mystics and saints. Service of one another is the logical path for us all, and as family members, workers and leaders, each role in life becomes our service.

This service is the expression of gratitude, which requires a discipline of generosity, awareness, and practice. Life in this realm of solitude becomes a game. One of seeking out those who may be served by a smile, a listening ear or a compassionate heart. Generosity starts and reaches completion in generosity of spirit, but funding the buskers of the Glastonbury High Street also works for me. Giving in every form is the pathway of effortless belonging whether it is charitable work or picking up trash. The rewards are obvious within one's peace of mind.

Though this stage of being, may sound like an unreachable state of tranquillity and non-attachment, a simple attitude of acceptance can change a life in transit. Beyond everyday stress, the non-doer is just showing up and without excessive control, a new disposition develops. Letting go of outcomes and self-image as something to defend, is the state of grace where the *Lanka* says samsara is nirvana and nirvana is samsara, suffering is bliss, and bliss is suffering. Acceptance and imagelessness is a matter of perspective, attitude, and learning to play by new rules of engagement with the connecting intelligence or whatever you may choose to call it.

The power of letting go on a continual basis can't be overstated. It is faith in our connectedness and surrender to the flow of life. My words may seem to imply a greater power or divinity of the living intelligence, but in a not-separate awareness, greater anything is relative and dualistic.

Any words that separate say something is less than and something is not sacred or divine. My acceptance is for a power and intelligence, which we experience as it's vehicles if we can just tune to a higher awareness.

Said another way, letting go of outcomes allows for the wave action of mutuality or entanglement. In declining preferences, we create a magical ease in life as being disappointed loses grip. Being irritated almost disappears and being offended becomes a point of shame. Trusting the benevolence of existence is the magic ingredient and may require developing a new relationship or understanding the natural attractions inherent in our living intelligence. This relationship is where good works or truth, honesty, and generosity come into power.

Manifestation

Such statements as "all means to their work are provided, through vows of devotion and surrender," may also seem far-fetched, beyond our rationality, for sure. Still, it is directly related to surrendering ownership or non-grasping. The catalyst for what is basically the power of manifestation, is commitment and practical understanding. We may manifest many things, but it is no longer the ego doing it.

In relaxing one's hold on life, the primary mechanism is mindful awareness, or being fully present in every moment. It was well said in the book, *Be Here Now* as the gift of my late friend Ram Dass. By observing gratitude and acceptance without controlling, our love and desires reinforce the certainty of life's interconnected interdependence, to become more stable over time. My late teacher, Swami Satchidananda, also had a very Zen way of placing "letting go" in an everyday context when he said, "Make no appointment, have no disappointment!"

Control is Attachment

This is what we confuse as non-attachment. You've heard that what we own isn't the problem, unless we identify and limit ourselves with that ownership. But struggling to control and have our own way is the real attachment, as it disturbs the quiet pond of effortlessness and muddles what just is. Rather than non-attachment, it should be called non-interference.

Non-interference lets the network of entanglement express its living intelligence. Not disturbed by trying to control, life's natural balance and harmony can do their thing. These are two quantum discoveries bouncing off each other, where observation disturbs entanglement. When you try to control the outcomes, subconscious intelligence is disrupted from its subtle wave of communications, as mutuality is disjointed by the loud voices of preference, opinion and judgment.

A family member needed support during substance abuse recovery. In trying to understand, I found an exceptional view into the raw, immediate form of spirituality presented in Alcoholics Anonymous. So, I stayed awhile. One of the best examples of real magic came to me after reading and applying *The Sermon on the Mount* by Emmet Fox.[38] It's a very Christian book by a somewhat outlaw minister, but it holds the most beautiful understanding of the Beatitudes and offers a magical mindfulness practice like Japa Yoga, but in Christian terms.

In this practice, we simply put the mind to work, saying a prayer or mantra. Emmet might recommend "God is love" as the focus during a family difficulty or "God is truth" during a contract negotiation. My favorite was "God is life," which I would use when fishing alone off the coast of Galveston. I caught some beauties! However, the critical point of the practice is to let go of an agenda, focusing on the greatest and highest good. Not to argue what that meant for the fish. The *Lanka* has a whole chapter on not eating meat, so I'm defending nothing. I choose not to explore many parts of the *Lanka* beyond my thesis of a non-separate reality.

In my work experience using Emmett's approach, I led a group of men and women to receive the highest corporate recognition for continuous improvement. All the while, I was secretly getting me out of the way, to access the living intelligence among the group.

Non-interference and non-discrimination are expressions of mindfulness, suchness, and acceptance. In a selfless committed attitude shift, choice evolves as an awareness of intention, without the need to micromanage details. This perspective of intuitive receptivity is a unique way to encounter life and observe synchrony.

---

[38] Fox, E. (1994). *The Sermon on the Mount.* HarperCollins Publishers.

The big question is how letting go of outcomes can possibly work. It was the center of my late teacher's message, which stuck to me in my twenties. Swami Satchidananda taught that nature as a living intelligence has attraction to certain actions, thoughts and intentions. This attraction is the magic element which facilitates entering synchronicity. It can be seen in our own experience, as we are attracted to loving people and especially inspired by those living in higher values. With nature, it is the same.

The living intelligence is attracted to, and supports the non-violent peace maker, the completely honest and unreservedly generous people, in ways which transcend logic. Said another way, a pure heart in peacefulness, total commitment to truth and the complete absence of greed, has a magical effect in everyday life. In the presence of such a person, angry people will forget their anger and wherever they go, such enlightened one's bring peace and happiness.

But it's much more than a wonderful way to recognize enlightenment. What is said, by a completely truthful person, will become reality and the world's wealth will be laid at the feet of the person, who has banished greed in all its forms.

Manifestation is the function of resonance or entangled energy attracted to life sustaining frequencies. And the more pure the source frequency or person's nature, the more powerful the wave function which creates as it inter-acts. So as we are truthful, honest, and generous, we create the attractive resonance and energy gathers in our field. Reacting in the way Buddha, Patanjali and Swamiji describe things happen not by our doing, but by our being. We also see this manifestation around us in small and great ways, if we only look.

My friend and creative writing teacher before he got famous, Joe Vitale was part of the video presentation *The Law of Attraction, The Secret*, which presented this power of manifestation as a function of positive thought, within their frame of reference. And as one thing is connected to everything, it holds great truth. But many examples beyond manifestation, can be seen in the global influences of masters like Gautama Buddha, St. Francis of Assisi and Jesus of Nazareth, among countless others. And as religion has tried to communicate, we needn't be perfect to acquire benefit. But the more pure the intention and behavior the stronger the energy.

Of course, Swamiji gained his wisdom from ancient teachings and in this case the source was Patanjali's Yoga Sutras. He taught the Yamas and the Niyamas, which start in these aspects of attractive energy and go onto right choices and behaviors. But mostly, Swamiji lived in the magic and peace, which was palpable in his presence. As I lived with his Sanga for a few years, I naturally experienced myself as a better person.

Furthermore, Swamiji would say that fearlessness comes from non-violence in one's deepest self. Life becomes completely open in truthfulness, wherein actions and their results become subservient to truth.

The attractive force, in this view, is that if no lie comes through you, honesty as a field of resonant energy wants to be with you. It interacts as a wave of mutual entanglement within and around you. So what you say, think, or intend will come true through the field interaction of resonant propagation.

In another sense, Swamiji presented the perspective that when you stop running after things, they will run after you. Things come automatically.

No white lies,

cause no-one else to lie,

or say nothing.

Follow truth and truth will follow you.

Complete honesty attained,

all wealth comes.

But truth includes non-greed and generosity.

Its resonance so pure,

Accept anything without gratitude,

it is stealing.

Small theft, great theft, no difference.

Stealing ideas or credit

equals stealing diamonds.

In this discipline,

we do not run after the person, place or thing,

before long it runs after us.
If nature knows we aren't greedy
we gain her confidence.
If we accept and give with equal gratitude to loss or gain,
we are like the river rather than a dammed up pond
which becomes stagnant.
Even to steal usage is a trap.
If we have fifty garments half of which we don't use,
they should be freed to someone without.
Hideously not demonstrated
culturally, politically, financially
and in business practices.
Sadly, demonstrated in my own life,
My abundance is sometimes embarrassing.
Do my best.
Smile at everyone.
Eventually they smile back.
Serenity is contagious.
Be an activist.
Plague everyone with joy.
A carefree life is possible
In a well-controlled mind.
Free of our own control,
anxiety, desires or possessions
lose their power.

Truth, OWM

I am reminded of a lovely thought attributed to many sources including Gandhi and Mother Teresa.

Live simply so others can simply live.

Next we will circumnavigate the Seven stages of Awareness or Seven Kinds of Self-nature. These are not really separate places, though we are usually stuck here or there. These kinds of self-nature are starting points, centers of gravity where we rest.

Individual connection with innate knowledge becomes most possible in a mind not bound up in cascading thought. For this reason solitude, time to reflect and relax are the great gifts we give ourselves, to best be ourselves authentically.

CHAPTER TWENTY-THREE

SYNCHRONY: A DIFFERENT VIEW OF CONSCIOUSNESS

The *Lanka* begins with the premise that our dysfunction and disease are entirely due to a delusion of being separate from one another and creation itself. Then it goes on to explain how this happened via the ego-creation story or the Five Aspects of Sentient Beings. Awakening, it explains, is an awareness which identifies beyond sense consciousness, beyond identification with thought outcomes. Like the first thought, our self-nature or subconscious choice begins to identify with our higher self and the true nature of joy. But this isn't so easy, as the full awakening must occur within our deepest selves or the subconscious. But that's the opportunity.

With this idea as a starting point, it should be no surprise that the stages of awareness are levels of escaping this delusion, providing a progressive path to ever greater oneness and the experience of synchrony. Synchrony is an awareness of mutuality or the shared experience of energetic entanglement between people, animals, plants and creation itself. Referred to as perceiving the suchness or essence of all things, it is recognizing the mutuality of shared existence. So what hurts you, hurts me and what heals you, heals me.

The stages begin with narcissistic sense-consciousness and find completion in perfected oneness or Buddha-nature. These centers of conscious awareness or, as the *Lanka* calls them, the Seven Kinds of Self-nature, tie together the journey of consciousness into effortless belonging.

> *There are seven centers of conscious awareness or Seven Kinds of Self-nature:*
>
> *Collection as narcissism, relationship, not belonging, formless consciousness, non-dual rationality, certitude, and perfect awareness.*
>
> *Lanka,* **Chapter 2, section V**

Unlike most of my transcriptions of the *Lanka*, these seven centers of conscious awareness have been developed by expanding the single word Sanskrit descriptors: *Samudaya, Bhava, Lakshana, Mahabhuta, Hetu, Pratyaya,* and *Nishpatti*. This presentation is a simple map created from an enigma indicated by D.T. Suzuki. I only presume to define them as the culmination of my theory that synchrony or effortless belonging is the outcome of awakening to our Buddha-nature. For me, they are useful in opening questions about what may yet be done while examining our road to completion. It was an application of poetic license, sifting through hundreds of definitions and synonyms to fix the vision that evolved in my study. With no presumption of academic knowledge, these are the whispers of intuitive inspiration and contemplation.

Samudaya; Collection, Possession, and Self-interest

Collection, possession, and self-interest (*Samudaya*) are raw ego, self-centered, narcissistic, oblivious to others, and the least aware aspect of our lives. But it is also the survival instinct, source of bravery and determination. This is a pure survival skill and probably the strongest current in our species' memory, because it goes directly back to animal self-protection. As humans we usually grow beyond this stage in adolescents. However, its important to understand that self-interest is the basis for sense-consciousness universally.

In function, it is a collection of competing desires: gathering beliefs, experiences, things, and masks to protect ourselves in a materialistic world. Hiding shadows of fear, self-doubt, loneliness, and regret, the first stage of perception is limited by blaming others for our misfortunes and subconsciously seeing oneself as a victim or predator. As this aspect dominates our lives, we are oblivious to all other possibilities, living in physical reality as all there is.

Suffering is another name for Samudaya. Life is beyond control, tossed about by circumstance, emotion, and the consequences of self-interest and compulsion. At one extreme, collection is basic egocentric, self-serving nature. On the other, it is the icon of grandiose individuality, the psychopath lacking conscience and compassion, which we see applauded by ignorance.

Bhava; Relationship, devotion, tribal consciousness

Relationship (*Bhava*) as self-nature is the second least aware stage of our awareness, which lives in relationship to others, collecting feelings, emotions, security, and social acceptance while caught in physical existence. Still, this stage also begins our blooming into devotion, loyalty, self-sacrifice, and empathy as we start to see beyond ourselves. The challenge is to see beyond "us and them" then control the habits of justification, insecurity, negativity, and envy.

Bhava also means our wheel of birth and death or being caught within cycles of complacent compulsion, lacking the will to change or accept accountability for suffering. It is this awareness within us that fears and fights against change in all its expressions and locks us into comfortable habits of mindless entertainment. This is also common for humanity, sleepwalking through life due to family ties or tribal self-interest.

At one extreme, Bhava is tribal instinct justifying all sorts of behavior, war, atrocities, and most of the external suffering of humanity. But on the other, it is familial devotion, the foundation of cultural stability.

Lakshana; Not-belonging, revolution, rebellion

Not-belonging *(Lakshana)* is individuality awakening or our inner revolution, sometimes confused with the narcissist because standing apart is not unusual. But the motivation is more like teenage angst. It is recognized by rebellion, dissatisfaction, being different, and not fitting into domestic conformity.

This characteristic of inner revolution is the beginning of awareness beyond beliefs and labels and allows us to see other possibilities. No longer able to fully fit in or belong, we suffer significantly under the cultural limits of stories, beliefs, opinions, and preferences. But now, as our path begins to open, self-determined willpower and growing open-mindedness are possible.

The great risk is adopting one set of imagined beliefs for another. At one extreme, this individuality becomes rigid and defensive, having created an alternative non-conformist disposition. At the other extreme, inner revolution embraces not-knowing to become available for higher realities. Exploring the unknown is the key to the lock.

Mahabhuta; Formless Consciousness, spirituality

Formless consciousness (*Mahabhuta*) is our emotional awareness of formlessness and the subconscious network of life. It is the beginning of awakening. Recognizing consciousness, spirituality, and ego, we begin to develop our intuition and synchronistic understanding. But this can emerge in many ways: superstition, religion, spirituality, or the still quiet voice within. Riding the waves between imagination and experiences of primal awareness, we may still suffer from the delusion of identity, the mistaken belief we are no more than these thoughts, emotions, and feelings.

However, we may also see our earlier stages, sometimes imagining enlightenment or stages beyond. Here we can actively find a path as a blossoming of generosity and gratitude. The challenge is to see beyond false-imagination, to observe life just as it is, beyond preference and dualism. One extreme is closed-in, fear-driven, dogmatic beliefs, but the other may be completely genuine spirituality and an intuitive connection bordering on the magical. Letting go of desired outcomes and accepting fortune and misfortune with equal gratitude is a magic elixir for formless awareness.

Hetu; Non-dual Rationality

Extreme objective awareness of nature as the reflection of non-dual formlessness, *(Hetu)* non-dual rationality throws out imagination and most of what may be understood as spiritual. In this dark night of the soul, meaning and purpose beyond our subjective delusion grasps the full ferocity of nature and existence. Still suffering, we may cling to physicality and our identification with thought. The challenge is to refocus naked awareness on empathy, compassion, humility, and gratitude. It arises in respecting the differences and perfection of everyone's path. To avoid isolation, serving others without the need to change them becomes paramount and declining judgment extremely valuable. This is finding balance between being and doing.

But we can see our other stages. Emotional suffering, much curbed, recognizes grace as moments of primitive purity in pain and pleasure. The extremes of non-dual rationality can be seen in two yogic perspectives I've only heard described. One viewpoint denies reality and the value of physical existence altogether, while the other sees everything as Divine, orchestrating the dance of mutual entanglement for our growth and conscious evolution. A middle way may be Zen's loving path of objective not-knowing.[39] However, letting go of identification as the doer can lead to a powerful breakthrough.

Pratyana; Certitude, grounded experience of Nirvana

Certitude is the awareness through direct experience, reclaiming objectivity, innate wisdom, impermanence, and Mind-only in the simplicity of suchness or not-knowing. It *(Pratyana)* is owning the primitive, profane, and Divine as ourselves. Here we may live in the stream of synchrony, a conditionally fluid reality, tranquil in connection but still working on disentanglement from our collections, shadows, and domestications. As the integration of all preceding self-natures, certitude is the final thrashing floor of life. Living between the struggles of objective awareness and loving-kindness, effortless belonging is possible, but expectations cease in the old way, replaced by the mindfulness of mutuality. The golden grain of awareness, separated from self-definition, releases personality, both mine and others.

But as life may be abundantly pleasant, the challenge may become letting go of the desire to create a little distance from life's joyous cacophony, to see things just as they are. As mind chatter becomes less apparent, the choice of further penetration, letting go, and imagelessness itself has no great appeal. It's fun to be in this world and enjoy its pleasures, being

---

[39] Bernie Glassman is very well known for this mindfulness

and doing with everything just as it is. Without the drama of labels and boundaries, we may aid the great project that is relieving suffering. Also, since death is synonymous with imageless freedom, what's the hurry? While the causal world unfolds as one living field, why not come back and help? This may be the final trap, but it's definitely why I've chosen to lay this all out to the best of my ability.

Nishpatti—Perfect Completion, enlightenment, Buddha nature

Perfect completion is ecstatic imageless freedom, having consumed our collections in the fire of awareness and merged the subconscious with awakened consciousness *(Nishpatti)*. We may regard the inner and outer as Mind-only, beyond predictability and definition. Here we live beyond collections, belonging, not-belonging, insecurity, security, imagination, judgment, and accomplishment. Imagelessness has replaced personality and rationales. We may indeed become the reflection in the pond. These are the perfect mirrors among us, rare and conspicuously hidden. No further description applies as it is clearly beyond my purview.

As the *Lanka* upholds the completion of consciousness as being the avenue by which we escape the wheel of reincarnation. I'm not sure that description is so useful in the 21st century. Given the current trajectory of species extinction, it seems a shame to give up so close to an evolutionary tipping point. I think we need more formless consciousness, non-dual rationality, certitude, effortless belonging, and willing Bodhisattvas to crank up the fire for everyone's relief from suffering. For me, the goal is synchrony.

Synchrony is the awareness of a living, entangled creation, where energy itself vibrates with consciousness and intelligence. Enlightenment is a quiet mind, and freedom is found by simply letting go of individuation as our identity and preference as its tool.

CHAPTER TWENTY-FOUR
THAT'S ALL, FOLKS

The *Lanka's* gift to me is understanding the struggle of our clueless cultures and how there is no-one to blame. I will spend my remaining years contemplating this gift as I've spent my life seeking it. But, realizing the mutuality of entanglement, I can relax. The mind may never fully grasp right understanding. But to see it, to experience it even for a moment, breaks all bounds of judgment and doubt.

As a tear drop is indistinguishable from the ocean, effortless belonging is the conscious aspect of the not-separate living intelligence. Consciousness is the expansion of awareness into ever greater levels of synchrony, to eventually become the living intelligence which is our oneness and allness.

I set out to grasp what the delusion of being separate could mean. Like most penetrating concepts, it seemed to be a metaphor. But as I gathered together my peculiar gifts of life experience, I saw a wave-fabric reality of synchronicity, normally unseen below the events of my life. But the *Lanka* offered me the keys to grasp an undiscovered land. It is the subconscious penetration into the primordial source of self.

The famous experiment in Berne tested sexual attraction through young women choosing the body odor of young men. But it revealed so much more about our human potential. It demonstrated that the mind barely fathoms the depths of our own natural connection to the subconscious and its inherent awareness. Much of what we've mislabelled intuition is non-linear intelligence, the power of our subconscious mind. This awareness dwarfs what we think we know because it needn't rationalize a not separate perspective. It is the not separate aspect of mind, where the non-dual is perceived as natures synchrony, beyond judgment, opinion and preference.

Science may have labeled the girl's instinct for healthy breeding, as a container of inherited traits, without looking further. But that pigeon hole fails to recognize the advanced intelligence of each young woman's subconscious resources. Natural selection, which we mostly grasp as survival of the fittest, is actually a function of entangled mutuality. The girls didn't have to know, guess or apply a woo-woo intuition because the subconscious is completely wired into the non-dual and simultaneously informing the conscious mind. The subconscious is the field aspect of living entanglement. What we don't grasp is that the entanglement or the mutual life force is not only our oneness. It is our true self.

You may not comprehend a not-separate reality, but your subconscious mind functions as an aspect of the not-separate subconscious. It is in this way, you have access into the repository of all knowledge, if only you can get out of your own way.

I'm grateful and proud of you, having made it to this point of my writing. It could not have been easy because a dyslexic engineer is no friend of prose and my wandering logic doesn't try to prove anything. My purpose is only to leave you with more questions. Like an open door, maybe it will entice a little curiosity.

I think it was Maezumi Roshi, who once blew away a group of fledgling yogis at Satchidananda Ashram[40] when he shared an esoteric version of the Bodhisattva vow:

> *I vow to awaken for the sake of all sentient beings, knowing there is no enlightenment and no-one other than myself, to have compassion for.*

Unknown

From a novice yogi's point of view, this vow challenges dualistic understanding in several ways. It removed the self centered goal and challenged the question of why I was living as a monk. It left me no room to be a martyr or saint. Enlightenment was disavowed. Simply not being asleep, not being caught in my own made-up story of who I think I am, was everything my path had to offer. Swamiji just laughed.

For all I knew, the whole world could be enlightened, just watching me stumble through life like a sleepy child. So, of course, there was no one other than self, to have compassion for. In my cluelessness, I was left only questions.

Anyway, we've denied the existence of ancient science long enough.

---

[40] Pomfret Connecticut, Satchidananda Ashram, 1974

We've labeled it metaphysical and simply ignored it, but that goes back to the frailty of living only by what we think we know.

The *Lanka* isn't talking about supernatural speculations. It is, first and foremost, talking about practical psychology from a thousand years of penetration by some of the best minds ever to grace this planet. Though, my speculations, on physics and biology supporting the concept of not-separate reality, are just one viewpoint, it rings true to what everyone experiences when they sleep, dream or meditate. The challenge is to go beyond what we've been sold as miracle, mystery and authority.

Vital to my perspective as a householder, a father and a husband is understanding the possibility of living in a fully awake manner, without becoming a monk or hermit. It is a gift of my scientific materialist upbringing, which demands answers even though I'll be branded a lunatic, heretic and god knows what. All I can do in bidding you fare-well is to express how it seems to work best for me.

Devotion for me is not a religious separateness. It is engaged joyfulness and the endless challenge of attitude adjustment and perspective maintenance. It's objective is a disciplined discernment or the objective control of my subjective thought. But this is not ordinary mental control. My objective mind cannot rigorously keep from lapsing into the notion that I am the outcomes of thought. It's the most natural thing and occurs in every instance when I'm not focused on mindfulness. It can't be controlled with effort. It must be surrendered to good natured humor and replaced with loving awareness.

In this way, letting go or detachment is rejoicing in the synchrony of interdependent co-arising. Trusting the living intelligence is the magic elixir. It is letting go and letting God, if those are your comfortable labels. But not needing to control and realizing I'm not this mind, is seeing reality for what it is. There is no need to renounce life's joys and sorrows. Detachment is fully embracing the relationship with my deepest self and listening to its expressions of the living intelligence.

Effortless belonging, as I've tried to connect with consciousness, is available when two people share this understanding and path. My wife's greatest gift is this one thing, her ability to join the path every morning, noon and evening by having the love of life in her heart. Waking up happy is conscious discipline.

Ultimately the choice is up to you. If it doesn't happen naturally through trauma, psychotropic drugs or near-death experience, you can do as I've done and recognize that life becomes the teacher, and everything is the teaching. If you're very lucky or down right ruthless as I have been in searching out my earth angel, you might learn that effortless belonging is a sustainable life style. It is also the greatest gift you have to give.

More than this, I don't have to give. I've tried to share a vocabulary, which is approachable but maybe different. Its discernment was necessary for me to grasp what it means to penetrate the primordial subconscious mind. But actual penetration can best be described in nature walks, gardening, dreams, or semi-conscious inspirations which spontaneously occur on the edge of routine daily practice, a ceremonial necessity for me.

Grasping vast concepts like Mind-only, suchness, imagelessness, and letting go the outcomes of thought, may seem impossible, as they run counter to our logical self-creation. More familiar references like emptiness, impermanence, and the non-dual also run counter to rational materialism but we've heard them before. But this is how I could understand the role of the subconscious mind and its connection with everything and everyone, energetically.

My point in all this, is to serve you with the only thing I have, my experience. And so I'll share what personal secrets I can. I've found my best friends and teachers in transcendental literary works. By that I mean, works transcending the logical mind. Usually, it is in what I don't understand; books like the *Hsin Hsin Ming, The I Ching,* or maybe *Zen Flesh, Zen Bones.* My inspiration has come from books like *Zen Mind, Beginner's Mind* because they punch holes in my logic while having no vested interest, nothing to sell, and no one to join or follow. I've barely been involved with Zen Schools because maintaining the sanga, creates Dostoyevsky's dilemma. My excuse was to keep the bowl empty for penetration of the *Lanka,* though these traditions must be given credit for sustaining Zen's wisdom.

It is also not my intention to introduce miracles, then obscure them in mystery, to create my authority. It's a fundamental trap of communicating, we can all fall into. It is the most natural thing but it's very important to me, not to become cynical yet maintain my discerning awareness. But then, my path has been about pioneering an ancient trail, which was all but lost many times. So a myopic concentration was needed to exclude many outside influences.

You have to find what works for you, then stick with it for a while. Swamiji suggested to study a body of work, like Zen, for twenty years, then see where you are before branching out to something new. In writing this book, I've shared a few books, teachers, and even media that has inspired me. You might call it my collection and probably have started such a list yourself, maybe without knowing it. As life goes on and years pass, it's important to remember and often retrace the steps that have added the greatest value to your awakening.

For an eternal optimist or old curmudgeon like me, an exciting aspect in my view of physics is our entangled energy tipping point. Because it doesn't have electromagnetic limitations, the entangled energy shared through species evolution experiences mutuality. It is a wave propagation at the subatomic level and if my speculations hold water, when species awareness reaches a certain frequency, spin and momentum, an entangled resonance will shift the collective awareness simultaneously across the species. This has happened many times in human history as others have explored.

Life's synchrony, verified quickly in the starling flocks gracefully undulating across the moors, is all around us in millions of ways. It is there for our delight, if only we choose. But this pattern is the growing awareness of interdependent co-arising, oneness, and mutuality. It is beyond imagination as an intelligence, observed in everyone's childlike sense memory. It is the experience and influence of beneficial circumstances that brings each of us along our path, culminating in this inevitable moment.

No Story

The objective fact is that it takes most of our energy, mental and otherwise, to maintain the story of our illusion, our image to the world, not to mention our self-image. After being introduced to a different vocabulary and hopefully a few surprises, you may be wondering where to start.

A process of simplification takes the next step, when it points to a no-story-freedom and its empowerment, minimizing waste, chaos, and illness.

Simplification occurs in letting go the bony grip of labels, story, and all the stuff of collection. Meditation practice is the pivotal key, but rather than rush out and find the first teacher, you might want to introduce you first, to yourself. If your need is critical and urgent, I recommend a pause. I use a trick, when the noise if overwhelming. I jump start my connection and immersion by retreating into nature.

Resetting the mind can be helped with the natural processes of retreat. In the song, *A Horse with No Name*, written by Dewey Bunnell, recorded by the band America in 1971. They sang about remembering one's name in the solitude of the desert, which is essentially the concept. Swamiji used to have ten day silent retreats. The retreats were structured for silence and no visual contact with others. Aloneness can be created for this purpose of touching solitude, but it takes dedication by all concerned. Yogaville, Satchidananda Ashram, Virginia was still having such retreats on my last visit, about ten years ago.

But when nothing else seems to be working, getting away from people, technology and artificial stimulation is the quickest way to reset the system, in my experience. Remote trekking for a period of nine days has often allowed me to let go of my story, as it rapidly loses relevance to my immediate circumstances. With no more than survival food, water and camping equipment, contact with others can be avoided in most parts of the world. And with nothing but maybe a good book, meditation and exercise the mind quiets in a way not available in the busy-ness of life.

When there's no need to defend, define or represent in any way "who we think we are," relaxation occurs. The story falls away like a wave, unreinforced and not recreated, it just loses its hold. The energy becoming available may feel like personal freedom, but it's only a holiday. If done right the clarity can be a useful starting point. It takes the nine days of solitude, as referenced in the song for the grounding of my mind. I've tried to do this annually, up until my daily life stabilized. Also, during this retreat, asking four questions from an old friend helps.

What do I want to be?
What do I want to do?
What do I want to have?
What am I willing to give?

It's up to you. When the noise ceases, in submission to immediate experience, a naturally occurring suchness arises, and that's a connection with our own primitive purity. That connection is naturally occurring, and the access is simplicity and solitude.

> *Some understand belief and identification with the world as the cause of suffering while not understanding that all belief, identification, and experience are only creations of the mind itself.*
>
> *Alarmed by material consequences and turmoil, some may seek blissful detachment as nirvana.*
>
> *But all views of nirvana are also flawed, because views depend on subject, object, duality, cause and effect.*
>
> *Without delusion within nirvana there is nothing rising, nothing falling and no room for belief.*
>
> *So, in identification with habitual thinking, no matter what the goal, one may only wander around confused that nirvana is not found anywhere.*
>
> **Lanka, *Chapter 2, section LXXIV***

Sudden awakening is not always sudden and not always at the feet of a master. As masters are rare and often not in South Texas or the West Country of England, I recommend getting on with it yourself. There are plenty of paths and teachings, as I've tried to point out in the dozen or so that have given me so much. Though one size might fit all in some cases, I've never found the size that fits my peculiarities and disposition. So, we've created a sanctuary on a hill and make a practice sharing our joy of life every day.

> *I am only this awareness,*
>
> *yet a million things may disrupt it.*
>
> *I am not this body,*
>
> *until a shooting pain brings me to my knees.*
>
> *I am not this mind,*

until a misused word raises the fangs of argument.
I am not these thoughts,
until a button is pushed on who I think I am.
I am not the subconscious,
until threatened and the tiger takes control.
Truth disturbs my invested collection.

I am only this awareness,
when mind is undisturbed,
when body is free of needs,
thoughts are meditative,
and the subconscious is heard.

I am only this awareness,
between thought, needs and compulsion.
But the investment lies in wait.
This is my practice.
These are life's gifts.

The lesson of truth is only this awareness,
Seeing not-two, not-knowing, not needing to know, and observe.
The lesson of need is only this awareness,
face the need, care for it, end it and observe.

The *lesson of compulsion is only this awareness,*
embrace it, forestall it, cease the reaction and observe.
The lesson is only this awareness,
grateful for truth, need and compulsion,
observe, recognize, adapt and learn.

Suchness is only this awareness,
the natural state of who I am.
Truth changes the outcomes of thought.
Thought patterns change subconscious collection.

I am loving kindness beyond boundaries,
no self and no other-than-self is only this awareness
Mind-only, responsibly creating, healing and changing.
Truth shifts my nature of being.

Healing is only this awareness,
no prejudice, no discrimination,
letting go of outcomes, seeking the highest good,
devotion to truth and compassion above self-interest.

Freedom is only this awareness,
acceptance without preference,
no place held for insult, resentment or fear.
Truth is freedom, construction the cage.

Awakening is only this awareness,
beyond body, mind, thought and compulsion.
Listening, you are living intelligence.
Creation is truth beyond right and wrong,
no-thought is this awareness.

My mantra, repeated over and over
I am only this awareness
Seeing I am not the outcomes of thought.
Listening is to set aside thought and its outcomes.

Saying, contemplating, perceiving
I am only this awareness.
Free from compulsion
Free from beliefs
Free from preference
Free from judgment
Present right here, right now,
I am only this awareness.
Truth is not creation nor conception,
it is only this awareness.

Only This Awareness, OWM

Establishing a new sense reality is the product of Mind-only. Taking total responsibility for everything we see and experience as a product of our collection, we can see our power to recreate life with ourselves. It is the first practical step to non-conceptual awareness. Finding the solitude within oneself is to hold the world at arm's length and observe life, without being sucked in again, not to be caught by who we think we are.

The big step is effortless belonging, through relinquishing self-will to subconscious inspiration, learning to live in a natural flow of intuition. Where logic doesn't work you can understand the freedoms. Good fortune and discipline leads to the primordial subconscious but it will be surprise that awakens you.

Lastly, I offer you a window into what reading the *Lanka* might be like, if written in understandable terms. Following is the transcription of Chapter One, a parable about Ravana's development through six stages of awareness. All the characters in various guises demonstrate aspects of ourselves and our circumstances.

It has been a long ride and this is all I meant to say. I hope you've enjoyed the ups and downs along the way, with a few surprises. Pleasant journey.

Gone,
Gone,
Gone beyond,
Gone beyond beyond,
All hail the awakened.

Buddhist mantra, Unknown

PART III
LANKAVATARA SUTRA, CHAPTER ONE,
Transcribed Sequentially

CHAPTER TWENTY-FIVE

THE AWAKENING OF RAVANA

This story came out of India about eighteen hundred years ago, when Yoga and the Hindu Cosmology were still intrinsically part of Buddhism, hence the school's name of Yogachara. The story's location in Sri Lanka allows us to imagine beautiful flowing clothes and tropical surroundings. The characters and references are most similar to the Hindu classic, the *Ramayana*, still performed and revered across the Hindu world. As a little-known sequel to the Ramayana, it presents Buddhism and especially the *Lanka*'s science before it was transplanted outside of India.

I recommend reading the whole story without referencing the footnotes. By skipping the explanations, you will gain an intuitive imprint of the text itself. Then return to my notes if the impression is unclear.

The first chapter of the *Lankavatara Sutra* emerged about a thousand years before Zen's development in Japan. There are only three main characters, plus the narrator. Then, of course, there's me, the storyteller. Everything I say will be in standard text. Everything transliterated from D.T. Suzuki's translation will appear like all the previous transliterations in earlier chapters. My comments (marked with an asterisk) mainly explain embedded meanings. This is a sequential transcription of the *Lanka*'s first chapter, from beginning to end, so there will be no notes giving the chapter or section.

The three main characters represent stages of awareness. The Separated Self is that aspect of us that arises from false discrimination, clinging to the belief in physical reality alone, and identifying oneself as body, mind, or thought. The Higher Self is that aspect of us that is aware of relativity, Mind-only, and our dualistic trap. This awareness is called Right-knowledge. Finally, the Awakened Self has perfected awareness and transcendental knowledge, which is our Buddha-nature.

First, the show's star is the Separated Self; his name is Ravana, King of Lanka and King of Man-eating Demons (all destructive human forces). He is also an overlord of the nature spirits and has ten heads, which traditionally means: over-educated in all fields of knowledge, including sciences, arts, literature, and religion. Ten heads also suggest he has ten faces and ten personas. I've tried to point out what attitude or persona is talking to you in the story, or it can get somewhat confusing.

The second character, Buddha's closest companion is the Higher Self, Mahamati, whose name means the highest wisdom and represents everyone's moment-to-moment challenge of awareness. Though he has a minor part in this story, his dialog with the Buddha comprises everything after the first chapter within the remaining nine chapters of the *Lanka*. Ravana disappears altogether after the first chapter. Though this little story is less esoteric and meant for a wider audience, it is still a bit like shock therapy.

The final character is the hero of the story, the Awakened Self. The Buddha, who has more names and titles than can be counted is represented mostly with the title.

> *Narrator:*
>
> *Om! greetings to the three treasures of transcendent knowledge, the community of truth, and the Awakened Ones. Greetings to those awakened beyond intellect and those on the path of selfless enlightenment.*
>
> *This story is the beginning of the Lankavatara Sutra painstakingly recorded from the master of transcendental wisdom; relating the oneness of all things, beyond ego, personality, and separateness.*
>
> *We have heard that the Awakened Self, Buddha, once dwelt in the ancient principality of Lanka; on the peak of highest human understanding, decorated with the jeweled bouquets of man's most significant achievements; high above the ocean of Alaya, the repository of all knowledge, memory, and experience.*
>
> *With him were innumerable beggar monks, masters, and a host of selfless Bodhisattvas, having come from all the awakening realms to serve the blessed Awakened One.*
>
> *His company were masters in their own right, led by the higher self, Mahamati. Authorities in all forms of mind-body discipline, every kind of meditation, meditative consciousness, and spiritual bliss, they held*

the ten paranormal powers and six clairvoyant discernments. As the consecrated disciples of awakened beings, they understood the perceived world as psychologically, physically, and energetically the mind's creation.

As disciples and teachers, they preserved and taught the practices, the principles of self-control in harmony with humanity's diverse psychological mindsets and expressions.

The Buddha's companions were grounded in the four noble truths and non-discrimination, accepting but discerning without judgment or false knowledge. Through Right-knowledge and perfected comprehension, they had mastered their relationship with the eight portals of consciousness.[41] *These masters embraced no-self and no-other-than-self.*[42]

This story begins with the Awakened Self deep in subconscious meditation, in the depths of Alaya. There he was met by the Leviathan King, Guardian of the Dharma, representing himself as the most terrifying sea serpent. With the faces of human perversion, psychopaths, and all the human atrocities we abhor, the leviathan was confronted by the Buddha's equanimity, tranquility, and non-conceptual awareness.

There was no fear and no revulsion, to which the sea monster was most unaccustomed. Because there was no judgment, the Buddha did not see who the serpent king thought he was, nor his role as ferocious gatekeeper. So, the illusion of appearances dissolved.

---

[41] The eight portals of consciousness include the five senses: sight, hearing, taste, touch, smell, and three aspects of mind: subjective, objective, and subconscious.
—Subjective mind (*Manovijnana*): includes thought, will, ego, attachment, and especially identification with belief, thought, opinion, and judgment.
—Objective mind (*Vijnana*): provides logic and discernment.
—Subconscious (*Alaya-vijnana*): gives access to the personal repository of knowledge, memory, experience, emotions, instinct, and shadows (karma).
Alaya is indiscriminate and not conscious. As such, our subconscious is our constant living connection to innate knowledge but is individually filtered and distorted.
[42] The *Lanka*'s application of psychology and philosophy equates to behavioral un-conditioning, with constructs to create a healthy perception of reality. The three aspects of the mind point to the possibilities of integrating our shadow, our logical brilliance, and our passion for life by consciously connecting them.

After seven days of revealing the great way in the subconscious depths of the psyche, the Buddha emerged and was welcomed by all the liberated daughters of the Serpent King,[43] the Lord of Gods and the Creator of the Universe.

Surveying the world and the ocean of Alaya, the Awakened One smiled and said, "The awakened ones, who have gone before, are worthy of our praise. Because they taught, for all to understand, that the subconscious is our access to the ocean of all knowledge. This doorway opens to imagelessness, transmission, and self-realization, secure in the heart of Noble Wisdom. It is beyond any rational understanding, even those of higher consciousness, who still identify with personality or self. Now, I will also share this great way to awaken Ravana, Lord of Lanka, ruler of the nature spirits."[44]

Ravana, the Separated Self, who was the enabler of all destructive forces, heard the Buddha's intention and was deeply moved by the invisible force of his presence.

The Buddha considered the subconscious shadows of human nature, alongside divinity, nature, and creation. Rising up to full awareness, he observed the waves on the ocean of knowledge as his companions' mental agitation. He observed their accumulation of thought, experience, and feelings constantly being disrupted by the external world.[45]

---

[43] Daughters of the Serpent King represent our shadows. Depicted as Nagas, sea serpents, or snake people, they serve to illustrate everything we disown about ourselves. Not limited to the memory of poor behaviors and bad choices, they also include judgment misaligned with our true selves. Greater dissonance between waking and subconsciousness means they have more power to act out. As such, shadows sneak out until the differences are integrated.

[44] Nature spirits are the Yakshas, ancient tribes, or even elemental beings, but in this context, I take them to be the human population. Because Ravana is effectively each of us, king of our self-destructive tendencies, the Yakshas are his humanness. Left to our own devices, we are genuinely nature spirits in both negative and positive contexts.

[45] This image of waves related to the agitated mind is also a cornerstone of yogic thought, practice, and literary history as described in *Patanjali's Yoga Sutras* (200–400 CE). Here the Buddha recognizes the agitation of waking consciousness when viewed from meditative awareness.

Buddha was still deep in this reflection when Ravana swelled with enthusiasm and exclaimed, "I Must go and invite the awakened one to Lanka. In these dark times, it will serve his purposes to help us, delighting both the Divine and humankind."

Gathering his entourage into a magical transport of flowers, Ravana, Lord of Man-Eating Demons, arrived where the Buddha was standing. Alighting with all his retinue, they paid homage to the awakened self by circling him three times from left to right. Musicians played lutes inlaid with lapis lazuli,[46] using blue sapphire picks. Held by priceless yellow ribbons, the instruments were swung to the side, as together they all sang poetic quatrains. Accompanied by flutes, perfectly arranged on an ancient scale, they recreated the morning praise of deities.

Lord Ravana with attendants singing:

1. "The remarkable truth, innate knowledge, the universal mind, self-existent, beyond separateness, surpassing rational judgment, undefiled and pure, revealed in stillness. Master, show us this path."

2. "Buddha, Sugata,[47] incarnation of Vishnu, who dreams the universe into being, returns, enlightened, flawless, he embodies transmutation and dissolution of the illusory selves. He who enjoys universal mind as the original and authentic self. May you come to Lanka. Now is the opportunity, Beloved Holy Man!"[48]

---

[46] Significant metaphors and symbols are integrated within the text. Lapis Lazuli and blue sapphire picks indicate spiritual resonance and the flamboyance of Ravana's ego, as the yellow ribbon is supreme intellect. This paragraph is also about traditional ceremonies, honoring the sacred with rites symbolic of the most excellent gifts.

[47] Gautama Buddha is held to be the ninth incarnation of the Hindu god Vishnu (Sugata in the text), making him an Avatar, or incarnation of God. The title, *Lankavatara Sutra*, likely comes from this. The Buddha is also frequently referred to as Bhagavan or the great charioteer, as Krishna was also a previous incarnation, strengthening the ties to Hindu cosmology.

[48] A holy man is from the Sanskrit term "Muni" used in the text, but it is also associated with silence. This is important for two reasons. First, Buddha, unmoved by flattery, pomp, and circumstance, reveals Ravana's frustration at not being shown his entitled deference. Second, the silence is non-conceptual awareness, well beyond Ravana's conception.

3. *"Awakened Beings in the past came to live and teach in Lanka. Their disciples taught their powers, abilities, understandings, and disciplines.[49] My people are the nature spirits, with all the same limitations and potentials. Master, reveal to me the great way and they will hear your teaching."*

Narrator:

Lord Ravana changed his tune to a more refined poetic rhythm and meter as he continued to sing.

Ravana's intentions are revealed as not so bad, but he betrays his self-interest in bravado. Buddha is unmoved as Ravana's tone literally changes tune and becomes a little more self-important. The next part of the story are songs repeating previous actions with Ravana's enhancements.

Ravana:

4. *"The Buddha returns after a week in the realm of life's formless beginning, in the depths of Alaya being as home, even the leviathan king was transformed, now he emerges, his feet dry on wet sands."*

5. *"Recognize Lord Ravana, who not unlike the Buddha, has his magnificent entourage, celestial dancers of cloud and water, the hosts of elementals, nature spirits, and mankind, attended by all the high councilors of wisdom."[50]*

---

[49] The original text alludes to spiritual powers in statements about owning forms. They are natural extensions of deeper subconscious awareness, that look like magic to us.

[50] The characters in the original sloka, with Ravana, hold meanings describing the abundance of nature and power, in life-giving female spirits of cloud and water, nature spirits, and masters of ancient wisdom.

In D.T.'s translation, Sanskrit names are left untranslated to convey meanings and references to the *Ramayana*. Sometimes they've been more important than the description to convey meaning. These characters are our aspects, which describe our natural magnificence, limited as we are to see it.

The Awakening of Ravana

*6. "Magically, my company is transported
to where the lord Buddha has emerged
grandly disembarking from a chariot of flowers!
I humble myself, greeting the blessed awakened one,
offering homage, we all present ourselves."*

7. "It is I, Lord Ravana, the most learned king of destructive desires who approaches.[51] Please accept me kindly with all of Lanka, and those who dwell here."

8. "On Lanka's bejeweled heights of intellect, knowledge, and tradition[52] your forbearers revealed the innate knowing of universal mind."

9. "Bring your entourage, so that stark reality may be revealed on this pinnacle of human knowledge. Lanka is gathered and desires to hear your teaching."

---

[51] Led by self-interest, Ravana continually reinforces the story he tells himself. It's very tiring, and his uneasy peace begins to show. Ten-headed Ravana brags about his mastery of science, art, literature, and religion. But his reference to himself as King of Man-eating Demons is about self-will and ownership of destructive human nature. We can safely assume that Buddha was neither impressed by all the pomp and splendor nor enticed by association with Ravana. Based on boasting and flattery, the Buddha stands silent and undisturbed, so Ravana's tone now becomes more imploring as his frustration mounts. Ravana, King of Lanka, continues trying to convince the Buddha of his just request.

[52] In many places, the story recognizes the brilliance of humanity as the adorning jewels of Lanka. Advances in culture and technology were held in high value by the ancients. Here Ravana speaks of innate knowledge and stark reality as the rational goals of objective understanding. It indicates a goal of the *Lanka*, embracing the universal mind within the stark reality of life. This disciplined intuition is subconscious integration.

Buddha is still unmoved. So as pleasantries and a little boasting didn't work, Ravana assumes a more presumptuous, demanding tone.

10. "The Lankavatara, celebrated by the Buddhas, reveals conscious tranquility in subconscious harmony, though not established by any system of belief nor religious doctrine."[53]

Ravana, King of Man-Eating Demons, continues with no effect:

11. "I remember the Awakened Ones who have gone before, encircled by followers, recounting the Lanka. You too will reveal it!"

12. "Future Buddhas and their descendants will also have mercy for the nature spirits. Their wisdom, intellect, and knowledge will be shared by these guardians of enlightenment. Lanka is humanity's jewel. Great accomplishments encircle it, providing wealth, culture, art, beauty, and protection."

13. "See the nature spirits, my people. They are free from compulsive desires, contemplating awakening and giving alms to past Buddhas. They have faith in your highest wisdom, determined to direct each other to practice."[54]

Narrator: Ravana, Lord of Intellect becomes frustrated in rationalization.

14. "Also, there are future generations to consider, hungry for true understanding. We depend on your council. Come to Lanka's highest peak where all can appreciate your teaching."

---

[53] This verse is a rare instance where a book refers to itself. Still, many things are unheard of, misapprehended, or hidden in the *Lanka*. This sloka points out the path, beyond all rational systems, never to be grasped intellectually.
The distance continues to grow between the Buddha and Ravana. So, the student changes tune once more, recognizing that guilt and shame don't seem to be working. His exasperation builds.

[54] The nature spirits or humans appear in folklore as wild people, sometimes as sorcerers and witches, associated with mischief, like elementals or fairies. The human propensity to discipline others rather than ourselves was humorously evident in this section. The basic trap is their belief in physical reality alone.

15. *"Even the demons of destructive desire, led by my good-natured brother live here, committed to the highest truth, they want to understand your illumined experience".*[55]

16. *"In the past, even the demons of desire have diligently given alms to the Buddhas and will do so again today. Out of generosity and kindness, come to Lanka and bring your followers."*

Ravana, Lord of the Apparent World gives up in light of the Buddha's unresponsiveness:

17. *"Mahamati, please take all I own in this life.*[56] *Accept the companionship of the life-giving spirits, my wisdom, my knowledge and all my accomplishments, along with the just rewards of a righteous ruler."*[57]

---

[55] Some symbology, such as man-eating demons (Rakshasas) and Ravana's lovable drunken brother (Kumbhakarna), comes through its historical reference unclearly. Good and evil don't apply here because it describes forces in the human psyche subject to awakening. The drunken brother, for instance, was also considered so pious, intelligent, and brave, that the King of Gods was jealous. This allegory may help understand why the Buddha would encourage these demons, nature spirits, and wild humans toward awakening.

Still, the Buddha is unmoved and patently non-responsive. Finally, thoroughly exasperated, the Separated-Self throws up his hands, realizing he must establish a relationship through decent behavior or the higher self, Mahamati.

[56] This first step is symbolic of sitting still to listen to our innate wisdom or higher selves. A crucial turning point, Ravana abdicates attachments, giving them to Mahamati, his higher self. But it's nowhere near an honest abdication. As in all things, words are cheap.

[57] Giving up the fruits of righteousness is letting go of outcomes; crucial to recreating one's reality. Thus, the second premise is setting the highest intention and accepting whatever comes in gratitude. It is devotion to life-force and the elemental magic of co-creation.

Having made one step, Ravana finally reaches the only argument that could sway the Buddha. Ravana humbles and commits himself.

18. *"I surrender myself completely to serve the Buddhas and their descendants. All my possessions, I lay at their feet, great holy man,[58] have compassion for my miserable state!"*

Hearing this, Buddha responds directly:

19. *Buddha, the Awakened Self, Master of Desire (subjective mind), form (objective mind) and formlessness (subconscious mind)[59] said, "King of Nature Spirits, this realm of intelligence and abundance has, in deed been visited by great visionaries in the past."*

20. *"Having compassion for you, they exposed your understanding to the truth of their own self-realization, as will the enlightened also proclaim the great way to future generations."*

21. *"Indeed, great masters of discipline, have attained the shelter of faith-mind, tranquility, by observing the world from non-judgment. The master of nature spirits, can also find it within himself through the love and wisdom of avatars and the enlightened."*

22. *The Awakened Self, Buddha, silent and tranquil, then boarded a magical transport of flowers, offered by Ravana. The mood and tone changes as Buddha accepts Ravana's request.*

---

[58] This holy man is again Muni, with his characteristic silence. The Buddha recognizing both humility and commitment turns for the first time to acknowledge Ravana, not fooled that this is anything more than a first step.

[59] "Lord of the Triple World" was the title used for Buddha in the original translation. It is a reflective term contrasting cosmic reality with aspects of mind, but it also indicates the Buddha's dominion over illusion. It conveys that all three aspects of the mind are almost entirely dominated by self-will or desire. All children grow through this stage and hopefully out of it. The degree of growth determines the level of suffering and enlightenment.

23. Enroute to Lanka, the entourage, Ravana and Buddha are honored and entertained with song and dance by the beautiful female spirits of cloud and water, source of all life on the earth.[60]

24. In the heart of dazzling Lanka, the celebration of male and female nature spirits revealed Ravana among them, honoring the Awakened Self.

25. Their innocent wisdom and knowledge of children,
like a net of precious jewels was offered.
Ravana gave as alms of adornment, to honor the Awakened Self and his followers, all the wealth of science, religion, literature, and art.

26. The Buddha with his entourage of enlightened men, acknowledged these gifts and shared their reality of truth as a unified consciousness, with everyone at their own level of comprehension.[61]

27. Mahamati, the Higher Self, was then honored as the greatest orator; honored and persistently questioned by Ravana along with all the people. Ravana, attempts to coax Mahamati into calling upon the Buddha on his behalf, demonstrating his impatience and frustration.

Ravana addresses Mahamati:

28. Mahamati, you are blessed to converse with the Awakened one on discernment of subconscious integration. My nature spirits, Buddha's entourage, and the wise men, all want to hear from him. Yet he

---

[60] As an analogy to single human experience, the Buddha's group have traveled from head to heart, serenaded by life-giving spirits, on their journey to feeling; the results of Ravana's admitting his need.

[61] Unified consciousness is introduced to highlight the *Lanka*'s underlying persistence that awakening is only part of the story. Noble Wisdom is also the focus. Almost as next steps, self-realization is reflected as loving-kindness and imagelessness is identified as unified consciousness. Having traveled every path and learned every lesson, rather than disidentification, imagelessness identifies and empathizes with everyone. Transmission is the *Lanka*'s physics as the resonance of our thought to attract awakened ancestors.

remains silent. We, as one, ask you to request this teaching of the Buddha."

29. *"Mahamati, you are the most articulate and persuasive among us, as befits your arduous Yogic discipline. Trusting in your virtue, I plead you to seek the all-inclusive teaching.[62] You can do this."*

Mahamati, the Higher Self, replies:

30. *"liberated from the enlightenment of mind, doctrine and discrimination, the mistakes of rational men are no more. The truth of Buddha-nature, once cultivated, is flawless, leading to subconscious enlightenment and unified consciousness."[63]*

31. *On hearing this, the Buddha manifested the innumerable mountain kingdoms bejeweled with intelligence, abundance, and wealth, with the most valuable objects and attainments of a material world.*

32. *Buddha, Ravana and all the nature spirits appeared standing above every kingdom as Lords of the Earth.*

33. *So, the Buddha, Ravana, and their companions were recognized as the highest authority in each kingdom; attended and served by the ruler of every land.[64] Ravana, the Separated Self is stunned and*

---

[62] Ravana's demand for teaching is thinly veiled rationalization, where any logic, including the *Lanka's*, is only of value in leading to the non-rational.

[63] This focus on the subconscious is somewhat unique to the *Lanka*. It explains the underlying necessity and purpose of practice. Starting as the thought of loving-kindness, it attracts other higher thoughts such as compassion.

Mahamati neatly tied up Ravana's dependence on mind mechanics. However, moved by Mahamati's correction, Buddha proceeds to give Ravana what he's asking for, though unable to admit it even to himself.

[64] Each mountain kingdom represents human nature, responsible for their own life but over lorded in this image. So, Ravana is presented with humanity and all its creation at his feet, representing our most egoic desire of having everything our own way.

amazed when the scene changes to fulfil his secret, most grandiose desire; to be lord of the world.

34. Here stood the King of Man-eating Demons, Ravana, together with all his kingdom of nature spirits worshipping him. The Buddha, the Awakened Self conjured even the city of Lanka countless times, for all to see.

35. Every aspect was perfect, even the palace and royal pleasure gardens appeared on every mountain kingdom peak. Then also Mahamati, the Higher Self, was seen appealing to the Buddha, just as Ravana had desired.

36. To complete every wish Ravana expressed, the Buddha disclosed the great way for all beings to understand. In each kingdom, he revealed the truth according to each individual's ability, intelligence, and circumstance.[65]

37. When the teaching was complete, everyone and everything except the Separated Self disappeared, leaving Ravana, the great nature spirit himself, alone in his head with no Buddha, Lanka or world.[66]

Ravana goes mad with questions:

---

[65] The illusion of ego, complete for Ravana, is an analogy for human learning. It appears that his every wish is granted in one moment. This pattern is how our enthusiasm starts loving the car, house, marriage, and all acquisitions. Then the sloka says something significant about individual capabilities, as teaching must be delivered in a manner best suited to each. This is like saying we must approach a teaching repeatedly as we change in our ability to grasp it.

Having given Ravana the dominion he desired, the Buddha let his ego expand to its maximum excess and aggrandizement. This inflated illusion provides the perfect opportunity for Ravana's bubble to be burst.

[66] Now, Ravana doesn't know what's going on, and the mind is scrambling. This explosion of illusion is fantastic because the Buddha has taken Ravana on the greatest roller-coaster ride. It is an analogy not unlike our own lives. As we mature, our childish delusions and dreams are created to be dissolved or destroyed in maturity. It is meaningful as everyone encounters life with a choice of gratitude or cynicism. This is the crucial choice, determining what life contains.

38. "Tortured by, What was that, and what does it mean? Am I hallucinating? What about everybody else? Did they see my grandiose desires? It was real, the city, the people and all the kingdoms! Even the Buddha was teaching us, as I asked."

39. "Where are the kings and princes of humanity, or the host of enlightened beings and God men? Was this a dream, a delusion, or a spell cast by spirits?"

40. "Maybe I have some kind of physical impairment, or it was some kind of mirage. If it's not my own wishful thinking, maybe it was the ghostly image of something that once existed?"[67]
Ravana reflects in shock, horror, and awe, which leaves him at a rational emptiness, in the clarity of unobstructed lucidity.

41. "Ravana's awareness disentangled, "It's all the mind's creation. I have seen and experienced the drama of life's highest lesson. Not understanding this, others are confused in false-imagination and fail to recognize the pattern of oneness behind form."[68]

42. "In this realization, there is neither one who sees nor that which is seen. It is not taught, for it cannot be spoken. Even the Buddha, his actions and his truth—are nothing, but what the mind creates."

---

[67] Teachers often use extremes to shock their students into sudden awakening. As I described previously, when I was given the name Gurudas by Swami Satchidananda. It was like the loud thwack of two hardwood sticks slapped together, with my ego in the middle. My reaction was the same as Ravana's.

[68] This sloka points to oneness intrinsic in a world of synchrony. It is the materialization of thought and intention. Being formless, the Awakened Self reflects no light, operating from the depths of our subconscious. So, when thinking-desire-will, logic-form, and nonlinear-formless minds are still, the light is coherent. So, like a hologram, the pattern of synchronicity can be refracted to visibility.

43. "Others having shared this experience, do not see the blessed one through belief. The Buddha cannot be seen. The fully enlightened one may only be witnessed prior to perception, thinking and doing. Only then do the Buddhas show themselves, when the mind is not agitated nor conflicted in doing or being."[69]

Narrator:

Lord Ravana rose from his deep thought, sickened by his deluded perception, identification, and arrogance. Turning back from these impediments, he recognized himself as the architect of the perceived world and the creator of his reality. Transformed and awakened for the first time, he discovered his mental attachment to self as both distorting his perception and creating his reality. He relaxed into suchness, abandoning opinion and judgmental thought. Ravana's good karma opened understanding to replace what had been only his advanced knowledge. For the first time, he saw everything just for itself, without reflecting on others' beliefs or opinions. His own innate wisdom emerged, independent of rationalization, argument, and the judgment of others.[70]

Ravana mastered the disciplines of yoga, whereby he could embody the paths of right action, right understanding, devotion, physical discipline, mental control, and Noble Wisdom. Familiarized with all varieties of spiritual practice and the stages of development, he learned the principles of mastery.[71]

---

[69] Doing and being represent the three poisons that blind humanity as anger, greed, and delusion (separateness). Failing to trust a living intelligence, we miss synchrony's pattern and presence. Only in duality, in the world of suffering, is an awakened-enlightened-self anything special or separate.

[70] Masterhood, per the *Lanka*, could be defined as being 100 percent independent of outside influence. It is the self-determined side of the *Lanka*'s psychology. Solitude recognizes 100 percent responsibility for the past, present, and future; no blame means no attachment and no dependence. The second aspect of this solitude is letting go of self-image, where external things no longer affect our state of being. Others' view of us becomes none of our business; it still exists but isn't our problem.

[71] This section depicts the Buddha was a Yogi, and where Buddhism likely held yoga as central to its practice in ancient times.

Ravana was happy to cast off his habitual ways of thinking, going beyond the distorted reality of memory, surrendering his story and the attachment to "who he had thought he was." With this applied perspective, he was free from the three poisons of greed, anger, and delusion. The certainty of his direct experience overrode all previous knowledge, dispelling the arguments of all philosophers and intellectuals. Fully understanding the subconscious as the Womb of Enlightenment,[72] the path of awakening and self-realization, Ravana grasped his awakening to full life.

Suddenly, he heard a voice from above, "Certainty is to be yours."[73]

Buddha addressing Ravana:

"Excellent! Lord Ravana. Your commitment and dedication are examples to others. Seeing the awakened and everything without the limits of belief or disbelief, you validate the truth of your own purpose.

"As you have experienced, apparent reality is going beyond the exclusions created by will, memory, thought, senses and awareness. Going within, do not tie yourself to doctrine or accept the world's view at face value. Avoid the seduction of your achievements, including this understanding or even transcendence, which is the limiting goal of others.

"Avoid demeaning witticisms and all distinctions of separateness as in entitlement or self-interest. Do not pursue fame, glory or power and especially do not seek supernatural and clairvoyant powers, which may arise naturally with practice."[74]

---

[72] The Womb of Enlightenment or subconscious is critical linking still mind (*dhyana*, *chan* or *ZaZen*) meditative practice as the vehicle of harmonization, enlightenment, and self-realization.

[73] Of course, the voice from the sky is the Awakened Self, the Buddha.

[74] This counseling is a synopsis of the *Lanka*'s behavior theory, intended to point out and establish inner seriousness, solitude, and humility. Taken all together, these precepts focus on alleviating opportunities for self-deception. The guidance is to develop a lifestyle without the added disturbances of denigrating influence. Mindfulness that comes out of this awareness is a powerful instrument of change, without trying to do or change anything.

The Awakening of Ravana

"Ravana, Mind-only, discovered by the Yogins, renders the habit and rhetoric of belief as oblivious baggage, eliminating the basic fearful views of life. This triumph, called the Great Turning Back,[75] uncovers the higher-self, beyond the limits of worldly identification. Thus, thoughts of self-obsession become repulsive and shameful. In this mindfulness, nothing in life needs change, but everything changes as the awareness shifts to one's core being, the higher self. Such are my children, and this is the great way, through which you must pass, in realizing your true self."

The Awakened Self continues in a fatherly tone:

"What you have seen and understood cannot be undone, so it will work slowly on your awareness. In the quiet space, which is mindful practice, recognize the constructions called truth. Don't be drawn into the traps of naive spiritual ambitions for abundance and fame. You can not give what you do not have, and when you have, that awakening serves others not you. Realize that embedded in doing are the ideas of separateness, which blind us in the torrent of creation and desire. Herein we are rendered oblivious to and disconnected from the perfection of living intelligence.

"Life, when seen as something to control or own, is ignorant of intuition and incapable of mindfulness. So, the intrinsic magic of interdependent connection goes unseen and beyond experience. If you hold up beliefs as reality, you will be trapped in judgment and opinion, endlessly frustrated in the cycles of acquiring, achieving, and comparing one's worth to that of others."[76]

---

[75] A sudden awakening, the Great Turning Back is the focal point of Ravana's experience and the shift that opens his new perspective verifying the source. Awareness and experience of Mind-only manifest as the exquisite knowledge of trusting intuition and objective awareness to recognize and identify reality.
Ravana, moving from the separated self, is converging into the higher self, and for the moment, he knows that he does not know. He has a lucid moment.

[76] In the Buddha's awareness, there is nowhere to hide. He points out how we are trapped, devoted to our story, while self-interest arises as entitlement or victimhood. This view is the stark reality Ravana asked for earlier, looking life squarely in the eye. Something magical occurs with this shattering or turning back of an egocentric mindset. Nothing changes, but everything is different.

"Understanding reality, as the creation of one's mind, leads to extraordinary realizations and achievements. Conviction and certainty follow, to the extent of one's unselfish intentions and dis-identification; seeing the manifestation as only waves of formlessness.[77] This attainment is an exquisite magical thinking, leading to the most incredible and magnificent life."

Buddha said:

"The veil is lifted, as obsession with self fades. Noisy internal dialog subsides, absent the defense of one's beliefs. The struggle ends with the irrelevancy of external causes. [78]

"Beware of paths thinly masking self-interest as bait. The consequence of the slightest separateness or self-importance leads to endless cycles of false hope and misery.

"Congratulations, Lord Ravana, you have correctly embraced awakening."

Narrator:

Ravana thought, "If only I could see the Buddha again[79] to answer all my questions on disciplines and systems of belief. In sustained clarity, resonance, fully realized, untouched by even the duality of enlightened beings and students, his is the certainty of effortless belonging. Where we seek an intuitive penetration of life, to him, it is the immediate knowledge of being. Effortless and undisturbed, his compassion begets

---

[77] Magical thinking, usually considered idiocy in modern cultures, is the exquisite awareness of Mind-only, seeing into the formless essence or interconnected suchness of all things. The Buddha also indicates two advanced stages of spiritual development as conviction and certainty, being non-dual rationality and certitude.

[78] The condensed script of everyone's spiritual development, the Buddha reframes the perspective of Mind-only into tranquilization of being offended or disturbed by external causes. He warns of self-interest backfiring, wary of teachings with worldly purposes.

[79] Here, Ravana faces every seeker's dilemma of an environment for sustainability. When the Ravana whispers from the shadows of uncertainty that everything is undefined and insecure, we all feel insecure. At a loss to let go of "what we think we know" and reconsider or doubt our conditioned beliefs is the universal dilemma. But, we must empty the cup to have it refilled.

his supernatural power. Beyond needs, wishes, and desires, in the non-dual reality of suchness, he knows all minds. Dwelling within everyone, he seemingly does nothing, disregards all appearances, and yet nothing is lacking in his perfect composure and teaching.

"Maybe, unattached to the outcomes of effort, welcoming all life lessons in gratitude; maybe then I can fully see him, learn what I need, or at least hold onto the understanding I've gained so far? In this way, I may progress in non-judging, mindfulness, right understanding and Right-knowledge."

Narrator:

Buddha heard Ravana's willingness and materialized the world as before. Once again, Ravana saw the splendors of creation, but now the Buddha also bore the thirty-two traits of perfection;[80] beams of light shone from his third eye and from his heart. A blue and gold aura extended ten feet in all directions. Transported back in time, the awakened one was again giving a great discourse on the resonance of thought in non-conceptual awareness. Enraptured like children listening to stories of elves, fairies, and goblins, the crowd gathered close.

The Buddha's eye of wisdom warmed with joy. Then a knowing smile emerged like the most glorious sunrise. The Awakened Self then roared a deafening laugh that rivaled anything ever heard in all the realms of heaven or earth.[81] His body blazed with the light of a newborn sun at the beginning of a new age.

---

[80] The traits of perfection describe the body of a fully enlightened being, which is mostly about adaptations for powerful swimming in the ocean of the subconscious. For example, traits of perfection include webbed toes, fingers, and arms down to his knees. Along with the aura and light from his third eye, the marks of excellence even describe reduced body hair, a curl in the middle of his forehead (the sign of a Hindu god or goddess), and long earlobes, to mention a few.

[81] This laugh blew everyone away because it was entirely out of character for the quiet, elegant, unattached behavior for which the Buddha is known. The Awakened One reverts to his customary composure, acting as if nothing unusual has occurred.

The Gods and Guardians of Creation took notice, and with the Bodhisattvas, they were shocked, surprised, and concerned.

Narrator, the group thoughts:

Questioning in themselves, "Why would the most ineffable, enlightened, powerful, and dispassionate being in the world behave in such a way? Allowing himself to be consumed with passion, first with the smile, then to bursting with light, as he produced the most tremendous laugh ever known in all planes of existence.

Though this was surprising enough, now he acts as if nothing at all has happened? How can Ravana's accomplishment in discipline, understanding, and demeanor move the Buddha from his expression of equanimity to this most passionate of behaviors?"

Narrator speaking of Mahamati:

Mahamati, The Higher Self felt the concern and stress of the enlightened crowd while taking pity on Ravana, who had previously asked for his intercession with the Buddha.

He considered future generations, who would likely misinterpret the Buddha's passion because of their obsession with manifestations and spiritual power. It is only natural to wonder why the Buddha, with his supernatural awareness, would suddenly explode with laughter and light.

So Mahamati asked, "Master, why did you laugh so immoderately? What was the cause of your gigantic rapture?"

The Awakened Self anticipating this reaction, was fully aware of the questions and even the rationale of Mahamati's concerns. Turning to the Higher Self:

The Buddha replied, "Very good, Mahamati. Your choices are exemplary, as always. You see the world with the clear eyes of selfless intention. Your only desire is to illuminate the understanding of those clinging to confused views of past, present, and future. And so, you ask me this question, as should all wise men seek clarity for others, as well as for themselves.

"My amusement and roaring laughter were in anticipation of Ravana's next question. Asked of my forbearers, we can appreciate and acknowledge its character, value, and comprehensiveness. I don't mean to make fun of Ravana nor his question, because it is necessary that he ask. However, its answer is beyond rational inquiry and even meditations limited by dualism. And, most certainly, our curious, inquiring, over-educated descendants will also ask future Buddhas the same question."

The Awakened Self turned to Ravana:

"Ravana, you have my permission to ask your questions but understand your responsibility is to listen with an open, uncluttered mind. Look within your heart, and I will satisfy your need. Concentrated listening is required because your greatest lessons will arise in the awareness of your own reactions. Recognize these thoughts and emotions but do not give them free sway. Listen intently, setting all else aside, so you may contemplate what is given, as your own wisdom arising.

"Rest in meditative consciousness, tranquil in the company of right understanding.. Surpassing bliss and understanding, be unbound from limits of perception and manifestation. Discipline yourself in mindfulness, free of reaction and material desires. Pursue the highest truth within yourself as intuitive penetration of the subconscious.[82] Behold no-self and no-other-than-self. In this way, sustained by the power of awakening, all will accept you eye to eye.

"Intuition beyond imagination is sensing the field of co-arising and responding in accepting awareness. Set yourself in the way of practice, which your needs will reveal as changing potential. Buddhahood and the purposefulness to all beings will be yours.

---

[82] A pillar of Buddhism, the *sangha* or company of truth, focuses on human potential and provides acceleration. Still, like a householder's practicality, it is what we surround ourselves with that matters most. By extension, Ravana himself becomes the sacred space of practice. The "highest truth" comes out of Sanskrit as the character traits of constancy, renunciation, and reality just as it is. Fully grasping the concept of non-doer engages us completely, letting go of expectations and outcomes. Philosophically, in a world where we measure ourselves by accomplishments, good or otherwise, it may feel like sacrilege.

"Don't confuse this with enlightenment of the conscious mind; this is Mind-only."[83]

Narrator:

Having received permission, Lord Ravana stood apart from his worldly wealth, immediately enveloped by even greater opulence and lifted into the air. Surrounded by heavenly beauty, showered with jewels, incense, flowers, banners, crowns, and ornaments of all sorts, he was beyond anything known in creation.

Music played eclipsing that of gods, shadows, spirits, sorcerers, half men, serpents, and mankind, with instruments created beyond all realms of pleasure and awakening.

Bejeweled in brilliance, everyone was adorned as to their nature, with high honors displayed on great banners standing higher than the trees.

Ravana made offerings to the Buddha of this heavenly adornment and returned to his seat, which now rivaled the sun for glory.

Smiling in deference, Ravana asked, "The ancient awakened ones answered these questions within the limits of their enlightenment. However, duality has never been explained by a Buddha of the silent, primordial depths; the subconscious.[84] *Such Buddhas, absorbed in bliss, shun trivial matters; since they neither judge dualism nor instruct on it. Please disclose your vision in our struggle to disentangle from duality. Your imagelessness belies your comprehension, and we would love to hear your thoughts."*

---

[83] The Separated Self, Ravana, is suddenly not only in the spotlight but also surrounded by wealth on a cosmic scale; Ravana is once again overwhelmed by the power of his desire's creation.

[84] Here, the story distinguishes this teaching from others because the Buddha of Silence points to the *Lanka*'s primary thesis of Mind-only, as it begins the story with the Buddha rising effortlessly from the subconscious ocean of Alaya. This distinction of silence offers no beliefs, no doctrine, no rules of conduct, and no forbidden desires, only non-conceptual awareness.

However, to be asked a question by the Buddha puffed up the Separated Self in Ravana, giving him the courage to challenge the bedrock of suchness as seen by his pomp and circumstance returning.

The Awakening of Ravana

Buddha asked, "What is it you understand about duality?"

Narrator:

"Ravana, Lord of All Destructive Forces, once again in all his worldly glory, now wore a necklace strung on the thread of power."

Ravana said, "We have been told, to embrace the non-dual,[85] one must abandon truth and untruth. Why must definitions be relinquished? How is it even possible? Truth and untruth may be easy because they are vague abstractions. But how can we dismiss the function of our awareness to perceive the world?

"We understand the delusion of duality as the divisive discrimination of circumstance and the isolating fear of others. Oblivious to universal mind, we objectify life and misidentify ideas of what is real or not. Duality is like the floaters in one's eye, misunderstood to be clouds on the ceiling. Duality also belongs to the realm of abstraction, conjecture, and intellectual creation. Poorly defined, immature and obtuse, this is apparent and true. How can one even fathom abandonment of duality as truth or untruth?"

The Buddha's tone seems to soften at this point, like a father with a confused child.

Buddha softly voiced, "Ravana, seeing people paralyzed in life experience, entangled by habitual likes and dislikes, leaving themselves in constant dissatisfaction and turmoil, this is apparent and true. Why do so few recognize their self-imposed suffering?[86]

---

[85] This is heart of the parable. Ravana is asking, "This is the nature of existence. How can I let it go?" As the knife cannot cut itself, the collective subconscious field is impossible to grasp or understand, and this is Ravana's point. Said another way, we are not in the soup; we are the soup, so we can't see it.

[86] Describing the human condition, the Buddha equates the value of one's life to tragedy and the waste of constant worry until examined, understood, and taken into control. We believe our value is authentic, although everything we cherish will perish in time and no-thing has any worth when we face our end. The Buddha is hammering reality, as we see it, as merely the machinations of belief, which we glamorize in pretense.

"Preferences, judgment, and understanding, evolved in similar habitual discrimination. They only lead to naïve and relative truths and untruths. This is beyond most people, being oblivious and unaware of their limitations.

"Noble Wisdom is far beyond sleepwalking. But then, for you to give up at mere words would also be a tragedy. Life energy is wasted worrying for those who believe only in what they can see and measure. Minds, bounded by senses and circumstances, have giving away their control and are cast about on the whims of others and happenstance. The wise recognize this as the behavior of children."

"Fire burns indiscriminately with no regard to consuming shacks, houses, castles, parks, or forests. But colors of flame and ferocity vary depending on the structure and the energy of that being consumed. This is apparent and true. Why is it not understood that our equality as human beings does not mean our sameness in comprehension? It is in clinging to petty, ignorant desires that the argument of truth and untruth comes into being.

"As one fire expands and becomes many, a single seed produces one plant with all its component parts. The stem, leaves, flowers, fruit, and branches share a common life and yet are each individualized; no two are the same.

"External life grows in the same way as internal life. From who we think we are, we develop obsessions with the body, emotions, perceptions, thought, and consciousness. Even intuition from this bias of self is false-imagination.

"As we can cling equally to healthy and unhealthy things or experiences, these compulsions grow from desire, form, and formlessness.[87] What we

---

[87] This whole section speaks conditions as they usually are before a choice is applied, except for a few points. First, these stanzas talk about diversity and equality but not sameness, as everyone is unique. It says truth is a relative thing, which always has many sides. The external and inner life is equated to organic diversity, and even intuition is doubtful based on self-interest. Also, desire, form, and formlessness are the three worlds, our subjective, objective, and subconscious, respectively. Hence, the stanza ties us back to Mind-only by pointing out our compulsion of choice.

perceive to be happiness, appearance, expression, and conduct, are all arising continuously around us but beyond our control.

"So, it makes sense that our identification with consciousness is experienced differently, dependent on what we can verify in a physical world. We see things as good and bad, better and worse, pure and unclean. Not only are there infinite variations on the conditions and forms of life in general, but also the inner experience and realizations of everyone vary extremely, even as he or she treads the well-established path of good practice.

"Do you think we create our own great chasms, between truth and untruth, in our compulsive world of self, characteristically enslaved by discrimination? You bet we do?"

The Awakened Self continues:

"Lord Ravana, the separation and distinctions of truth and untruth are only products of prejudice and opinion.

"What do we commonly believe as truth? They are judgments based on memory and opinion, which have been handed down and defended by those most invested in their perpetuation.

"This pre-judging leads us to believe that truth, understood to have value and meaning, comes from an ultimate source or cause, but these notions should always be questioned. Such truths can generally not be upheld as certain reality because they are only characteristics and features by which a thing is recognized.

"Clinging to this perspective comes from regarding your own projections as reality. These thoughts are self-limiting containers, products of our belief and imagination, conceived in need, desire, and limitation without our full awareness. They don't exist separate from our prejudice because their substance is not independent of our projection.

"To understand things from this perspective is known as detachment or abandonment."[88]

The Awakened Self:

"Okay then, Ravana. What are untruths? Argue as you may; untruths are only beliefs or the prejudice of dislikes and disagreements, which cannot be proven or disproven as they come from no ultimate cause. As you said, truth and untruth are abstractions and projections. Lacking physicality and verification, their reality or fantasy is unreliable.

"This is known as abandoning truth and untruth.[89]

"So, why are truths beyond verification and comprehension? Very often, they are just imaginings, like unicorns, the Easter Bunny, Eeyore the donkey, or a horned camel, for that matter. Sometimes we also imagine truths from wishful thinking, like the heartfelt longing of a barren woman to have her own child."

"But the essential nature of all truth is unreachable, and so we say they must be taken on faith. However, such faith is usually the veil of control by others, and truth should not be thought of as certain because truths and untruths are only the façade of something and not the real thing itself.

"Truth or untruth should be promoted only if it makes sense at all and never imposed as substantive reality and especially as boundaries to limit understanding.

---

[88] The sutra describes delusion as the most fundamental mistake, where habitual reality is entombed in a shroud of our own making. However, seeing this is stepping beyond normal limits to a stage of awakening. Mind-only as mindfulness is a state of observation, a waking meditation, and perspective, which merely observes, "What am I creating now?" This questioning, discerning perspective opens life to possibility.

[89] Absoluteness is another word for non-dual. Here the Buddha indicates the next stage of renunciation. It is in freeing oneself from having to be correct. It recognizes that absolute truth must always be legitimate for everyone, everywhere, and for all the time. In this idea, doubt, argument or disagreement, and thoughts, by definition, cannot be truths. So, truths as we know them have no distinctive character; they are only appearances of belief. Truth only exists where we connect or become our awakened selves.

"The fanciful and unreal are given an artistic value in our thinking; it is easy to detach it from its substantive reality where detachment or abandonment makes sense.

"As certainty of these formless unrealities fades, letting go of things arising from discrimination and prejudice is the natural evolution of understanding. This perspective is known as abandoning truth and untruth.[90]

"Lord Ravana, your question is now answered."

The Awakened Self eyes Ravana to see if he is getting it. He looks a little shaky, but he is wide awake.

The Awakened Self:

"Now Ravana, remember we were playing with words in the first place, and you said these questions had been asked of other enlightened beings in the past, who answered them. When you speak of the past, it too is just another concept, which divides and defines it from future or present, just discriminations of time."

"Living in a serene reality, the enlightened do not judge because they go beyond discrimination and pointless rationalizations, which include time, space, and form. However, the enlightened do represent reality as separate appearances of form, space, and time, but only for the benefit of sentient beings, as a context for suchness and humanities' peaceful wellbeing."

---

[90] This step is the third renunciation, abandoning the illusion that truth or untruth is viable discrimination. To reach beyond belief, we engage doubt and the benefit of the doubt equally. Doubting what the mind creates begins with judgment, feelings, perception, will, and the senses. This doubting is just to let things be as they are, without labels. It can be called suchness, thusness, or maybe not-knowing. Interestingly, this non-obtrusive path must start with trust or faith, which we have associated with devotion in a religious context. If you must believe, believe in listening, or maybe that joy reflects one's ability to express loving-kindness. Suchness in this view is the recognition of Mind-only in quiet observation.

"Suchness itself is also just a discrimination, but lacking prejudice, it is also non-conceptual awareness, and as such, it is discernment at the highest level."[91]

"It is from this place that the Buddhas teach causeless, formless being beyond the discriminations of time, space, and form because that is their essential state of being."

"They may also seem to have magical powers, like they may know every detail of your life or appear in multiple locations simultaneously. But to them, it is hearing, seeing, or moving without the limits of discrimination by their subtle resonance, evolved from love and an untainted intuitive insight. They live in and have as their essence transcendental wisdom, which is noble in that it includes imagelessness, transmission of the dharma, and self-realization."

"The Buddhas do not judge or discriminate, nor can they be judged or understood according to identity, personality, or ego. Why is it the enlightened do not judge thought itself? Because discrimination only emerges in the identification with a separate self, a soul, or a personality."[92]

"How do the enlightened go beyond judgment and opinion? They dwell in their boundless selves beyond the subjective, attached mind.

---

[91] When speaking of suchness, it demonstrates belief, using the objective mind's focus and detaching the subjective mind's habitual control. Its final goal is the revulsion of dualistic belief, to reprogram the subconscious. In this puzzle, the objective mind's understanding is not understanding at all; it is a discipline in breathing deeply and listening without the mind's chatter.

[92] This image of the enlightened is the thesis and example of pure suchness and detachment as described through the stage of imagelessness. Its reflection is like the still pond of Zen. Seeing no-self and no-other-than-self in all things and all others, it was never so bright for the mind to grasp and ponder. It is interesting to hear about psychic or clairvoyant powers as natural awareness, just much less self-involved and much more in-tune.

Not-Two. Not this, not that. Such thoughts can frighten people because they have no comprehension, but it's a very long road to imagelessness, and no one goes further into the unknown than they choose. Stepping beyond suffering into belonging is universally acceptable, but effortless belonging requires some awakening because it is a devoted love embedded in wisdom.

Unbounded from self-will and ownership, their thought is free in each moment to draw from Alaya, the living field of all life, the source of all knowledge, and the dharma itself."

"Though the subjective attached mind is meant for the material world, where cause and effect predominate, entanglements overpower us with form, appearance, conditions, and value. These separate us from our true potential. Therefore, discrimination and also non-discrimination must ultimately be transcended."

"Lord Ravana, the lives of most human beings are mere images of what they could be, lacking sensibility and a real awareness of life. Everything in their world of appearance is devoid of significance because the people lack meaning and purpose. They cannot be taught because no one is interested, until they have cause through awakening."[93]

"However, all this can change in the flash of a moment, magically transformed, though not understood as possible by intellectuals and those limited to judgment and discrimination."

"Seeing beyond appearance and judgment is to see truthfully. Seeing otherwise is to depend on likes, dislikes, prejudice, and the fear of losing a make-believe image."

"Grasping this, repulsed by that, jumping to conclusions, and living in an unspoken fear, we become entangled in mental agitations, only waves, and foam on a vast ocean."

"These images we create are only shadows of our true selves, like confusing oneself with one's reflection in a mirror or like believing the echo in a valley is your real voice."

"Clinging to shadows, we defend our beliefs, which include truth and untruth. Not recognizing our own projections, we continue in a life dictated by ignorant desire and never know peace."

---

[93] Consequences are the necessary aspect of individual free will, which keeps us focused on "what's in it for me?" "Having cause through awakening" points out the sequence adopted in this book, where the first part is dedicated to one concept and what truly makes us happy. Awakening from our sleepwalking through life is a prerequisite to every fulfillment.

"Peace is oneness. Knowing our greater-self, as a focal point in the living field, is to know, no-one as separate from anyone else.[94] Oneness gives birth to the highest bliss, diving into the womb of enlightenment, the subconscious, Alaya. Here lies the realm of imagelessness, transmission, and self-realization."

The parable's focus clearly presents the mind with enough perspectives to choose to look closer without forcing open the door. It is all choice. One would think that a text on the consciousness of being human would start with meditation. Barely mentioned, its allusion appears in the next to last sentence, "diving into the womb of enlightenment… Alaya."

Lastly, one might wonder what happened to Lord Ravana, the nature spirits, and all destructive forces. Well, Ravana got an upgrade to become aware of his higher self; he has the choice to step into it or not. But fortunately, one can never step in the same river twice (Heraclitus), so something in his fabric of being is changed, and that, of course, is also referring to us all.

We have a choice, including disposition, understanding, prejudice, propensity, and circumstance. Compulsion and habit are the challenges we face to recognize we are not these collections of things, experiences, feelings, memories, and especially not these thoughts. That's a tough one, and Ram Das may have said it best, "BE HERE NOW," utterly present in this moment.

---

[94] The oneness of consciousness, perceived in the physical world, is the experience of the living Gaia, the living earth, which is most evident in sentient beings but extends unperceivably to the atoms.

BIBLIOGRAPHY

[Note: highlight indicates a correction needed to footnote; highlight over XXX indicates I couldn't locate the information.]

Alberts, B., Johnson, A., Lewis, J., et al. (2002). *Universal Mechanisms of Animal Development. Molecular Biology of the Cell. 4th edition.* Garland Science; 2002. Retrieved from https://www.ncbi.nlm.nih.gov/books/NBK26825/

Allen, C. (2003, revised ed. edition). *The Buddha and the Sahibs.* John Murray.

Annikha, P. (2012, January 20). "Dark Matter" (PDF). *CERN Physics.* Retrieved from https://arxiv.org/pdf/1201.3942.pdf

Bell, J.S. (2004). *Speakable and Unspeakable in Quantum Mechanics* [Physicist John Bell depicts the Einstein camp in this debate in his article entitled "Bertlmann's Socks and the Nature of Reality," p. 143]. Cambridge University Press. Retrieved from https://doi.org/10.1017/CBO9780511815676

Benson, K. (2008). "Prajñatara: Bodhidharma's Master" (PDF). Retrieved from https://wiki2.org/en/Prajnatara.

Blue Mountain Center of Meditation. (1987, reprint edition). *Upanishads* (translated by Eknath Easwaran, 1961). Nilgiri Press.

Britten, R.J. (2002). "Divergence Between Samples of Chimpanzee and Human DNA Sequences is 5% Counting Indels." Proceedings National Academy Science. Retrieved from https://www.pnas.org/doi/10.1073/pnas.172510699

Castaneda, C. (2010). *The Teachings of Don Juan, Carlos Castaneda* (audiobook). Recorded Books.

Chen, I. (2011, September 6). "How Accurate Are Memories of 9/11?" Scientific American. Retrieved from https://www.scientificamerican.com/article/911-memory-accuracy/#:~:text=We%20then%20went%20back%20to,percent%20accurate%20at%20survey%20three.

Chondron, P. (2005). *Getting Unstuck* (audiobook). Sounds True.

Collen, A. (2015) *10% Human: How Your Body's Microbes Hold the Key to Health and Happiness.* William Collins.

Dass, R. (2013). "Being Love." Ram Dass. Retrieved from https://www.ramdass.org/being-love/

Descartes, R. (2008). *A Discourse on the Method.* Pomona Press.

Dispenza, J. (2007). *Evolve Your Brain, The Science of Changing Your Mind.* Health Communications, Inc.

Dumoulin, H. (1998). *Zen Buddhism: A History, India and China.* Macmillan Publishing.

Dyer, W.W. (2014). *I Can See Clearly Now.* Hay House Books.

_____ (2004). *Pulling Your Own Strings.* Arrow Books.

Einstein, A. (1906). "Theorie der Strahlung und die Theorie der Spezifischen Wärme" [Planck's Theory of Radiation and the Theory of Specific Heat]. *Annalen der Physik.* Retrieved from https://onlinelibrary.wiley.com/doi/10.1002/andp.19063270110

Einstein, A., Podolsky, B., Rosen, N. (1935 May 15). "Can Quantum-Mechanical Description of Physical Reality Be Considered Complete?" *Phys. Rev.* 47 (10): 777–780. Retrieved from https://journals.aps.org/pr/abstract/10.1103/PhysRev.47.777

Formaggio, J.A, Kaiser, D. I., Murskyj, M.M., Weiss, T.E. (2016, June 23). "Violation of the Leggett-Garg inequality in neutrino oscillations." *Phys. Rev. Lett.* Retrieved from https://arxiv.org/abs/1602.00041

Fox, E. (1994, reprint edition). *The Sermon on the Mount: The Key to Success in Life.* Harper Collins.

Fronsdal, G. (2016). *The Buddha Before Buddhism: Wisdom from the Early Teachings.* Shambhala Publications Limited.

Garfield, J. L. (2002). *Empty Words: Buddhist Philosophy and Cross-Cultural Interpretation.* Oxford University Press.

Gilbran, K. (1923, reprint edition). *The Prophet.* Alfred A. Knopf.

Goswami, A. (2011, revised edition). *Quantum Doctor: A Quantum Physicist Explains the Healing Power of Integral Medicine.* Hampton Roads Publishing.

Gumbrecht, H.R., Harrison, R.P., Laughlin, R.B., Hendrickson, M.R. (2011). *What Is Life? The Intellectual Pertinence of Erwin Schrodinger.* Stanford University Press.

Hancock, G. (2015, reprint edition). *Magician of the Gods.* St Martin's Press.

Hanh, T.N. (1999). *The Heart of the Buddha's Teaching.* Rider

_____ (2021) *Peace is Every Breath* (audiobook). Penguin Audio.

_____ (1991). *Peace Is Every Step.* Bantam Doubleday Dell Publishing Group.

Hanuman Foundation. (1971). *Be Here Now.* The Crown Publishing Group.

Hartley-Parkinson, R. (2019, June 26). "UK Population Rises to 66,436,000 and Migration Is Biggest Factor." *Metro.* Retrieved from https://metro.co.uk/2019/06/26/uk-population-rises-66436000-migration-biggest-factor-10074103/

Heinlein, R.A. (2012). *Stranger in a Strange Land* (audiobook). Hodder & Stoughton.

Hensen, B. et al. (2015, October 21). "Loophole-free Bell inequality violation using electron spins separated by 1.3 kilometres." *Nature.* 526: 682–686. Retrieved from https://www.nature.com/articles/nature15759

Ji, S. (2020). *Regenerate: Unlocking Your Body's Radical Resilience Through the New Biology.* Hay House.

Jung, C.G. (2009). *The Red Book* (edited and introduction by Sonu Shamdasani 2009; translated by Mark Kyburz, John Peck & Sonu Shamdasani, 2009). W.W. Norton and Company.

Kalupahana, D. (2006). *Mulamadhyamakakarika of Nāgārjuna: The Philosophy of the Middle Way.* Motilal Banarsidass.

Kornfield, J. (1995). *Roots of Buddhist Psychology* (audiobook). Sounds True.

Kwiat, P.G., et al. (1995, December 11). "New High-Intensity Source of Polarization-Entangled Photon Pairs." *Physical Review Letters.* 75: 4337–4341. Retrieved from https://journals.aps.org/prl/abstract/10.1103/PhysRevLett.75.4337

Laszlo, E., Houston, J., Dossey L. (2016). *What Is Consciousness: Three Sages Look Behind the Veil*. SelectBooks, Inc.

Laycock, D.C. et al. (1989). *Skeptical—a Handbook of Pseudoscience and the Paranormal*. Canberra Skeptics.

Lee, K.C. (2017, May 22). "Diving Deep into the World of Emergent Gravity." Ars Technica. Retrieved from https://arstechnica.com/features/2017/05/emergent-gravity-and-dark-matter-explained-by-excited-universe/

Lee, K.C. et al. (2011, December 2). "Entangling Macroscopic Diamonds At Room Temperature." *Science:* 334 (6060): 1253–1256. Retrieved from https://pubmed.ncbi.nlm.nih.gov/22144620/

Houston, J. (2004). Jump Time. First Sentient Publications.

Loundenbeck, T. (2016, August 30). "These are the World's 10 Worst Problems According to Millennials." Science Alert. Retrieved from https://www.sciencealert.com/the-world-s-most-dire-problems-according-to-millennials

Maas. M. (editor). (2014). *The Cambridge Companion to the Age of Attila*. Cambridge University Press.

Masters, R.E.L & Houston, R. (1989). Mind Games: The Guide to Inner Space. Dorset Press.

Ming, H.H., Clarke, R.B. et al. (XXXX/DATE). *The Third Chinese Patriarch of Zen: Love, Serve, Remember* (digital MP3). Hanuman Foundation

Maugham, S. (2012). *The Razor's Edge* (audiobook). Audible Studios.

Nairz, O., Arndt, M. & Zeilinger, A. (2003, March 11) "Quantum interference experiments with large molecules." *American Journal of Physics:* 71; 319–325. Retrieved from https://aapt.scitation.org/doi/10.1119/1.1531580

Overbye, D. (2017, February 20). "Cosmos Controversy: The Universe Is Expanding, but How Fast?" *New York Times*. Retrieved from https://www.nytimes.com/2017/02/20/science/hubble-constant-universe-expanding-speed.html

Peters, S. (2012). *The Chimp Paradox: The Acclaimed Mind Management Programme to Help You Achieve Success, Confidence and Happiness* (audiobook). Random House Audiobooks.

Pine, R. (2012, reprint edition). *The Lankavatara Sutra.* Counterpoint.

Ray, H.R. & Anderson, S.R. (2000). *The Cultural Creatives.* Harmony Books.

Reps, P. (1999). *Zen Flesh, Zen Bones: A Collection of Zen and Pre-Zen Writings* (audiobook collection). Phoenix Audio.

Rinpoche, C.T. & Caspar, M. (2015). *Cutting Through Spiritual* (audiobook). Audible Studios.

Ruis, D.M. (2018, reprint edition). *The Four Agreements: Practical Guide to Personal Freedom.* Amber-Allen Publishing, Inc.

Sadhguru. (2020). *Death: An Inside Story.* Penguin Ananda.

_____(2021). *Karma: A Yogi's Guide to Crafting Your Destiny.* Harmony Books.

Sadhguru & Vasudev, J. (2003, reprint edition). *Mystic's Teachings.* Wisdom Tree.

Sankaracarya & Prabhavananda S. (1978). *Crest-Jewel of Discrimination: Viveka-Chudamani* (translated by Christopher Isherwood). Atlantic Books.

Satchidananda, S.S. (2019). *The Yoga Sutras Patanjali's, Sri Swami.* Integral Yoga Publications.

Schrodinger, E. & Penrose, R. (2019). *What is Life? With Mind and Matter and Autobiographical Sketches* (audiobook). Tanto Audio.

Sheldrake. R. (2011). The *Presence of the Past: Morphic Resonance and the Habits of Nature.* Icon Books.

Shimoff, M. (2008, reprint edition). *Happy for No Reason: 7 Steps to Being Happy from the Inside Out.* Free Press.

Siddha Yoga. (2010). "Glossary of Siddha Yoga Terminology" (PDF). Siddha Yoga. Retrieved from https://www.siddhayoga.org/glossary

Siderits, M. (1988). "Nagarjuna As Anti-Realist. Journal of Indian Philosophy." Volume 16(4): 311–325. Retrieved from XXXX/URL

Siderits, M. & Katsura, S. (2013). *Nagarjuna's Middle Way: Mulamadhyamakakarika* (Classics of Indian Buddhism). Wisdom Publications.

Shunryu Suzuki, R. (2011). *Zen Mind, Beginner's Mind: Informal Talks on Zen Meditation and Practices.* Shambhala Publications Ltd.

Smith, V.A. (1901). *Asoka – the Buddhist Emperor of India. Rulers of India Series* (PDF). Oxford at the Clarendon Press. Retrieved from https://en.wikisource.org/wiki/Asoka_-_the_Buddhist_Emperor_of_India

Strong, J. (1989). *The Legend of King Aśoka: A Study and Translation of the Aśokāvadāna.* Motilal Banarsidass

Suzuki, D.T. (1978, reprint edition). *The Lankavatara Sutra: A Mahayan Text.* Shambhala Publications.

_____ (1999). *Studies In the Lankavatara Sutra.* Motilal Banarsidass.

Tanahashi, K. & Levitt, P. (2014). *The Essential Dogen: Writings of the Great Zen Master* (audiobook). Audible Studios.

Trimble, V. (1987). "Existence and Nature of Dark Matter in the Universe." *Annual Review of Astronomy and Astrophysics:* 25: 425–472. Retrieved from https://www.annualreviews.org/doi/abs/10.1146/annurev.aa.25.090187.002233

Trungpa, C. (2014). *The Myth of Freedom and the Way of Meditation* (audiobook). Audible Studios

_____ (1984). *Shambhala: The Sacred Path of the Warrior.* Shambhala Publications Ltd.

Trungpa, C., Clark, C., Lief, J. et al. (2014). *Training the Mind: & Cultivating Loving-Kindness* (audiobook). Audible Studios.

Walsch, N.D. (1998). *Conversations with God Book 3: An Uncommon Dialogue.* Hodder & Stoughton.

Wilber, K. (2014). *The Fourth Turning: Imagining the Evolution of Integral Buddhism.* Shambhala.

_____ (2014). "The Fourth Turning of Buddhism: Opening Address" (video). Integral Life on Vimeo. Retrieved from https://vimeo.com/138409463

Weizmann Institute of Science. (1998 February 27). "Quantum Theory Demonstrated: Observation Affects Reality." Science Daily. Retrieved from https://www.sciencedaily.com/releases/1998/02/980227055013.htm

Wilhelm, R. (1989). I *Ching or Book of Changes.* Penguin Books Ltd.

Zukav, G. (1990, reprint edition). *The Seat of the Soul: An Inspiring Vision of Humanity's Spiritual Destiny.* Rider & Co.

Lightning Source UK Ltd.
Milton Keynes UK
UKHW011032031222
413263UK00001B/20